RE-THINKING AMERICAN EDUCATION

RE-THINKING AMERICAN EDUCATION

A Philosophy of Teaching and Learning

Second Edition

J. GLENN GRAY

Preface to the Second Edition
by Elisabeth Young-Bruehl

WESLEYAN UNIVERSITY PRESS
Middletown, Connecticut

To my daughters,
Lisa and Sherry,
unwitting educators.

*This book was originally published by J. B. Lippincott Company,
and reprinted in paper by Harper Torchbooks in 1972. It is
reprinted here by arrangement with Harper & Row.*

All inquiries and permissions requests should be addressed to the Publisher,
Wesleyan University Press, 110 Mt. Vernon Street, Middletown,
Connecticut 06457.

Distributed by Harper & Row Publishers, Keystone Industrial Park,
Scranton, Pennsylvania 18512.

Library of Congress Cataloging in Publication Data

Gray, J. Glenn (Jesse Glenn), 1913-1977.
    Re-thinking American education.
    Reprint. Originally published: The promise of wisdom.
Philadelphia : Lippincott, 1968. With new preface. Includes index.
    1. Gray, J. Glenn (Jesse Glenn), 1913-1977. 2. Educa-
tion—Philosophy. I. Title.
LB875.G824P76 1984   370'.1   84-5273
ISBN 0-8195-6106-1 (pbk. : alk. paper)

Manufactured in the United States of America
Wesleyan Paperback, 1984

PREFACE TO THE SECOND EDITION

J. Glenn Gray's books, which he wrote slowly, in a plain, unpretentious prose that perfectly presents the concreteness and simplicity of his thinking, always arrived ahead of their times. This story of untimeliness began during the Second World War, in 1941, when Gray sent *Hegel's Hellenic Ideal* into a philosophical milieu antipathetic to Hegel and everything German thought was assumed to stand for. The book was reprinted twenty-seven years later, under the title *Hegel and Greek Thought,* and is now accepted as a milestone toward the 1970s' American reception of modern German philosophy.

The most important episode in Gray's publishing story began in 1959. After nearly fifteen years of pondering his experiences as a soldier during the Second World War, he finished *The Warriors: Reflections on Men in Battle.* This book, a beautiful hybrid, part philosophical treatise, part reminiscence, part meditative essay in the American transcendentalist manner, part field manual for soldiers on the horrors and fascinations of war, was published to little acclaim and no commercial success. Its faithful circle of admirers and the rare-book dealers kept *The Warriors* in small circulation until it was reissued in 1967, with an introduction by Hannah Arendt. The time was then right. American readers were ready to think about the experiences of Second World War soldiers as they tried to understand a new war that cast the past principles and future possibilities of their nation deeply in question. Copies of the book were passed around on American campuses and many made their way to the battlefields in Vietnam. "Like many Americans," Gray wrote in a 1970 foreword to a new paperback edition, "I have been trying to come to terms with the particular horror of the Vietnam War and the violence, chaos, and emotional perplexity these horrors have occasioned—or reflected—in our own land."

During the years *The Warriors* was finally finding its public, Gray finished *The Promise of Wisdom: A Philosophical Theory of Education.* When this book was published in 1968, only one national magazine offered a review, or, rather, a brief notice—very laudatory. Several thousand copies of the hardbound and paperback editions were sold; a Harper Torchbooks reissue in 1972 made the book available for university philosophy and education courses; and then it went out of print in 1978.

The Warriors had first appeared in a relatively quiescent time, when few wished to reflect on men in battle. Ten years later, a nation divisively, disastrously at war needed the book. *The Promise of Wisdom* arrived during that tumultuous time of need, when few were willing or able to reflect calmly, philosophically on education. One can only hope that now, sixteen years after the first publication of *The Promise of Wisdom,* and seven years after its author's too early death, this book will also receive the concerned and careful readings it so deserves. Hegel's famous dictum that "the owl of Minerva flies only at the dusk" has lodged itself deep in our discontents. But we should not be too quickly persuaded that the promise of wisdom is fulfilled only after folly has had its march; there is a cautionary tale in J. Glenn Gray's untimeliness. Minerva's owl can take flight too early, and in forms unfamiliar both to those who expect nothing from philosophy and to those who await the Absolute.

J. Glenn Gray's reflections on education reappear, under the title *Re-Thinking American Education,* at a moment when the unwisdom of our national educational policies has become obvious. For years, educators have tried to bring the worsening crisis to our attention; now their worries are receiving both widespread publicity and the dubious attention of political campaigners. And educators must, thus, worry anew—about whether the crisis will be addressed for the wrong reasons with the wrong means.

In *Re-Thinking American Education* there are no prefabricated remedies for our schools and universities: for their economic straits and their perpetuation of our society's inequalities and injustices; for their curricular disarray and disciplinary chaos; for their new versions of old "melting pot" cultural complexities and their efforts to meet the challenges of advanced technological civilization. What Gray offers, rather, is a thoroughly constructed framework of the questions about education that must be asked as we consider the crisis of our schools. Education and schooling are not the same; we cannot say, much less achieve, what we want for our schools until we ask what education is, whom it is for, how teaching should be practiced, and what should be taught. These are Gray's simple, fundamental questions.

The manner in which Gray considers these questions is informal, conversational. His easy familiarity with the history of educational theorizing and the influence of his two close philosopher friends, Martin Heidegger and Hannah Arendt, are apparent in this book, but his language is neither difficult nor technical and his commitment to concrete thinking, and to the interplay of reflection and self-reflection, calls upon the reader's capacity for imaginative participation in the book's project: a philosophical theory of education. Education is an ascent "from information through knowledge to wisdom"; a philosophical theory should describe and analyze the ascent; and a book presenting such a theory should follow its course. This one does.

In recent years, we have been fortunate in this country to have excellent histories of American education, fine critical works on the schools as social institutions, lively debates on testing, special education, bilingualism, curricular reform, affirmative action, and so forth. But we have not had philosophical reflection of the caliber offered to earlier generations by John Dewey and Alfred North Whitehead. This is not because there has been no heir to those great writers; it is because we have not paid attention to J. Glenn Gray's work. He knew—the introduction to his book tells us—that in our time we have to question why we need a theory of education; that we have to overcome preconceptions about the impracticality of theory which have become more, not less, entrenched since Dewey and Whitehead's time. There are complex historical reasons for the current resistance to theory—and they are part of the current education crisis.

Re-Thinking American Education begins with an introductory therapeutic approach to our resistances. It concludes with a vision of education "in school and out of school, in learning and in teaching" that grew in the writing: "Gradually it has become clear to me that the search for an education is man's age-old search to become at home in this world." That this vision was articulated in a time not receptive to it is something to ponder; that the time could now be right is something to be hoped; but the timeless simplicity and meaningfulness of the vision is something to marvel at and be grateful for.

Elisabeth Young-Bruehl

ACKNOWLEDGMENTS

It is a privilege to acknowledge in print my debt to those who have helped me in the writing of these pages. In 1961-62 the Guggenheim Memorial Foundation provided me a fellowship and the Wesleyan University Center for Advanced Study a material and human environment for preparing the first draft. Henry Allan Moe and Victor Butterfield are the men within these institutions (rather were at that time) whom I wish to thank for these gifts of time and circumstance. The Hamburg-Amerika Gesellschaft granted me in the summer of 1963 a modest scholarship for study of German education; there the responsible man was Walter Stahl of the Atlantik-Bruecke. Louis T. Benezet and Lloyd E. Worner, successive presidents of Colorado College, have aided and abetted me at every turning. Jeannette E. Hopkins, editor-friend, likewise deserves my gratitude. My students, who reacted in philosophical journals to these ideas as the book was in process, have been a constant source of second thoughts and consequent revisions. I want to thank Mrs. Donna Werner for patient effort in typing my often chaotic manuscript. But my greatest debt is as always to my wife for guarding my solitude and rescuing me from discouragement.

February 12, 1968   J. GLENN GRAY

CONTENTS

RE-THINKING AMERICAN EDUCATION

INTRODUCTION

SOME TIME AGO one of my daughters' teachers called me on the telephone to inquire about a course at my college in which she wanted to enroll the following summer. "Is it all theory," she wished to know, "or will it be of some real value?" This veteran teacher went on to decry the theoretical study of education. In her mind, the term *theory* was clearly associated with a body of abstractions that had no relation whatever to the urgent needs of her children in the classroom.

Since I have been teaching a course in educational theory for several years, her polemic made me thoughtful about current meanings of the word *theory*. Derived from the Greek *theōria*, "a beholding," "a spectacle," from a verb meaning "to look at," it is a close equivalent of our word *vision*. And *vision* has both a literal and symbolic connotation in English, as it did in classic Greek. Hence, a *theory of education* means a direct looking at the educational process and an imaginative attempt at understanding it as well. Understanding is the active and constructive goal of the enterprise; looking is the prior, receptive, and necessary means. When I first undertook to teach the course, I decided that the theory of education was simply a reflective viewing of the means and ends of the process as a whole and, insofar as possible, as a unity.

Why, then, did this teacher attach such a negative meaning to the word *theory*, which I have long regarded as designating one of man's noblest activities?

I finally concluded that our opposition consists both in a radical difference in understanding what the word theory means and also in what we consider to be important in learning and teaching. Our difference as teachers is rooted in semantics and in substance too.

For my daughter's teacher, the word *theory* clearly signifies a body of abstractions, in the literal sense of something "drawn out from" or separated from an organic whole. These abstractions, as far as she could see, bear little or no relation to the concrete and vital problems with which she is daily confronted as a teacher. In this sense of theory, I must admit that she is largely right. For certain purposes, abstracting something from its living context in order to study it more clearly in isolation is useful, even essential. We do this when we view the economic practices of our society, its religious rituals, or its artistic forms. But education is, of course, much more than schooling and so intimately bound up with other aspects of our culture that such abstraction is not only difficult in the extreme but would also falsify the resulting theory.

However, for me the word *theory* denotes something quite different, namely the general principles of any subject matter. Since these words "general principles" are important in the chapters to follow, I would like to define them more exactly now.

General derives from the Latin word *genus*, meaning "class" or "kind" as opposed to "local" or "individual." Hence, it has a very different meaning from *abstract*, despite the fact that *general* and *abstract* are frequently confused in popular speech. The abstract is always the opposite of the concrete, whereas the general need not ever be. A general principle is one intended to apply to the largest possible group of phenomena, and if it is a good principle it will leave out nothing essential to the understanding of this group. Indeed, the general, in this sense, is likely to be more concrete than the particular instance, for it reveals the particular in its larger context and its vital relations.

As one of our great modern philosophers, Hegel, taught *only* that which is general is concrete, for the particular is isolated and thus abstract. To look at any phenomenon, whether it be a schoolboy or an atom, apart from its belongingness in a vital whole, is to be abstract. Part of the very being of schoolboy and atom consists in their position and participation in a larger context. Relatedness is essential to our reality. Unwittingly, we fall into abstraction often just when we think we are being concrete and specific. The teacher who refuses to generalize about his subject matter or his pupils by insisting on the unique quality of each particular is guilty of this. A moment's reflection would teach him that the very language he uses in this insistence on uniqueness (indeed the concept of uniqueness itself) is general.

The other word I want to dwell on for a moment is *principle*. In contemporary usage it is a fairly vague word, but it should not be. Again, a look at word origins is instructive. For the ancient Romans, a principle meant something that is at the beginning in the sense of a foundation. Hence, a *principium* in Latin is primary, not simply in time, but in substance as well. It is that without which a spectacle or a subject matter or an institution cannot be or be understood. A principle is a primary structure around which and by means of which single and isolated things are grouped and organized. By means of this structure, they derive their relations and unity and the possibility for a beholder to understand them. A theorist is always in search of these "beginnings" or foundations, since without them there can be no orderly advance in grasping the significance of any spectacle. In a temporal sense, he may not start with them, but for intellectual vision he does not get very far without principles.

The search for such principles in the subject matter of education is the purpose of this book. It is theoretical in the sense of vision, not only in the first half, which concerns definitions and purposes, but also in the latter half, which analyzes practical problems of teaching and learning. I will focus on the general, since the spectacle of American education is much too complex and diverse for anyone to view or re-view it in other than general principles. But I will avoid the abstract. The general is what lends interest to the theories of education, whereas the abstract is likely to be deadening and dull.

To return to my daughter's teacher, a different understanding of the word *theory* is not the only thing that separates us. Beyond this, lies a chasm in our evaluation of the importance of theory vis-à-vis practice. As I listened to her on the telephone, I remem-

bered Justice Holmes' remark that theory is the most practical
thing in the world. John Dewey, who mentions this in a book
titled *Problems of Men*, adds that Holmes' remark is "pre-
eminently true of social theory, of which educational theory is a
part." Quite clearly this teacher did not think so. Insofar as she
had been exposed to what passes for theory of education in some
courses on education, she is easy to forgive. However, her attitude is too widely shared among teachers and many other professional people today. And this is a serious weakness. Such
people are not really educated, because they lack any vision of
what they are trying to do. They tend to be interested only in
"how to" courses, in the "know how" as contrasted with the
"know why," in means, not ends; in skills, not principles; in
details, not wholes. They commonly lack a clear understanding
of the relations within their subject matter and the relations between their own specialty and other fields of knowledge. Such
people are technicians, not true professionals, whether they are
physicians, engineers, lawyers, ministers, or teachers. Perhaps the
lack of interest in theory is especially great in the teaching profession because of the difficulty this calling has had in getting
itself accepted as a profession, except at the college and university level.

I sense a great change here in our time. In view of our brief
history, it is not surprising that we Americans have been primarily intent on doing rather than "seeing," on action rather
than understanding, on building a society and a nation rather than
searching for its hidden principles. In any event, there is no
piety in polemicizing against our practical bent, for we have
had many blessings from it and have given much help to the rest
of the world because of our genius for practice.

What we need now is more theory, above all in education.
This will doubtless come, for our nation is increasingly aware
of its deficiencies in this area. So long as the preservation of our
society required that formal education be mainly vocational,
theories of education were relatively unimportant. Now that automation is relieving us of routine work and threatening to take

over much of the non-routine work, the situation is radically different. To put it more constructively, now that the problems of earning a livelihood are becoming less central, we have time for more important and less necessary concerns. At the beginning of Western civilization, according to Aristotle, men began *to wonder* as soon as they had a little respite from the tasks of caring for their physical needs. Educational theory, like philosophy itself, begins in astonishment and wonder that things are as they are.

There are other reasons why the need for educational theory has increased. Once we were fairly self-contained as a nation; now the whole world is more or less a neighborhood—and for much of this neighborhood we have somehow assumed responsibility. Once woman's place was conceived to be in the home, ministering to husband and children; now women are in offices, legislative halls, industries, and the professions—and often bewildered about their "place." Once Americans were for the most part under the guidance of religious convictions, from which they drew their moral ideals. Now we are adrift religiously and morally, at the very best pluralistic and doubting.

This list of fundamental changes could be prolonged without effort. But the changes mentioned suffice to show the growing need for theory and why a book on the theory of education does not need to be justified. If such theory is pursued in the right spirit—in search of the general and not the abstract—absorbing interest in vision will be apparent, and Justice Holmes' dictum will become a commonplace.

It is true, of course, that not all theory is self-justifying. Though educational theory as an attempt to see the whole process in its interrelations is on the way, there is no assurance that it will be worthwhile theory. For that undertaking, imagination is required, hard thinking, more research, and all the experience and criticism we can bring to it.

Most of my readers, like myself, have enjoyed and suffered from attempts at education in and out of the schools. This experience must remain a primary source of theory. But much can be learned from others and from those in the past who have re-corded their ideas. The history of educational theory is a vast reservoir that we have hardly begun to draw upon. Those who hold that this reservoir is largely useless because of the revolu-tionary nature of the contemporary world can hardly be right.

Of course, the task of building an adequate theory of education for a society changing as rapidly as ours is immensely compli-cated. For all we know, our society may not only be changing radically; it may also be nearing catastrophe. Since we cannot know this, it is folly to presuppose it. Simple wisdom dictates that no one can make a pretension to finality or completeness in educational theory. What we can claim is to be genuine searchers for a vision of education which will give significance to our voca-tion as teachers and human beings.

A little earlier, I quoted John Dewey as saying that educational theory is a branch of social theory. This raises the troubling issue of the relationship of educational philosophy to philosophy in general or, more precisely, to what has been traditionally con-ceived to be the proper subject matter of philosophy. In our recent past, educational philosophy has been mainly pursued, in the academic world, by departments of education and scorned by departments of philosophy. It is common to hear, as I did re-cently, a teacher of philosophy declare: "I know nothing of educational philosophy." It did not seem strange to him that two of the most respected philosophers of our heritage, Plato and John Dewey, built their own philosophies explicitly around the theory of education. This professor claimed to know a great deal about both and furthermore considered them as central figures. How philosophers, particularly teachers of philosophy, can manage to teach these and other great thinkers without concern for relating philosophy and the theory of education is puzzling.

We dare hope that this, too, is changing in our time. Part of the confusion arises from the unthinking identification of educa-tion and schooling. When Dewey writes that educational theory is part of social theory, he is referring to formal education, which we call schooling. But elsewhere he makes clear that the theory of education, in the wider sense of the term, is to him identical with philosophy itself. And when Plato asserts that societies will have no rest from their turmoil until philosophers are kings, the context of his entire masterpiece, *The Republic*, leaves no doubt that by *kings* he means little more than educational rulers. Philosophers are teachers of "the vision of truth" and as such, and insofar as they are truly lovers of wisdom, they ought to "rule." From Plato, Dewey derived his conception of philosophy as education. The recent tendency of philosophers in America to concern themselves once more with educational theory may testify to a recovery of this ancient conception of philosophy.

This does not imply that all theory is philosophical, any more than it implies that all educational problems are problems for philosophy. There are many theories that have little relevance for problems of education and many practical problems of education that require special skills and action more than philosophical reflection. But it does mean that education, insofar as it is concerned with the ends of living, is philosophical in essence. And philosophy, insofar as it is concerned with the good life, not only as a private quest but as a social goal, is theory of education. Educational theory that is a critique of our school system may not be specifically philosophical, but surely any thoroughgoing proposal for the reconstruction of the means of schooling for the next generation has philosophical presuppositions. Hence, philosophical theory is involved not simply in questions of goals and purposes of education, but also in the large problems of practice as well. For example, the current debate over ability-grouping in the schools, though a question of means, raises the most far-reaching issues of theory. Philosophical queries properly enter almost every phase of the educational process, from the problem of definition to the question of education's role in the world community that we hope is emerging. In short, philosophy is far short of being everything, but it is somehow involved in nearly everything that concerns education.

In what follows I have used a rather simple principle of organization. First, I deal with the definition of education by asking *what* it means to be educated. Second, I develop those purposes and goals of education that appear to be predominant today, in response to the all-important question: *why* be educated? The remainder of the book is devoted to the issues of educational practice which appear to be philosophical in essence and implication. They are divided into: *whom* we should teach, the able or the average; *how* we should teach (the issue of method); and *what* we should teach (the issue of curriculum). Finally, I take up two problems of the relation of school and society in answer to the question: *where* is education headed in our day? These simple interrogatives seem to introduce the important philosophical considerations of educational theory and practice.

Philosophizing has rightly been called the art of asking simple questions for which very complicated answers are required. In education the answers, no matter how sophisticated, are rarely satisfactory for very long or to very many inquirers. The issues of education are simply too complex and difficult for most of us, prisoners of our limited experience, to resolve. The longer I teach the theory of education, the more I long for the old simplicities of metaphysics! Our vision, at least mine, is too narrow for the kind of comprehensive theory the subject matter requires. But a contemporary philosopher has justly remarked that "to ask questions is the piety of thought." And I trust that what follows will be judged to be pious, however short it falls of being wise.

Part I

A DEFINITION OF EDUCATION

To educate man is the art of arts, for he is the most complex and most mysterious of all creatures.
—Comenius

1. THE PROMISE OF WISDOM

WHAT IS EDUCATION? At first blush the question appears uncomplicated; in reality it is highly perplexing. Stated another way: What is the condition of being educated? Or less abstractly: Who is the educated person?

At the unreflective level, the answer to the last question is likely to be: One who has completed a course of study at an educational institution. Nowadays such an answer would probably specify a college degree; earlier a high school diploma would have sufficed; by the end of this century a Master's degree may well be necessary. But a little reflection makes such an answer suspect. Education and schooling are not at all the same thing. Most of us have known individuals with little formal schooling who seemed to us unusually well educated—in a very common usage of the term *education*. And we have also known others who hold advanced degrees yet are uncultivated and insensitive. We are forced at once to make a distinction between *schooling* and *education*. Though the two often go together in the same person, perhaps increasingly so in our age and country, there is certainly no necessary conjunction between them.

Why is this so? Why do we refuse to call the merely well-schooled man or woman educated? Why is learning, even immense and highly specialized learning, not sufficient in itself to make a person educated? Throughout Western history there has been a reluctance to believe that schools can provide the ideal education or that schoolmasters are models of the best educated men. At the same time, few have denied that the greatest learning has been incorporated in the schools and that schoolmen usually command the best in scholarship. Insofar as this derogation of learning is not a manifestation of anti-intellectualism, what can be its source? I think it lies in the genuine insight that education is more than information and more than scholarship. But what is this "more"?

In Goethe's *Faust* there is a satire on education that contains a clue to the answer. Faust is a doctor-teacher at the beginning of the play, much revered in his community as a learned and wise man, but he is convinced that he really knows nothing at all. Studies have devoured his youth and middle years, kept him cloistered in musty library and laboratory, and in the end brought him to despair and the verge of suicide. Faust is not a narrow specialist in medicine or chemistry. He is one of those universal Renaissance men who have studied jurisprudence, philosophy, and theology in addition to the sciences. All his studies have had a similar effect: to leave him feeling empty, sceptical, and without vitality. And his students have contributed to his dejection.

Goethe introduces us to two of these students. One is a freshman, without a name but with the characteristics of the eternal freshman. He is attractive enough, respectful in the presence of this man of reputation and learning, though repelled by the ill-smelling laboratories and dusty books. His fun-loving spirit feels cramped by the academy. Trees and grass and long summer holidays seem much more real than the scholarly environment. He begins:

> *Please, sir, assist me. I have come*
> *With the best intentions, good health, and a little money.*
> *My mother didn't like to have me leave her.*
> *I want to learn something here that's practical.*

Here is one charge against the academic world that the satire makes: it is filled with youth who are interested in success rather than knowledge, who are motivated by what a course of study can do *for* them rather than what it can do *to* them. Whatever else the educated man may be, he is not one who pursues art and science for the sake of their commercial benefits. On this occasion Faust, under the guise of his Satan's mask and in a cynical mood, runs through the curriculum with his advice, making devastatingly amusing comments about law, theology, the sciences, and philosophy and finally counsels his own major specialty, medicine. Here the student's insistence on the practical is rewarded. Though medicine has no cures for the ills of mankind, the populace does not know it and prefers to trust the physician's arts rather than nature's curative powers. Armed with his title and self-confidence, a doctor can easily win the hearts of his patients, particularly the women "with their everlasting aches and groans." With impunity he can handle their bodies, unlace their corsets, and steal many a pleasure forbidden to other men.

> *That's better now. The How and*
> *Where one sees,*

cries the student, and decides immediately on his major course of study. As he leaves enraptured, his counselor ironically autographs the books extended to him: *Eritis sicut Deus, scientes bonum et malum* (You shall be as God, knowing good and evil).

This misconception of the purpose of learning is so pervasive that it can dominate a whole culture. In neophytes it is forgivable and can be combated by wise teaching, with the result that students who begin with pragmatic and egoistic motives may realize in time that education is for its own sake, that knowing, however useful it may be to society, should be pursued by the knower as an end in itself. Yet there is so much emphasis on material ends that in all schools teachers no less than students forget that schooling is for the sake of education. The recurrent emphasis on the three R's is put there usually by a commercial spirit, which is innocent of any conception of what education is about, wanting reading, writing, and arithmetic for the sake of gain. At the moment, the best argument American educators can muster against the drop-out plague is that incomplete schooling leads to unemployment and lowered life earnings. This motive is important, of course, and schools must serve the practical needs of the society which sustains them. But the acquisition of skills by which to earn a livelihood, however necessary, falls short of the meaning of education. If not resisted constantly and in every generation, such a spirit can effectively destroy the concept of education, causing schools to degenerate into training institutes.

The second student in *Faust* is the graduate assistant, Wagner, whose name has become a synonym for pedantry. Though ostentatious display of learning may seem to be at the opposite pole from commercializing it, the two are not so far removed in essence. Indeed, Wagner, like the Freshman, may once have appeared before Faust's desk, rosy-cheeked and impatient to learn the knowledge of good and evil. But scholarship has converted him into an insufferable bore. Goethe portrays him as "content to paste phrases together by the hour" and "to work up a little stew from others' feasts." Inflated by the waste baskets and attics of scholarship, Wagner feels vastly superior to the unschooled multitude outside the walls of academia. Convinced that the time in which he lives is far advanced over other epochs and asininely self-confident, he asserts the perennial creed of the mediocre learned man: "Much do I know—but to know all is my ambition."

Again and again he interrupts his teacher's musings, drowning Faust's creative moods with irrelevant chatter, pseudo-scholarship, and proverbial lore that he mistakes for wisdom. As incapable of despair as he is of insight, Wagner is the prototype of that multitude in the schools—both teachers and students—who mistake shadow for substance. They not only extinguish whatever sparks their youth might have promised but also impede immeasurably the progress of others. They can spend years in contact with excellence and sensitivity and still confuse, as Wagner did, discourse with invisible powers, originality with clichés, inspiration with insipid chatter. Such students are capable of driving good teachers into drink and debauchery as such teachers have done to good students. The Wagners are perhaps more hopeless than the opportunists who decide on medicine in order to seduce women, or study economics to get rich, or become teachers from fear of competition in other fields. They have at least the possibility of change; the pedant is forever just what he is. Both types are equally far removed from what most of us mean by the term *education*.

What of Faust himself before his adventures outside the ivied walls, those adventures which have made him a symbol of modern restlessness and striving? Is he truly educated? One would hardly say so. He is possessed, to be sure, with the primary requisite of educated human nature, the passion for knowledge. But he lacks the required experience of the world to give that passion direction. A prisoner of books, learning, and his father's inheritance, he yearns for freedom to create his own life. His plight led Goethe to write:

> *What you inherit from your fathers*
> *Must first be earned before it's yours.*

As a scholar and a teacher, Faust lacks serenity and real wisdom. His knowledge has not brought him any fulfillment; it has not opened the world to him. On the contrary, he feels stifled in the confinement of his library and laboratory. Hence Goethe led him out of the life of scholarship, the Goethe who had himself found little satisfaction in his formal education. Faust learns to know the world of amorous excitement, governmental affairs, stock markets, drawing rooms, and battlefields, and finally the world of statesman and colonizer. At the end of this colorful career, the ex-professor sums it up as follows:

> *I only through the world have flown:*
> *Each appetite I seized as by the hair:*
> *What not sufficed me, forth I let it fare*
> *And what escaped me, I let go.*
> *I've only craved, accomplished my delight,*
> *Then wished a second time, and thus with might*
> *Stormed through my life.*

And after rejecting as foolish any concern with another life beyond the grave, he ends with this advice to the young:

Firm let him stand and look around him well!
This world means something to the capable.

Though Faust in his old age has gained some wisdom from his rather chaotic foraging in experience, we are still in doubt, I think, that he can serve as a model of the educated man. He has reacted violently against the restraints of scholarship and learning as pursued in the schools and universities but has failed to unify direct experience, the life of action, with *theōria,* that search for those "secret springs" which hold the world and man together. As Goethe himself admitted, after spending much of his long life on this great dramatic poem, *Faust* is no whole but simply the fragment of a great confession.

Faust can teach us who the educated man is not. He is not merely the learned man, though a learned man may also be an educated man. He is not the opportunist bent on worldly success, nor is he the despairing hero of the tragedy, who alternates between cynicism and ecstatic religious faith, weekends on Walpurgis and extravagant schemes for national reforms. Nevertheless, Faust and his students afford some hints into the condition of being educated. Education seems to involve both direct experience of many kinds and reflection on that experience; in some fashion it involves experience and knowledge and wisdom. We need to explore the relations of these qualities in order to discover, if possible, some hierarchy.

Some years ago I ran across lines of T. S. Eliot that have haunted me ever since. They are relevant to our search for an acceptable definition of the educated man.

Where is the wisdom we have lost in knowledge?
Where is the knowledge we have lost in information?

These lines are tragic as well as haunting. They seem to suggest that an educated man may lose his state of being educated, to become something other than he was. We like to think that, whatever else is true, education is a kind of ladder upon which we climb from information to knowledge to wisdom. Eliot laments that it is possible to descend the ladder, to have been once wise and now merely informed. The danger of such a loss makes it even more important that we discover the relations among these components of education: information, knowledge, and wisdom.

How do we commonly distinguish information from knowledge? Most of us are somehow aware of the difference; we have information in many areas where we know that we have no real knowledge. Particularly in this age of mass communications, our minds contain a jumble of information, bits and pieces bombarding us daily from all over the world. Much of it belongs in the department of useless information and is forgotten and re-acquired on occasion, often at night when one is trying to sleep and finds this floatsam and jetsam of information coursing, mysteriously enough, through consciousness.

Information may be as unsound as it is haphazard, since the dictionary reports there is no implication that information is factual. Knowledge, on the other hand, implies system and order, logical relationships of facts and a perception of their proximate causes at least and some of their effects. The Greek philosophers early made the distinction between knowing "the fact that" and "the reason why." By observing, many of us have information that such and such is so; far fewer know why it is so. The former comes from experience, the latter from art or science. All of us have some jumbled information about the chemistry of our own bodies; physicians and physiologists are said to have knowledge of it. Or we know something of the laws and regulations that govern our society; whereas lawyers and political scientists are supposed to have systematic knowledge of them. If this knowledge is extensive, physicians or lawyers can interpret the relations and applications of the principles of chemistry or jurisprudence to individual cases. They understand the why and the how as well as the fact that the laws are.

This early formulation of the difference between information and knowledge still endures, but there has grown up in the last century and particularly in this country an allegedly more rigorous definition of knowledge which would restrict it to that body of facts which has been tested and verified by strict scientific methods. *Knowledge* is a term that threatens to become a synonym for science itself and especially for mathematically measurable and exact science. And, perversely, as I see it, this conception of knowledge does not imply necessarily much acquaintance with the principles or theory underlying the subject matter but concerns itself instead with statistics, measurement, and the quantitative aspects of any subject matter. Its emphasis is on precision and exactness, not on understanding and on wholes or on interrelationships of a qualitative sort. In this narrow definition, knowledge is nearly identical with facts as isolated particulars.

It is hardly an exaggeration to say that, if this definition is to prevail, the distinction between training and education will largely disappear. There are individuals in our country who call themselves scientists yet make no pretense of knowing anything about the principles or origins of their subject matter or its relations to other fields. They command acquaintance of a body of facts and are skilled in methods of discovering the sequences of events within that body of facts and of measuring how frequently those events succeed one another. Such intense concentration on a tiny area of observed phenomena, the study of their surface and the manipulation of their parts, is of course necessary and valuable in a society as technological and as scientifically advanced as ours. For our material existence, such trained technicians are perhaps more necessary than scientists and knowers. But it is surely a serious mistake to confuse these technicians with scientists. The confusion of factual information with knowledge is akin to that between breadth and depth. A man may be highly specialized in one of the established disciplines and be a thoroughly educated man. Education does not consist in knowing something about many fields of knowledge. The specialist who is educated is one who is in search of the principles of his own field and how they relate to the principles of other fields. He will go far beyond minute observations of the phenomena themselves.

It is a great error to restrict knowledge to this narrow meaning of detailed acquaintance with exact scientific facts. Indeed, I think it an error to restrict the term *science* to the investigation of natural phenomena, as we Americans increasingly tend to do. *Knowledge* and *science* are equivalent terms if they are properly used to designate an ordered and systematic familiarity with any subject matter that possesses principles, together with an understanding of its relations to other subject matters. We could profit from the Europeans, who speak of the science of literary criticism, for example, or the science of history, with no implication of exactness or minute precision but definitely with an implication of insight into the principles of these inquiries. Some of our sad and silly wrangling over the role of the natural sciences as opposed to the humanities might well disappear if we learned to speak of the science of literature or music or painting and turned away from the equation of knowledge with verified information.

In any case, it is becoming increasingly clear that much of what the natural sciences once held to be exact and absolute fact is now seen to be imprecise and relative. We also possess large quantities of fact in new fields for which generalizations are being discovered; principles are coming into vision, so that we are able to guide future action and uncover new data. Many of these new fields of inquiry, especially in the social sciences, are obtaining knowledge that cannot in principle be verified in any exact way. Yet these subject matters are already organized, rich in theory, and capable of generalization. If we are wise, we will reverse the recent trend to restrict the term *knowledge;* we will restore it to the usage of previous centuries and other nations, namely, the systematic grasp of the principles of a subject matter and the ability to communicate these principles to others.

It is characteristic of one who is acquiring an education that he learns to make the passage from information to knowledge. The process is in no sense an automatic one. Gathering information in any field is reasonably passive and can be gained by reading, by keen observation, or by listening to informed teachers. But to organize and relate the information and facts thus gathered demands the active and imaginative participation of the learner. Knowledge is "being able to learn," as we often put it today. That is a phrase we would do well to ponder for a long time. Being able to learn hardly means being facile at acquiring information. For information, as we all know, easily leaves the mind unless it is ordered into a framework of related facts and they in turn are grounded in principles which can be used in guiding our activity. Unless we, as students, rise up, as it were, and become actively engaged in the process of our own learning, we will never obtain knowledge.

The idea of education as self-education has been repeated so often that it has become banal. But surely no principle of educational theory is less subject to challenge than this one. At some early point in his career every aspirant to the status of educated man must decide that he is in charge, that information and facts will only confuse and weary him unless he learns to exclude as well as include, to synthesize as well as analyze, to relate himself to the immediate world that is external to consciousness by responding to it rather than reacting or remaining passive. Being able to learn means being imaginative or being creative in a general sense. And this in turn signifies being constructive and reconstructive, synthesizing the impressions that flood into the mind with the principles already present to it. Only in activity are these principles brought to light. Vision or theory is not so much an acquisition as a discovery, one that each person must make for himself though countless minds have made it before him.

In an age like ours, characterized by a floodtide of new facts, it is not enough to gain insight into the principles of a subject matter once and for all. Our traditional fields are being transformed by the discovery of ever wider principles, by visions of new relationships. As everyone knows, the natural sciences are developing interstitial fields of investigation—areas between chemistry and biology, geology and astronomy, biology and physics, and so on. And mathematics, that gateway of the sciences, is, to the astonishment of everyone, undergoing a revolution in our generation. The situation in physics may well be prophetic of all traditional knowledge. Not so long ago the subject matter in physics was thought to be complete and closed, its major principles established for all time. Sir Isaac Newton had synthesized and set down what God had wrought in the material universe; henceforth students need only master the master. Now we know, even as laymen, something of the creative confusion that has entered the reconstruction of this bellwether among the natural sciences. Physics, as one of its contemporary practitioners remarked not long ago, "leaps from one lie to another by means of intermediate falsehoods."

If the situation is not so acute in most of the other fields, it is probably because they have not advanced so rapidly in our century. The term *research* has acquired fantastic prestige today, and many absurdities are promulgated in its name. Its currency testifies, nevertheless, to the new uncertainty that possesses us concerning the reliability of our received traditions. We have come to accept Goethe's wisdom that "he only deserves freedom and existence who daily conquers them anew." Now we are beginning to realize that something of the same sort is true for learning and scholarship. For it is not simply a matter of staying abreast of the new facts in the various disciplines to which we are devoted. Frequently these new developments require a reorganization of principles and a positive unlearning of what we have been taught since childhood.

As a consequence, knowledge is not only "being able to learn"; to a unique degree in our time, it is also being able to unlearn and to relearn throughout life. Well might Eliot ask resignedly: "Where is the knowledge we have lost in information?" For it is lamentably true that to stop searching for new theory, to cease reordering the traditions we have inherited, is to descend the ladder from knowledge to information. "The merely well informed man," Whitehead assures us, "is the greatest bore on God's earth." It is frightening to a keen and reflective mind to realize that age will not necessarily either increase his knowledge or his wisdom, however much his store of information grows.

If the distinction between information and knowledge is fairly clear, that between knowledge and wisdom is much less so. And advancing from the one to the other is so difficult as to elude most of us all our lives. I suppose many would not deny the title of "educated man" to the possessor of knowledge, interpreted as one who is able to learn and who has a growing insight into the principles of any subject matter. Yet we normally think that being well educated involves something more than knowledge. The age-old reluctance of the non-academic world to accept the scholar as the model of the educated man relates to the nature of this "more". What is this "more"? Many would answer: wisdom. Yet the question arises at once: What does it mean to be wise? If we can explicate the significance of the word, perhaps we have a chance to point to the possibility of its attainment.

In our Western tradition the term *wisdom* is commonly used in two senses, senses that were first distinguished clearly by Aristotle. There is a practical kind of wisdom—sometimes called *life-wisdom*—which enables a person to apply his learning and knowledge to the enrichment of his daily activities. In ancient Greece that man was wise who had achieved excellence or virtue (*aretē*) in the conduct of life. He was an artist in living, using the materials that were available to him from within and in his society, and molding the "good life" from them. Because his was a public society (where the term *idiot* was applied to the merely private person) the wise man was necessarily an effective citizen as well. Here knowledge was only a part, though an essential part, of wisdom. The capacity for happiness was another. Honor or reputation that came from serving one's state and age was still another.

This practical wisdom was usually construed as the consequence of ordering aright the various elements of one's psychological constitution or faculties. No one who came under the domination of his appetites, whether for drink or sex, money or power, could earn the title of being wise. Nor did the Greek thinkers or dramatists believe that the emotional life was in itself productive of wisdom. They regarded the positive emotions as highly desirable, to be sure, an indispensable ingredient of the good life. But to be fully wise in even the practical sense of the term a man had to bring his daily life and thoughts under the guidance of reason. Wisdom was that excellence or virtue which was the consequence of curbing the appetites and harmonizing the emotions under the control of reason. The other cardinal virtues or excellence of the Greeks, courage, temperance, and justice, and even holiness, were likewise the product of reason. Hence a man had achieved practical wisdom when he had ordered his activity by reason in order to realize his best powers, gaining maximum happiness for himself and contributing according to his abilities to the common life of his society or state.

With the increasing secularism of American culture, this early conception of practical wisdom is being revived. We tend to regard the wise man as one who knows pre-eminently how to live well or, as we rather curiously put it, "how to get the most out of life." We think of him as a happy man or at least one who has a clear surplus of happiness over misery. Though it is hard to believe that anyone in our chaotic times can transform his life into a work of art, we do call wise that man who has found his role and is effective in it, at the same time aiding others to be effective, too. Like the Greeks, we put emphasis on activity rather than passive contemplation, on mastery of passion, not subservience to it, and we tend to believe that wisdom is associated with a kind of satisfaction and serenity in daily life, which arises from a knowledge of self and of society. If we do not glorify reason, it is doubtless because of our inheritance of Christian and Romantic ideals and of Darwinian and Freudian theories, an inheritance that has undermined our confidence in human reason.

Despite these influences, it seems to me that the importance of the concept of liberal education in twentieth-century America testifies to a revival of the Greek idea of practical life under the control of reason. We certainly have a new appreciation of the difficulties of attaining to such practical wisdom, but the ideal, perhaps the dream of it, is very much a part of our reflective culture.

But there is another definition of wisdom, as old as Aristotle, which occasions confusion not merely in concept but in practice as well. According to this second definition, wisdom is the search for truth about the world and man's proper place in it. This wisdom is theoretical, as opposed to practical, the vision of the pure scientist or researcher, the philosopher and the man of great intellectual power, who are concerned with knowing things for their own sake. This sort of wisdom comes from study and reflection and is the product of leisure and freedom from the daily life of vocation and association with others of quite different concerns. Such theoretical wisdom involves long-continued intellectual discipline, inherited ability, and a passion for truth however unpleasant or impractical. It involves an objectivity that can come only to the disinterested, the researcher who has learned to suppress what he would like to believe in the interest of what really is true. This wisdom does not, as the Greeks poetically put it, "teach a man how to find his way home." It does not make him practically effective as a family man, citizen, or community leader. But Aristotle at least felt that it did make a man supremely self-sufficient and even god-like, for it enabled him to retrace the thoughts of God after Him.

This conception of wisdom is still very much with us and is an aim of formal education at its upper levels and its non-vocational curricula. We call it pure science or pure research. Many of our acrimonious quarrels in education over purposes derive from this difference about wisdom conceived as practical or as theoretical. The pure scholars, if one may call them that, want the accent in schooling to be on straining the minds of students early and late in the pursuit of learning the materials of our heritage in order to make them searchers and researchers for truth in whatever realm. They are not concerned with applications to the daily existence of their students, either because they doubt that this can be taught or because they believe that education is for the sake of truth. Education should lead to scholarship if it is not to be dilettantism.

The proponents of practical wisdom, on the other hand, are convinced that ideas and learning are to be judged by their fruits in subsequent living. They are for liberal education in the sense of freeing its products for effective action on the contemporary social scene and making them good parents, good citizens, and happy men and women. Implicitly they question whether more than a tiny minority are fitted for the life of pure scholarship, and in any case they consider theory to be valuable only as it relates to practice.

This distinction between practical and theoretical wisdom goes to the heart, I believe, of many conflicting theories of education and competing schools of educational philosophy. It separates those who are accustomed to thinking about the purposes of education and confuses them in their attempts to select models of the best in contemporary life. Accordingly, this distinction is much more fruitful for reflection than are most other conflicts in the theory of education.

It is obvious that both practical and theoretical wisdom can exist in varying degrees in any person and that to attain either in significant amounts is the task of a lifetime and can only be started in the schools. It is nearly as obvious, I think, that there is no necessary exclusiveness between the two kinds; no law of nature prevents a seeker after truth from being an effective citizen and leader in public life. Nevertheless, the limitations of most of us predetermine the directions our lives are to take, whether predominantly the life of pure theory or the practical life. In the former case formal education is surely more important. The pursuit of theoretical wisdom for those called to it is most easily launched in the schools. For the brilliant child who is exposed to a few teachers devoted to learning for its own sake can become infected first with the love of knowledge and then, as he matures, can make the leap to wisdom, that state of independence of judgment and desire where life is importantly governed by a disinterested love of truth.

Such individuals, always a tiny minority in any society, can become the scientists, artists, philosophers, creators in every field who discover new knowledge, establish new ideals more relevant to present times, and increase the grasp of mankind on the significance of its career in time on this planet. Though they may be deemed impractical, even foolish, in the ways of the world, and be, in fact, indifferent husbands, wives, or citizens, they are supreme in reaching wider principles and creating new syntheses. Many of these creative ones do not find it easy to renounce worldly success, the fame and fortune that their high talents appear to justify. Though they may discover a higher happiness in devoting themselves to ideal goals, they may feel bitter about the studied neglect by the majority of their contemporaries and about the indifference of their governments.

In our generation, the traditional attitude toward theoretical wisdom appears to be changing. America has not yet produced her share of such theoreticians, partly because of material needs of a new civilization, partly because of the pragmatic bent of our educational establishment. Now we are increasingly aware of the place of pure theory, particularly in the sciences, if only because of its practical relevance. Our motives for this change may be suspect. We are mortally afraid of being bested by our Communist adversaries, and the transformation of our educational emphasis in the direction of theory owes much to this political interest in triumphing over other peoples. Yet in our dawning recognition of the fact that one superb theoretician is much more valuable, even for our survival, than a dozen average ones, we may well be raising up a kind of person who can see beyond the immediate political struggle and can establish respect in the layman for the theoretical life.

Such a development is a highly desirable one for many reasons. Our culture still lacks dimensions of depth and richness needed to attract and hold the allegiance of potential allies of the democratic way. We alienate many who want to be our friends simply because Americans appear to be all surface, without depth. Our own best minds continue to draw most of their nourishment from Europe in science, art, and philosophy because of our comparative poverty in these fields. Moreover, we now possess the requisite leisure, thanks to our conquests in technology and economics, to support a rich and varied life of vision for those who are called to it, an advantage that perhaps no society has ever had before us. Without great strain our American society could free a good many of its most creative, theoretical minds to pursue their deepest interests without holding them responsible for practical results.

An even more important result of the growing respect for theoretical wisdom in American life may well be a clarification of the differences between specialization and such wisdom. Everyone recognizes that specialization is a necessary and inevitable effect of the complexity of contemporary civilization. Yet the *specialist*, in the narrow sense, is far removed from the creative theoretician. The latter is on the frontiers of learning; the former is lost in the labyrinths of his discipline. The creative artist, scientist, or philosopher will assuredly be specialized in his discipline, but his specialization will be, from the beginning, a means and not a goal; his learning will be an impetus and not an end.

At present, there is much popular confusion about the difference between specialization and wisdom. Many practitioners of art and science are themselves confused about what they are trying to do. Are they in search of knowledge or wisdom? How are the two related and how are they different? It is clear that we require more reflection in this age of the floodtide of knowledge to clarify these relations anew.

Even when theoretical wisdom is attained and distinguished from its semblances, an important problem remains. For these creative theoreticians require practical wisdom, too, more so in our time than ever before. Aristotle, who first made clear this distinction between the theoretical and the practical, hesitated before deciding that the theoretical life was the higher and more desirable for man to live. Unlike his teacher Plato, he refused to make such thinkers responsible for the political fortunes of society. They were self-sufficient and could well choose to be *in* but not *of* their society. Whereas Plato's best men, after years of study and trial, were required to devote their maturity to the conduct of public life, and only later allowed to pursue their first love in private vision, Aristotle's theoreticians were under no such restraint. Aristotle's ideal, and not Plato's, has triumphed in the centuries since, for the most brilliant thinkers have remained aloof from the practical and political affairs of the nations.

The danger in such a separation is patent in our times, since so much of the theoretical at present lies in the natural sciences. Our creative scientists are discovering, often with agonized consciences, that their most pure and apparently remote theories are capable of practical and destructive application by technology. Unless they assume some responsibility for the application of theory, the theoretical life may become its own destroyer. Hence the age-old cleavage between practical and theoretical wisdom has narrowed dangerously, perhaps disastrously, in recent decades as pure and applied knowledge have become interrelated as never before in history. In consequence, we need to combine in education the practical and the theoretical. Perhaps it is not important or possible to make the man of theory into a good householder or family man, really interested or able to deal with the more mundane issues of community life. But unless we insist in education on making him concerned with larger political problems and able to be effective in dealing with governments, we will forfeit his great contributions to the human career.

For the great majority of us, practical wisdom will continue to be the overriding goal of education, since only the few have sufficient ability and resolution to contribute significantly to new theory. The educated man as one who can make the advance from information to knowledge and then apply that knowledge to create for himself a meaningful career as a private person and also as an effective citizen of the communities of which he is a member—this will continue to be the practical purpose which motivates the vast majority of us. Education is not information and not knowledge; these are only means to effective, productive lives that satisfy intrinsically and carry significance beyond themselves. Nevertheless, the majority must somehow learn to tolerate and even cherish the theoretically wise who aim at different goals. These, in turn, must undertake the harder task of learning that their fate is integrally bound up with that of their more practical fellows, to whom they owe time, and effort, and understanding. The life of theory and the life of action are in our day mutually responsible for each other, however inconvenient such responsibility may be to both. We can now venture to answer the question with which we began. The educated man is one who is either practically or theoretically wise. If such a one is not to descend the ladder, he must keep constantly educating and re-educating himself. Education is a search and not a state of being. And though wisdom is inevitably dual in nature, as we have seen, a new necessity is upon us. Though we cannot unite the two kinds of wisdom, they must learn to support and to supplement each other.

Eliot's lines about knowledge and information and wisdom are preceded by a still larger question: "Where is the life that we have lost in living?" Perhaps an answer to this query can only be found if we look deeper into the problem of how in actual practice we make the advance from information through knowledge to wisdom.

It is one thing to say who the educated man is and quite another to lead an educated life oneself or help another along the path. There seems to be what Existentialists like to call a "leap" from the definition of wisdom to the practice of it. There is, I am convinced, a leap of this kind from information to knowledge and an even greater leap from knowledge to wisdom. Knowing does not imply doing; nor does the promise of education imply its practice. The reason appears to be that each stage of the educational process involves more and more of the individual's total being. A response of the whole person to the world about him is rare and difficult and demanding.

John Dewey once defined education as "a process of forming fundamental dispositions, intellectual and emotional, toward nature and fellow men." This is quite clearly a definition of education that aims at practical wisdom. Like Plato, Dewey developed his philosophical outlook around the idea of educating

youth, and this definition, as he recognized, is equally an expression of the aims of philosophy. Both education and philosophy
imply a relating of individual life to its larger social and natural
context that is far-reaching in effect and radically practical. Philosophy, as everyone knows, literally means the love of wisdom
and if one puts the emphasis on *love*, he is immediately confronted
with the essential incentive of education as contrasted with its goal.

We need to reflect on Dewey's definition. What is a disposition? The dictionary informs us that it is "a predominating bent
or constitutional habit of one's mind, as a cheerful disposition."
Education, according to Dewey, has the task of forming these
constitutional habits or predominating bents, which are both intellectual and emotional. Until and unless the process of education reaches this level of the human being, it has little real chance
of affecting fundamentally the way he conducts his life.

How little of what we experience in school and out really
changes our lives, either in the inner or outer sense! All of us
have known people with advanced degrees and in positions that
require genuine understanding who in all their personal relationships are nearly indistinguishable from the uneducated. Their
conversation is largely chatter or gossip, their inner lives petty
and narrow, their aims hedonistic and self-centered. And if we
are unsure about the true selves of our associates in this respect,
we can always find in ourselves evidence of the failure of education. Learning has simply failed to reach that disposition which
represents the fusion of our thinking and feeling selves. It has
made no real difference. Often we are tempted to despair over
ourselves and others. Can any experience change us? Are we not
simply given our dispositions by the accident of genetics? How
can the process of education hope to change fundamentally the
basic nature that each of us discovers in himself when he comes
to the age of self-awareness?

The full import of these questions is seldom faced squarely,
even by those of us whose lives are passed in the teaching vocation.
Perhaps we fear to face them, since no one wants to live without
hope. Nevertheless, clearheaded honesty would help to allay this

despair and is, in any case, necessary in order to examine the failures of education as well as its successes. For it is simply true that most of our learning, both formal and informal, fails to reach our dispositions and to effect any permanent change in us. And it is equally true that some education does effect such a change in some of us.

Most of us remember, when we reflect on the course of our careers, experiences that helped to mold our dispositions and altered significantly our relations to others, to the things of nature, and to the instruments and institutions of culture. Once we recognize that it is easier to fail than to succeed—that failure is tenfold more likely than success—we are in a position to measure fairly the real task.

Most of the findings of modern psychology support the belief that the younger we are, the more profound these changes in disposition are likely to be. More of them should occur, therefore, in school than in adult life. But the ignorance and indifference of those who teach make it inevitable that genuine education is frequently postponed till later life. Many older people, when questioned, will recall one teacher who changed the course of their lives decisively, one out of the myriad who instructed them, and our literature is filled with testimonials to the *few* great teachers of the past. But more of us, I suspect, have required a later love affair, a personal tragedy such as the death of our dearest friend, the triumphs and disasters of a more personal experience than school usually offers, to make us what we are. And many perhaps have seldom or never been reached in their deepest self, which remains a confused amalgam of nature and the nurture of their immediate social environment. The difficulty of achieving that practical wisdom, which is the aim of most conscious educational efforts, is rarely overcome early enough and often enough to reduce the role of chance in forming our fundamental dispositions.

Dewey's definition stipulates that our dispositions must be directed toward nature and our fellow man. What does this mean? Quite simply, it means that all of us are formed by the relations we sustain to our social and natural surroundings. As individuals, we are in situations formed by our physical and temporal location and by the degree of awareness that each of us has reached. My situation is not yours as yours is not mine, even though we may be approximately in the same location in space and contemporaneous in time. For our situations are formed by our inner selves as well as by the external world and the kind of disposition we possess shapes the character of the external world.

A large part of what we call our own being is not contained within our skins but is in our relations to the beings around us. Starting with our fellow human beings, each of us is formed by relations that are radically unique. As children, we are related to the members of our immediate family, first of all; it takes the infant a number of years to distinguish his self clearly from that of his parents. Soon he becomes aware of a larger circle of friends and acquaintances, as well as an indeterminate number of people who pass on the street or on the television screen with whom he never comes into an effective, two-way relationship at all, however close he may feel to some of them in imagination. The situation is hardly different as he grows into adulthood, except that he gradually loses the close relations with his family and gains others with friends and acquaintances, perhaps establishing a family of his own.

All of us are alike, however, in possessing a unique constellation of relationships to other human beings. Some of them move in the inner circle of our immediate situation; we can hardly imagine what kind of being we would be without family and close friends. Others are at one remove—business associates, colleagues, team or club members, casual neighbors—and form a kind of second circle of relationships through the chance of proximity. There is also a large circle of people whom we do not know at all, people we jostle in the subway, pass in our automobiles, read about in newspapers, see on television, ask directions of on a vacation trip, and so on.

These thousands of individuals with whom we come in contact in the course of years are, of course, constantly changing us as they themselves change. Our situation is never static. Some move from the center to the periphery of consciousness, while others who were on the horizon of our awareness become close friends, perhaps even our husbands or wives. A close friend in high school or college may perhaps drop out of sight permanently and be all but forgotten, though his or her influence may continue to affect us. The series of relationships we possess to the human world will change from childhood to youth to adulthood and to old age, but this series forms our situation in some measure and affects our fundamental dispositions—makes us what we are.

Our situation does not consist merely of this varying company of creatures like ourselves; it is also constituted of possessions, of things, implements, and tools that are here for our use and enjoyment, the creations of the arts and sciences, using both terms in the widest sense. We are surrounded from birth with the implements of civilization and must learn to relate ourselves to an almost infinite number of them. Their range is very wide, extending from the merely practical objects of the nursery to the ideal products of the fine arts, from the clothes we wear and the rooms we inhabit to the symphonies we hear and the most abstract books of science we study. None of us can escape being related in the most complex ways to these objects and things of our human environment, either as users, producers, or observers; and they form our fundamental dispositions more than we realize.

Beyond this human and man-made world, there is a much more extended realm which we call *nature*, not made by us and from which are drawn, directly or indirectly, the things our sciences and arts construct. This world of nature is both closer to and farther from us than are the products of our civilization. It is farther from us because it forms a variable horizon in a society as man-made as ours, so that millions in large cities may be hardly aware of the natural world at all. It is farther, too, because it extends beyond the creations of man, contains them as well as supplies them, and is much more. But it is closer because our bodies are natural and our minds, too, and we are always related to our bodies in a fundamental way, no matter how far our minds may carry us from the "merely" natural. The beginning and ending of our individual lives are also an effect of nature and serve to recall to us this fundamental situation of man, however likely we are to forget it in the labyrinth of the human and man-constructed world we now inhabit.

Each of us sustains a unique relationship and complex of relationships to these inescapable realms of the human and the natural; they are part of our dispositions, our situations, indeed our very being.

Because we are creatures of memory and imagination, part of our being is also the past and the future. We are never wholly in the present, except as infants, perhaps, for it belongs to our nature to be constantly transcending. We can live in memory in the past, our own past or the past of others through historical memory. We can imagine ourselves to be others, not merely as in a waking dream, but in a more substantial sense as well. A scholar, for example, through an extended study of a past era can become more intimate with it than with the present and gradually inhabit the world where his interests and affections lie. We also project ourselves into the future. Most of us have gone through periods when what had not yet occurred became more real to the inner life than what was immediately at hand. The "not yet" is as truly a part of our beings as the "no longer"! Our "nows" consist, indeed, of these and little else.

I find Dewey's profound conception of education ultimately inadequate because he does not sufficiently specify the *kind* of fundamental disposition toward nature and our fellow men that genuine education implies. In my opinion, the educated disposition is one that is forever in search of relations of closeness and intimacy toward its world. If our being is intrinsically part of this larger world, as I think it is, then fulfillment depends on the degree to which we achieve dispositions of care and concern for this world. The educated man, as I have come to understand him, is one who has fully grasped the simple fact that his self is fully implicated in those beings around him, human and non-human, and who has learned to care deeply about them. In contrast, the relatively uneducated man has not understood the self as a relationship and consequently is unconcerned and unrelated to what is part of his potential being. To be sure, the state of being educated is a matter of degree only, for education is an endless search and a process. Only to the degree that we become educated, do we gain relationships of depth and intimacy to the encompassing world.

Experience teaches us that this is no simple unfolding of our natural powers. We are alternately reconciled to and alienated from our nearest of kin, from friends and neighbors, from our various communities and nations. Likewise, we are able at times to feel a sense of intimacy with the instruments and objects of our cultural environment; at other times they are foreign and simply there for us, with no emotional investment at all. It is the same with the larger natural world. Who of us has not at moments believed himself protected and cherished, gay and irresponsible, in this world we did not make but to which we feel profoundly akin? But sickness and indispositions of a thousand sorts can quickly estrange us, to the point where the spirit in us seems lost in our own skin and nature a hostile stranger.

Education does not eliminate these moods of reconciliation and estrangement. These poles between which human life is tossed are inseparable from the human condition. Education seeks rather to use them as a means for fuller self-understanding. Hence, education is something we suffer from before we can profit. Indeed, suffering in many of its forms seems indispensable to the educated person, however unwanted and ultimately undesirable it may be. The educated man must first be estranged before he can know reconciliation; he must be driven into the confines of his own skin, before he can experience that aspect of his being which is a part of the larger world. Or to put it another way, we must first experience the contrast of inner and outer being as a painful reality before any reconciliation is effected. And this does not happen once for all. Most of us never finally heal over this breach. To become fully at home in our world is an unrealizable and vain ideal, dreamed of by certain idealists. But to renew the

struggle to achieve involvement and intimacy with this larger
natural and human environment is surely the fuller meaning of
the educational adventure.

Such a search for relationships with the fuller aspects of the
self and world is pursued in many ways, within and outside the
schools. Understanding is the one way to which the schools, at
their best, are devoted. Understanding is furthered through
knowing in the manner of the sciences, through esthetic enjoyment and communion, through participation in the progress of
inquiry, through reflection on these things, and doubtless in other
ways. Falling in love, in the many senses of that ambiguous
word, is another way of reconciliation. It furthers our education
in ways that nothing else can, provided that it does not become
fixed and exclusive in regard to the objects and persons involved.
Gaining perspective is still another; for, though a seeming paradox, it is nevertheless true that we can be really close to someone
or something only when we learn to see it or him at one remove,
critically and objectively. We learn to care for the world in
which we are totally involved, not when we are unthinkingly at
one with it in the fashion of animals, but after we have become
reconciled to it as individuals capable of standing apart from it.
The child loves his parents unreflectively as he loves himself, the
adolescent may love them in rebellion without knowing it himself. But the adult can gain a conscious affection for them only
when he recognizes their weaknesses and his own as part and
parcel of our common humanity.

It is difficult to go further in this general discussion without
becoming involved in the purposes of education, which are the
subject of the following chapters. But perhaps I should say a
word about the supposed difficulties of achieving education in
our contemporary world. Is it true that to become educated is
really more difficult in one age than in another? It would seem so.
Perhaps it is the myopia of our day that we think other generations have never had such problems in education. On the other
hand, it is surely true that the extreme complexity of our technological society makes the effort of relationship particularly

perplexing. Young people today are tempted into an unthinking conformity more readily than were their parents and grandparents. And at the other extreme, the temptation to withdraw into oneself and to lead a private existence is correspondingly great. These extremes, like many others, have a tendency to approach each other.

But if the difficulties are increased for our generation, it is also true that the means for genuine education, such as leisure, the availability of materials, the floodtide of new knowledge, and the models of education, have never been so abundant. Once we recognize that practical wisdom has always required an almost titanic effort to achieve, we will hardly believe that our own age has an overbalance of handicaps. Other epochs may well have felt more truly in charge of their problems. Ours seem to have gotten out of hand. But none has been so rich in resources for the development of practical wisdom; none has given the individual a greater margin of time or a greater store of resources for the forming of his disposition.

At all events ours is the only age we have. And it is the task of a philosophy of education to discover those principles which will help to reconcile the individual and his world.

Part II

THE PURPOSES OF EDUCATION

The existing practice is perplexing; no one knows on what principle we should proceed—should the useful in life, or should virtue, or should higher knowledge, be the aim of our training; all three opinions have been entertained.

—Aristotle

2. THE INDIVIDUAL OR THE GROUP?

FOR WHOM is education, the individual or society? Stated less abstractly, should young Americans be educated for their own sake or for the sake of their contributions to larger entities, such as the family, the local community, the church, the nation, or international organizations? Is an individual or a group the basic unit of society? What is the proper emphasis: on educating men or on educating citizens? Ought we to concentrate in schooling and in education on developing those capacities which we possess in common with others or on those which are distinctive and unique?

Such questions are deceptively simple. Most of us would answer by rejecting the disjunction. Does not everyone today realize that formal education at least is a social enterprise, to be supported financially by common taxes and by state and national governments? Then it follows surely that schools should try to develop those potentialities our youth have in common; they ought to be educated for effective public service. And since our country was founded on the doctrine of inalienable individual rights, both schooling and education must also be directed toward providing the young American with a rich private life, with skills and knowledge for realizing himself economically, socially, and culturally. Though his private interests and the public good may at times conflict, education should help him determine the proper priorities between self-seeking and the common good. Is this not, after all, the meaning of our democratic American faith?

Practically, we Americans dislike dualisms. We are reluctant to believe that there can be any lasting opposition between private and public, between individuals and groups.

During his term as president, Eisenhower, worried about

where our nation was headed, asked a group of our national leaders to study and prepare a statement of our goals as a nation, they began their report in confident tones as follows:

> The paramount goal of the United States was set long ago. It is to guard the rights of the individual, to ensure his development, and to enlarge his opportunity. It is set forth in the Declaration of Independence drafted by Thomas Jefferson and adopted by the Continental Congress on July 4, 1776. The goals we here identify are within the framework of the original plan and are calculated to bring to fruition the dreams of the men who laid the foundation of this country. (*Goals For Americans*, p. 1.)

Few of these leaders—and perhaps few of you who read these lines—recognize any inconsistency between the Declaration, the rationale of revolution, and the Preamble to the Constitution, the basis of political community:

> We, the people of the United States, in order to form a more perfect union, establish justice, insure domestic tranquillity, provide for the common defense, promote the general welfare, and secure the blessings of liberty to ourselves and our posterity do ordain and establish this Constitution for the United States of America.

Yet to a philosophic mind the purposes outlined in this Preamble sound quite different from the ringing words of the Declaration. To be sure, most Americans would say that these documents simply emphasize different aspects of our national existence. But are we really aware of how much of our short history revolves around the conflict of these private and public spheres? Have we ever really decided which functions belong to the private and which to the public?

It is certainly true that conservatives and liberals alike insist on the primacy of individual welfare as the foundation of American theory. But in practice conflict persists concerning the values of individualism and "socialism" concerning the priority of community or individuality. Though we act as dualists, we refuse to believe that duality cannot be overcome through persuasion and enlightenment. And we look to education with a faith nearly sublime to reconcile any discordance between personal fulfillment and general welfare.

If we have managed as a nation to live successfully with this unresolved issue to the present, there is no assurance that we can continue to do so indefinitely. For there is no doubt that the present age has brought new difficulties, practical and theoretical, to the bridging of the chasm between individual and community. Those of us who teach are increasingly troubled, if we are sensitive at all, by how self-evident the pursuit of private goals has become for myriads of our youth. In a day when public issues have become ambiguous in import and massively complex, the young person does not find it easy to become absorbed in them. Overwhelmed by the weight of numbers in the schools, a boy or girl awakening to self-awareness and the world finds it difficult to believe that what he or she believes or does can matter very much. Impersonality, bigness, standardization, mobility of population, shifting moral standards—these and other manifestations of our age make closeness to nature and to one's fellow men more difficult than ever before.

It is not at all surprising that the gap between individual and community should widen in a period like ours. Self-seeking has always held a primary appeal for most persons. History teaches that it becomes nearly the only appeal when social and political complexities become too great. When a vision of the future is dimmed, we concentrate on life in the present; when we find no hold on the world about us, we turn to ourselves. It is ironic, nevertheless, that in a period when our youth are more generously supported by public funds than ever before in seeking a formal education, sometimes supported nearly to the doctorate, they should feel so little responsibility for public life. Those who owe their society much should be correspondingly grateful, we feel, and eager to serve it. But in eras of confusion formal education seldom reaches the level of disposition sufficient to alter the direction of individual lives.

Can this chasm between private and public be bridged by a

systematic effort to indoctrinate young people? Communist educational theory in our century represents a conscious and continuing effort to do so. Soviet educators reject the proposition
that the individual is the essential unit of society and seek to
create what they like to call a new type of man. This new man of
Soviet theory will unhesitatingly put in first place, not his own,
but the interests of the group to which he belongs. Starting very
early in a child's life, Soviet teachers try to make the child responsible for his whole class in school, at least the row or portion
of the class to which he is assigned. Making full use of the principle of competition—Socialist competition—such teachers attempt to mold the child's character in ways that will make group
loyalty a primary motivation. They aim to make him feel as
proud and responsible for what his unit accomplishes vis-à-vis a
competing unit as for his own accomplishment. He is systematically encouraged to evaluate his group's progress and to report
failures in discipline as zealously as he confesses his own.

The details of this training in character of Soviet schools have
been often described and need not be repeated. Communist
theorists do not, of course, stop with the schools. They make
every effort to persuade parents that whatever authority they
temporarily have over their children is derived from society as a
whole. While attempting to wean the child from self-seeking to
group loyalty, they work to persuade the adolescent to pass beyond allegiance to secondary groups, such as family, school, or
vocational class, and to instill in him devotion to the ideals of
Communism itself.

It is too early to measure their success in this effort to build a
collectivist society. Their failure to overcome the selfishness of
individuals, on the one hand, and what we Americans consider
legitimate needs for a private life, on the other, is reported in the
press and in treatises on Communist culture. Soviet youngsters,
one hears, are pathetically susceptible to Western individualistic
patterns, fads, and fashions, even after years of indoctrination.
Yet impressive Soviet advances in nearly every field have been
sufficient to cause a revolution in our own educational practice.

Their experiment in seeking to re-direct human energies away from the private and personal is not exactly new in history. Western civilization has seen many such efforts, usually under the impetus of religious faith. Still, it has never been attempted on such a scale and with the means that modern technology has placed at their command. Every serious student of educational theory should feel impelled to watch with deep interest these attempts to remold human motives—with deep interest and with as much objectivity as he can muster.

Barring catastrophe, however, we Americans are not likely to follow the Soviet model. What we need is a philosophic analysis of the nature of individuality, one that is simple enough to be useful for educational theory and subtle enough to account for the new difficulties of achieving individuality in our time. We ought to ask ourselves afresh what it means to be an individual, how individuality is achieved, and how an individual properly relates himself to his various communities. In the pages that follow I will make this attempt.

First, I want to consider the common perversions of individuality. For the question of individuality is not one of isms but of ideals. There is a perverse individualism which justifies the egoistic impulses within us and attempts to base a creed on self-seeking and freedom from social regulation. There is likewise a perverse collectivism that subordinates individual uniqueness and creative energy to group goals in the interest of power or mindless harmony or herd pleasures. Both extremes hinder the growth of individuality. They are isms or ideologies in the sense that they are one-sided and abstract attempts to define the individual without reference to his context. Individualism ignores the role of the community in forming individuality; collectivism ignores the uniqueness of the individuals who compose groups. Both appeal in an age like ours because they appear to offer an escape from the pain of growth. They are shortcuts to salvation. Individuality and community, by contrast, are infinitely more difficult because they must be willed as well as constantly constructed and reconstructed throughout the course of life.

An illustration will clarify the distinction between individualism and individuality. Since the process of making oneself an individual is roughly analogous to making a work of art, I shall cite an opinion of the film-maker Ingmar Bergman. In a recent book he has expressed his disillusionment with individualism. Art, he asserts,

> lost its basic creative drive the moment it was separated from worship. Today the individual has become the highest form, and the greatest bane, of artistic creation. The smallest wound or pain of the ego is examined under a microscope as if it were of eternal importance. The artist considers his subjectivity, his individualism almost holy. Thus we finally gather in one large pen, where we stand and bleat about our loneliness without listening to each other and without realizing that we are smothering each other to death. The individualists stare into each other's eyes and yet deny each other's existence. We walk in circles, so limited by our own anxieties that we can no longer distinguish between true and false, between the gangster's whim and the purest ideal.

Then he contrasts this contemporary individualism, not with a political or economic collectivism, but with the religious community of the medieval artist.

> In former days the artist remained unknown and his work was to the glory of God. He lived and died without being more or less important than other artisans; "eternal values," "immortality" and "masterpiece" were terms not applicable in his case. The ability to create was a gift. In such a world flourished invulnerable assurance and natural humility.

I am not concerned with the validity of Bergman's charges against contemporary artists nor with his Romantic overestimation of medieval communalists. In the context of education, however, his assertions serve to define the goal of genuine individuality. We cannot return to medieval times nor would we want to, though all of us could use in our frightening age a little more of the alleged invulnerable assurance and natural humility of earlier individuals! Forming individuals, rather than individualists, within the confines of a community, rather than a collectivity, is, I believe, the comprehensive goal of contemporary American education. To repeat, it is a question of ideals and not of isms.

Let me begin by asking a simple question. What does the community contribute toward the development of our individuality? Then the reverse question will be in order. What does the developed individual bring to the community? By *the* community, I hasten to add, I do not understand some abstract unity such as society but rather a very concrete plurality, ranging from a family, a neighborhood gang, a sports club, a church group, and a school class to more strictly adult associations such as professional societies, military units, political parties, and the like. To avoid abstractions, one ought to think of the individual as himself or as some one he knows whose individuality is clearly differentiated. All of you who read these lines have been at various times involved in communities of one kind or another and presumably have reflected on what distinguishes you from any or all of them. In the course of a lifetime, all of us belong to a variety of communities, some very transient, others durable, some intimate, others more casual, some local and small, others national and even international in scope. They may possess all kinds of purposes or none at all save the impulse to gregariousness. Together with the relations we sustain to the world of nature, its creatures and things, and with the man-made world of houses and cars and clothes, etc., they make us what we are, above all in that aspect of our selves we call character.

Most obviously perhaps, these various communities give to each of us a sense of belonging. When a youngster can refer to *my* gang, *my* family, *my* football team, *my* school, and *my* teacher, he is acknowledging his place in the scheme of things. These groups give him a name and a function; they help him define himself and to make a start on the long journey of finding his place and role in the world. He learns only slowly to detach persons from their situation and location among things and creatures. In that, he is a better philosopher than adults, because a large part of our being lies in our surroundings, as I have indicated. His sense of identity grows as his attachment to places and persons develops, paradoxical as this may sound.

If we adults observed children more carefully and imaginatively and then had the wit to reflect on what we see, we would learn a great deal about the interrelationship of self and world. The fierce attachment of a boy for an old sweater, a football, or a machine, the fondness of a girl for dolls or stuffed animals with which she adorns her bed—without which some children find it almost impossible to sleep at night—are very revealing. The ease with which youngsters establish an intimate relationship with dogs, cats, horses, or almost any other animals indicates how elemental is our human need for attachment and how necessary in the development of individuality. Most of us quickly lose, as we grow up, a sense of closeness to such pets; and, worse, we forget what they once meant to us in the barely conscious struggle to feel at home on this uncanny sphere we call earth. Before we became conscious members of purposeful groups of human beings, we had to be unconscious members of far more intimate communities of objects and creatures, tied to us by immediate proximity in space and time.

These relationships are for children not at all utilitarian, and this simple fact makes them difficult for adults to understand. The notion of practicality and usefulness is a learned notion, one that is gradually acquired and fatefully acquired in the passage to grown-up status. It is fateful and unfortunate because it involves an abstraction, since the use of anything is only one aspect of its whole nature. It would never occur to a child to ask what use his cat or dog is; only adults learn to consider such creatures so abstractly. I have sometimes asked my daughter why she spends so much time carefully arranging a large collection of stuffed pets on her bed every morning and removing them at bedtime in a pattern so complicated that others could not reproduce it. The question puzzles her, and I have finally concluded that it is a silly question.

What happens to this sense of belonging nowadays when our

society has become so highly mobile that our youngsters must change homes and playmates, schools, landscapes, and even countries, so frequently? The only answer is that it suffers a severe setback and makes the climate of community more difficult. One of the reasons why Americans are, as I believe, on the whole less individualized than some other peoples is our mobility, our lack of rootedness, and our loss of family tradition. We parents, I know, like to exclaim at how quickly our children become acclimated to a new environment, how easily they find new playmates and seemingly forget old surroundings, the lost pet, and the favorite game. And it is true that their pliable natures do help them to adjust quickly to the new. But we forget how absolutely necessary this adjustment is to them, nearly as necessary as food and drink. Unless a youth can find a minimal feeling of belonging in a new environment, he will be unable to sustain emotional health, not to speak of growth toward individuality. For children have not developed adult capacities for postponing immediate satisfactions in the interest of future gains.

A youngster can be as dreadfully alone in crowds as can an adult and twice as disconsolate. He requires not the mere gregariousness that appears to suffice for animals, but things and people he can be familiar with, dependable features of the environment to which he can hold as once he clung to his mother's skirts. Twice my wife and I have taken our own children into a foreign country while they were growing up. During the crucial few weeks when they were adapting to a strange language and strange children's ways, they were bewildered. Without each other and their parents, our familiar words and presence, they could not have eaten, slept, or faced the streets and schools of a foreign land.

We adults might better understand this primal need for belonging if we reflected more on how dependent we ourselves are on little-noticed features of our daily situation. What makes us "like" or "dislike" a new job or school or residential community? Is it not a sum of little things, most of which are barely conscious of? Sometimes a smile from a casual acquaintance can change the quality of a morning. Or the way people nod or fail to greet each other on the street or subway can determine our impressions of a city new to us. A week of sunny weather can alter our disposition from vague hostility to an eagerness to explore a new environment once more. Or it may be a hundred other little events or chance occurrences. That indefinable sense of well-being depends on our closeness to our immediate milieu, and even the most self-aware of us can know only a fraction of the constituents.

Of course, there are exceptions. A rare person now and then can free himself from such dependence on others and the environment to a remarkable degree and at least approach self-sufficiency. It may be that in the distant future a different type of man will develop whose psyche will not be so sense-bound and situation-bound as ours. But until then the sense of belonging will remain for us a spiritual necessity if we are to become individuals as maturing adolescents or maintain individuality as adults.

It is evident that this sense of community can give to each of us an access of power, a feeling of importance and worth. That ten men can lift more than the sum of what each of the ten can lift singly is known to everyone; or that an athletic team which functions as a unit can triumph over an opponent whose team is composed of individual stars who are not united is equally a commonplace. Yet facts like these teach us that an organic group can raise the individual out of his impotence and make it possible for him to accomplish things of which he never dreamed himself capable. If we need assurance that part of our being consists in *being with* our fellows, this sort of experience ought to convince us. Our essential selves lie not simply within the separate confines of our skins, but in that larger self we call our family, gang, club, or community.

Today more than in earlier epochs, that individual who is cut off from effective participation in this larger self is overwhelmed by the realization of his powerlessness. As our population increases with catastrophic rapidity and organizations grow more complex as a necessary consequence, the isolated person can hardly escape noticing that he counts for next to nothing. In previous times, things were radically different, of course. But even Aristotle, more than two millennia ago, observed that the individual, however gifted and industrious, could achieve and know little when working alone, whereas in cooperation with others the sum of his knowledge and accomplishments could be impressive. If this was true in that almost infinitely simpler society, how much truer it is today!

In contrast, it is plain that the weakness of the isolated person is opposed by the enormous power of the cooperative individual. All the technological forces of our incredible age stand like an army of willing slaves at the beck of the man who is in charge of a smoothly functioning group. Intoxicating power, undreamed of in other times, is at the fingertips of many individuals today; others who may be potentially as able have probably never felt so helpless. The difference surely lies in union with or separation from others, in the capacity to belong fully to a group.

We should not forget that this access of power which derives from belongingness is not necessarily beneficent. Group egotism is no more tolerable than individual egotism and much more dangerous. The tightly knit family group often looks upon the larger community as a field for exploitation, and members of that family will commit deeds for the family they would not consider doing for themselves alone. Colleges can be utterly ruthless in defending their reputations at the expense of individuals or other colleges. All of us are conscious of the feelings of snobbery we possess in belonging to the "right" school, the "right" social class, country, or ethnic group. Few who are white, Anglo-Saxon, Protestants (called WASPS nowadays) can escape the secret pride in their majority status, nor can most Americans forget that (by an accident of birth) they are members of the most powerful country in the world. In asserting that a sense of power and importance is a quality that the group contributes to the growth of individuality, we should not foolishly believe that this is always or necessarily something desirable.

Apart from this moral neutrality of power, which I will deal with later, there is no question that belonging to a group is also the fount of all durable morale in the individual. The "we con-

sciousness" lifts us out of our primal helplessness in the face of
the enormous forces of nature; by its means we are able to forget
at times the brevity of our individual lives and to believe that the
tiny radius of time and place within which we pass our day is
incalculably expanded. For those who have been thoughtful
members of military units in time of battle, the experience of
morale has been felt in its most unmistakable form. The cheerfulness, the *élan*, the surge of power that comes to the well-trained
member of an elite unit when it overcomes the enemy are like
little else in his whole experience.

Community implies communication; and of all the benefits
which the group confers on the individual, the impetus and opportunity to communicate is probably the greatest. For individuality, as opposed to mere eccentricity, means that I am able to
say who I am and what I am about. It enables us to explain
ourselves, surely a primary need for human creatures. Where we
cannot get into communication with our kind, we cannot grow.
Without the opportunity to explain ourselves, we are driven into
aimless gregariousness, into blind conformity, or into withdrawal.
All of us have had the experience of not knowing what we believe until we have spoken it under the impulsion of a sympathetic listener. And since we are always becoming and are never
what we simply seem to be at any given moment, genuine conversation enables us to transcend our previous condition. Not
only is our horizon expanded by serious discussion, but also our
relations within familiar boundaries are subtly transformed.

We listen to others in a group to which we belong in order to
learn who they are. For real communication permits us to set the
limits of ourselves as truly as to transcend ourselves. The recognition that others think differently does not cut them off and make
us alien. Friends can become exhilarated by the revelation of
differentness. Relatedness to others does not involve sameness of
goals or similarity of thinking or outlook. Sympathy is discovered as much in the overtones and undertones of a discussion as in
what is actually said. A group of the completely like-minded can
lose all interest for one another.

To use a personal illustration, for several years I have been involved with a faculty group teaching an undergraduate seminar. We come from different disciplines and meet weekly over lunch to discuss the materials of our course, to change certain readings, and to discover new perspectives in books, many of which are classics of our culture. Our purpose is to keep the separate sections of our seminar, which is also composed of students from different fields of learning, lively, revealing, and suggestive for them. Gradually, our faculty group, composed of professors with very diverse beliefs, has become a real community, in which we are not afraid to display our learning or our ignorance, our doubts or our dogmas. We have learned to withstand hard challenges to the most cherished convictions. Our discussions are usually heated, and a frankness prevails that is not very common among proud professors. We differ sharply in our views about science, religion, literature, politics, and most other important subjects. Yet these sessions are high points in the week for most of us, even when we emerge shaken inwardly by a favorite opinion overthrown. For we are aware that long association in which we have communicated our deepest beliefs has changed us for the better. We can dispense with the artificial constraints of ordinary talk and investigate the unexplored shadows of our own and our fellows' philosophical faith.

There is a kind of mystery about communication that all our thinking and writing on the subject have not cleared away. Indeed, too much talk about it, one fears, is likely to impede its reality. Thoreau was near the truth of the matter when he once said: "We communicate like the burrows of foxes, in silence and darkness, underground." He and Emerson, close friends and very sensitive to one another's moods and dispositions, found themselves communicating in the mode of silence. Paradoxical as it sounds, silence does at times teach us much about our friends as well as ourselves, as anyone can testify who has sat in a Quaker worship service that was truly "gathered," as the Friends like to say.

It is a curious fact, on the other hand, that speech is frequently used to conceal one's feelings and the truth about our human situation. We are given to chatter, we human beings, superficially

resembling monkeys when we are nervous and unsure of ourselves. Much of our social life is spent in this masking of our real
selves, in the wearying search after an image acceptable to others.
One thinks inevitably of cocktail parties with their din, where
the alcohol frequently induces a false confessional that fortunately is not listened to or remembered. The dissatisfaction with
oneself and others after such attempts has been too often described in modern literature to be repeated here. It is enough to
recall the experience common to all of us of trying unsuccess-
fully to explain ourselves in words to strangers when a gesture or
a few words suffice for friends. It seems to be true that the need
for explanation is common, that being human involves being with
others in more than a gregarious sense. But the winning of a
relationship of community is far from guaranteed by the possession of language. The potentiality of our dispositions can be frus-
trated as easily as fulfilled.

Our youth suffer much from their formal education today, I
think, because of the impersonality that has overtaken us in a
crowded society. We have become increasingly dependent on
books for learning, and too much reading tends to make we who
are teachers incapable of easy and frank access to the minds of
others. Often we professors talk like books and are deformed by
our profession, so that students despair of penetrating our veneer.
This is surely one cause for the growing influence of peer groups.
Plato's insight into the priority of the spoken word in education
is surely truer today than ever before. He writes in the famous
Seventh Letter:

> There exists no writing of mine on this subject, nor ever shall.
> It is not capable of expression like the other sciences. It is only
> after long intercourse and a common life devoted to the sub-
> ject, that a light is suddenly kindled, as though by a leaping
> flame, and reaching the soul, it thereafter feeds itself.

Like other early educators Plato was rightly convinced that
there had to be a distinction between communication based on
friendship and intimate associates and that based on ordinary

teaching where teacher and taught are limited to what is actually spoken. But even the latter, Plato was convinced, is superior to the knowledge gained from books. The written word is dead, it cannot respond to questions. There is no easy dialogue with a book whereas reasoning is a dialectical process. And in the myth of Theuth (at the close of the *Phaedrus*) Plato questions the value of the invention of the alphabet, because it makes us forgetful of the fact that truth is a communal discovery and without dialogue the written word will serve to separate rather than unite men. It is, of course, futile to reject the education we obtain from books. Like many other aspects of civilization they are here to stay. Plato knew that also. But the point of his myth needs today to be pondered more than ever. We can only regain community in education if we learn that communication is near its essence. And communication is possible only where individuals are able to speak directly to one another, with enough intimacy to assure understanding beyond the logical sense.

Without such communication it seems impossible to grow. Even he who has become an individual cannot maintain individuality unless he has intimate converse with at least one of the circles in which he moves. The alternatives are simple and stark: withdrawal, a phenomenon all too common today; or conformity, which is even commoner. Both break off communication and end in the polar extremes of an irresponsible individualism or a featureless collectivism. Communication, on the other hand, liberates us from the fetters of our own narrow experience, while enabling us to reorganize that experience into larger meanings. It helps each of us to come to ourselves, in the old Biblical sense, by the unforced recognition that our ego is but a part of a larger whole from which it derives and to which it can contribute.

This suggests another contribution which the sense of community makes to individuality, namely, its readiness to sacrifice private goods to a larger cause. Alone, we always cling to what we have; we are possessed by getting and holding, by building up defenses against the external environment. As members of a group, however, we recognize almost unconsciously the need to give up our possessions and expend our powers in others' interests. At its best this spirit of sacrifice is known as generosity, surely one of the highest ethical qualities. It stems from the consciousness of overflowing powers whose expenditure does not imply loss in any absolute sense. We can work ourselves to the bone in a project to which we feel fully committed without feeling that we are owed anything in return. Sacrifice is best when it is not aware that anything is given up which we want to keep. Relationships of love and friendship call forth this impulse and form therefore the model of all communities. But, tragically, whole peoples are swept up in time of external war to voluntary sacrifice, even though their cause be unjust. Afterwards in the less emotional and clear-cut task of building peace, the same people have to be forced to sacrifice a modicum of their property in taxes.

Yet anyone who has observed reflectively this capacity in human beings to give themselves generously in pursuit of larger aims has learned something about the power and substance of the impulse to community. It can overcome at moments the very distinction between mine and thine in property holding. In a congenial family we approach this sense of community, which is the reason that so many social scientists cling in theory to family organization, despite all that can be said against it. They recognize it as the most likely condition for the development in embryo of the future individual from the child. Fulfillment for most of us comes as much in giving away as in getting, and without the careful nurture of generosity, the bestowing virtue as Nietzsche called it, happiness is difficult if not impossible. The isolated and lonely person may cultivate other qualities and sustain himself for a time, but unless he discovers a cause or a person on which he can lavish his substance, material and spiritual, he is nearly certain to die unhappy.

Nevertheless, sacrifice connotes deprivation and loss as well as generosity and it is unrealistic to neglect this pole of the relationship. Every human community to which we belong makes demands on us which run counter to our selfish impulses. For every group, from our family to the nation, finds itself threatened by conditions hostile to its cohesiveness and to hold it together requires exertion, patient labor, and conscious determination. None of us all the time and most of us rarely can be carried by feelings of enthusiasm and devotion to do our duty to the group. Hence, we learn soon or late the hardness and pain of group membership as well as its joys. We discover that what we do not willingly give will be demanded of us anyway and taken as a condition of our belonging. The freedom that such membership brings is not the freedom to do as we please, rather what the group pleases. Not self-preservation but group preservation becomes the over-riding consideration; and responsibility precedes privilege.

Yet precisely this unpleasant aspect of sacrifice can be its greatest benefit. For it puts steel in the soul and enables individuality to flower. Because membership in groups enlarges the individual's stake in existence, he finds it possible to put forth efforts in their preservation he would not be able to call upon as an isolated being. Many of us are kept going in difficult periods of our lives by the awareness that others depend on us and we do not want to let them down. Though such occasions are classically illustrated by perils of war, they are more common in everyday living. There is scarcely a mature adult who would not have given up the struggle of existence many times, had he not perceived that in so doing he would be betraying the interests of others less strong than himself. Sacrifice, therefore, accomplishes its function when it keeps us aware of our place and purpose in existence. It contributes in a curious way to the measure of happiness we experience and heightens that in morale which is more than mere intoxication.

These are some of the more important benefits that membership in groups can bring to the development of individuality. Without the experience of community it is as impossible to develop individuality, I am convinced, as it is impossible to quench our thirst by drinking sea water. Though individuality and community are always in tension and often in outright conflict, they are never polar opposites as individualism and collectivism constantly are. For individualism, as a theory, asserts that others are there as means and instruments for my private advantage and purposes. At most it recognizes their right to use me likewise for their own development, usually asserting that egoism is the only basic drive in human beings and concluding, illogically, that therefore it ought to be the standard for society. Collectivism, in opposition, asserts that the group is the ultimate reality and must accordingly be the starting point for all action and analysis. For collectivists a single person is an abstraction and not real at all, since he derives whatever force and distinctiveness he possesses from his membership in his collective. He is like an arm severed from the body or an isolated piece from a set of chess. Neither interpretation of human nature seems able to take account of the mutually supportive and interdependent relationships of individuality and community. Individualists will deny much of what I have said up to now. Collectivists will deny what remains to be discussed, viz., what the individual contributes to community.

It is difficult indeed to avoid the tendency to put undue importance on the individual or the group. In a sense all our Western history is an alternation from one to the other extreme. Waves of individualism have succeeded periods when institutions and collective theory were dominant. Though our short American history has been largely one of individualism, we too have experienced both. When I was a student at Columbia, John Dewey's ideas of education were still in the ascendant. It is, of couse, true that a deeper reading of his *Democracy and Education* reveals the individualistic nature of Dewey's thinking. Nevertheless, the early impact of his ideas was in the opposite direction and there was continual discussion of the communitarian components of education and democratic living. Now once again we are in a period when the individual is asserting his rights over society and the social bases of education are in dispute.

Persistent reflection on this problem should convince most of us that it is impossible to assert that the one exists for the sake of the other. What sense does it really make to say that the family, for example, exists for the sake of its members or they for it? Clearly they are there for each other's sake, and the one is not more basic or philosophically real than the other. What can be said surely is that though community is a prior condition of individuality, once produced an individual is always straining at the bonds of every group, tending to break them asunder in order to search for more satisfying associations. Without the group the individual cannot be. But it is equally true, that once in being he finds no unity or community finally satisfactory. His quest for community does not stop as long as he continues to grow; his rest in existing communities is forever temporary.

Where do we get the ability and insight to criticize the institutions and groups of which we are a part and which have made us what we are? The answer is not hard to find. At some point in his development, every individual develops the capacity for self-reflection. This enables him to transcend himself and become what the groups who fostered this reflection perhaps never intended. Reflection is able to envision an ideal that goes beyond any existing condition. It can not only make its possessor dissatisfied with himself, what he formerly was and now is, it can also make him highly critical of his social environment. To such an awakened one, all groups are likely to seem too conservative, cautious, and intent on self-perpetuation.

When self-reflection discovers nowadays the aid of scientific method and knowledge, it has a powerful instrument with which to evaluate its own origins. The natural and social sciences are not only aids to the discovery of new knowledge and wider principles of explanation, they are, in the first instance, powers of emancipation for the individual from the parochial bounds of his limited experience. He is nearly compelled to see the incidental and accidental limitations of his place in the larger drama of man as a late species on an insignificant planet. Our age is, more than preceding periods, one in which scholars and scientists range over wider fields and derive insights from societies formerly unknown. Hence any reflective youth, coming into contact with current science, is given a perspective with which to compare his own background. And since scientists are constantly in the process of examining and rejecting the received truths of science itself, criticism is today elevated, quite properly, into a principle in its own right. Not acceptance of the received, but examination with a view to discovering what is wrong with it, has become the basic assumption of a democratic educational theory made sophisticated by the new science.

Moreover, religious faith has always given an individual a place to stand over and above the groups which nurture him. Though we usually think of religion as a primary conservative force and emphasize the communal nature of its worship, it remains a fact that our Western faiths have been born in the desert as largely the products of single thinkers and owe their growth to a long line of heretics. When tradition and ritual threaten to overwhelm personal piety and direct communication with one's God, there is always someone to rise up and say, with Luther: "Here I stand. . . ." Though both religion and science have deep roots in communitarian thinking, it remains true that both also afford the reflective and recalcitrant individual much support for his urge to judge the groups to which he belongs. With the birth of reflection, therefore, comes also the power to transcend one's various communities and to assert the claims of the isolated self over any and all of them. Every teacher at the slightly advanced levels of schooling knows from experience that our youth take advantage of this power.

What are the essential elements which individuality contributes to life in community?

In the first place, group association tends to breed conservatism, that is, an interest in its own perpetuation which is at war with change. There is a law of inertia that pervades all such forms from the family to the international organization. All of us have experienced this inertia, this dead weight, and have been disgusted with it, for it tends to hold us to the level of the most inert members. Consequently, the first and last duty of the person who has developed individuality within the compass of the communities of which he is a member is to act as a critic of these associations. He could not have become what he is without them, but they in turn cannot become what they ought to be without his examination and attempted reconstruction of the bases on which they operate. This is analogous to the perennial criticism of father by son and mother by daughter, by which the rising generations earn the right to take command. Without it there is no growth. Many educational philosophers assert that the development of the critical mind is the chief task of all education, formal and informal. Though that seems to me an exaggeration, it is nevertheless an essential goal of any modern society. For criticism is a form of creativity that is inescapable if all our groups are not to become human ant heaps. And it is a function that is unavoidably individual, the product of the single person who has transcended a previous standpoint and gained perspective on the past and insight into a possible future.

Such critical evaluation of our forms of association is inevitably unwelcome. It demands an openness and willingness to change that are counter to all our traditional group instincts. These look backwards and cling to the forms, the machinery of organization. Our feelings prefer the minutes of the last meeting, and our analytic faculties search for precedents for any change. "The laws," wrote Goethe, "are like an eternal sickness of the human race." None of us need to be persuaded of the value of laws and precedents and minutes. What does need persuasion is that alone they are insufficient for vitality and the older we are, commonly, the more persuasion is needed. Hence criticism is a quality of which we can rarely have enough, particularly when it comes from individuals within the group itself. The caution ever to be heard is that it be constructive criticism. If that means that it be distinguished from mere complaining, we can well agree. But destructive criticism is often in order as well. Many groups outlive their usefulness and ought to be abandoned. How many organizations have we all belonged to that had no real excuse for existence! They survived by habit and the inertial effect of familiarity, inhibiting our growth and wasting our time. The courage to dissolve associations that no longer serve vital functions is a rare but needed courage, the consequent of a critical spirit.

Such a critical power is equally necessary for humanizing and sensitizing all forms of communal life. There is something inhumane and potentially gross about the vast majority of groups. It is doubtless the negative consequence of their positive virtues of instilling morale and enlarging our sense of power. The defects of these virtues are dangerous, for group egotism and selfishness can be—indeed have always been in history—much more ruthless and blatant than their individual manifestations. A person who would not cheat or lie or steal in an individual cause will frequently do so without qualms in a communal one. He has a seemingly good alibi, an excellent rationalization, for such conduct. The importance of preserving the organization gives him license to sacrifice conscience in the interest of a larger goal.

Again, I think, this characteristic of insensitivity to the claims of conscience pervades nearly all groups. The family can be and often is one of the most inhumane of all institutions. In the name of providing for his wife and children a man will often commit heinous deeds against all other "outgroups" or individuals and find a ready justification. We are constantly surprised that the most ruthless corporations and business organizations are controlled by men who in private life are models of correctness and consideration. And fraternal organizations, churches, colleges, and professional groupings are not very different. For the member who threatens their prosperity and strength by deviant conduct they show no mercy. They sacrifice the part without compunction in the interest of the whole and often exhibit a self-righteousness in so doing that is nauseating.

In this respect it is certainly true that the morality of groups can never approach the level of individual morality, as Reinhold Niebuhr has long reminded us. To an extent this is inevitable and necessary. Frequently, it is unavoidable that individuals must be sacrificed with or without their consent, most notably in defense of their country. But the careless and often callous attitude of the organization toward such subordination of individual rights and goods is the point at issue here. Unless every group develops genuine individuals and permits them to assume leadership, its actions are likely to be associated with a degree of group egotism and inhumanity that is utterly unnecessary. Only an individual can bear to be alone in the sense of communing with himself. And our groups must contain those who can bear solitude if they are to moderate and humanize the power that collective action makes possible.

The temptation of every group, in short, is to make higher claims for itself than events warrant. The larger and more powerful the group the closer these claims approach total allegiance. The function of individuality within these associations is to remind the organization of its role as means and not as end. As I see it, the end is always ultimately the full development of individuals, not organizations, however indispensable the latter may be to the achievement of the former. As the group restrains the unwarranted claims that the immature self makes for itself, so the developed individual must restrain the far more powerful group from riding over the legitimate but weaker rights of the persons who compose it. Such individuals have likewise the function to moderate the injustices arising from inevitable conflict with other, competing groups. That success in their efforts is all too frequently not attained makes the stuff of tragedy in human life. Individuals fall victim to superior force, even when they are upholding the claims of justice and right. Our historical records are filled with the pathos of unmerited suffering, of men acting like wolves to man.

To assert, as I have, that the end of group association is the free play of individuality means that I affirm certain inalienable rights of the person. Difficult as the doctrine of natural rights is to ground philosophically, practically it has been indispensable for every age till the present. The state may rightly ask me to die in its defense, the family to give up my ambitions of higher education to support my parents. Neither has a right, however, to demand that I perjure myself or renounce my claim to privacy or

alter my religious faith. Duties to parents, to country and to
every other form of association can never be absolute or abolish
my responsibilities to my own private self. Therefore, there will
be a tension and conflict in every developed society between
individuality and community, a constant struggle to determine
the things that belong to the one and those that belong to the
other. If the individual draws from the group his sense of identity, *esprit de corps*, his will for communication and willingness
to sacrifice, the group draws from the individual its powers of
renewal and adaptation to change, its humanity and humility, as
well as its consciousness of the limitations and bounds to all group
activity. This tension need not be destructive; under happy circumstances it can be creative, perhaps the source of all genuine
creativity.

If I am correct in the foregoing evaluation, the implications for
education are many, sufficient to fill the pages that follow. The
schools can at best seek to do their share in a task that concerns
every other institution in our society. For if the development of
individuality is the most comprehensive goal of our time and
must be preceded and accompanied by a deep-going experience
of community, formal education is only one of the means to
assure either condition. Nevertheless, schools are more and more
expected to provide the essential bulwark against the forces of
impersonality, standardization, rootlessness and discontinuity
which threaten us today.

Unless our youth find in formal education the time and leisure
for that unhurried building of relationships which modern living
makes increasingly precarious, they are unlikely to find them
later. Unless educational institutions lead the way in providing
intimate associations in classroom, halls, and dormitories, the rising generation is nearly certain to be thrown back upon itself,
made to feel insignificant, and tempted to gain identity by over-
conforming or by deviant behavior. We simply cannot afford in
education the mechanical, the bureaucratic, the mammoth organization that has long since imperilled our industrial, recreational,
and political life.

For even where young people are residentially stable and their associations not overwhelmingly large, difficulties of community are still formidable. The dizzying pace of social and technological change is all too likely to make the wisdom of the preceding generation seem largely irrelevant to the next. George Kennan has put this situation in somewhat apocalyptic form in the following sentences:

> Wherever the past ceases to be the great and reliable reference book of human problems, wherever, above all, the experience of the father becomes irrelevant to the trials and searchings of the son, there the foundations of man's inner health and stability begin to crumble, insecurity and panic begin to take over, conduct becomes erratic and aggressive. These, unfortunately, are the marks of an era of rapid technological or social change.

These are the manifestations of which sociologists and social psychologists write nowadays and it would be easily possible to multiply such quotations. But I see no need. If we visit our schools, we can observe how high school and college youth are tossed between the poles of collectivism and individualism. They are likely to be conformist in their extra-curricular associations and excessively individualist in their academic goals. As parents we may try to help them avoid such extremes, but many of us are uneasily conscious that we are not so different, being ourselves victims of these polarizing tendencies.

Nevertheless, in this transformation of society certain stabilities endure. Our youth want to be happy still and they desire to be productive. Though they may not consciously realize it, they desire that extension of the self implied in genuine community and the development of the unique and distinctive implied in real individuality. They resist the merely conventional and blandly abstract responses to their inquiries occasioned by their new situation. In our huge cities, they fight the tendency to become "asphalt animals." At some level they know that they lack that dimension of their being which earlier generations discovered in mountain, forest, and non-human creatures that complement the human species.

The task of forming individuality in our day is the task of humanizing and naturalizing an environment threatened with the loss of both by virtue of man's incredible inventiveness and reproductive powers. Our species is threatening itself, in peril of making its own continuance either undesirable or impossible, perhaps both. Yet because this threat to individuality is of human origin, it would seem possible that human beings could overcome it.

Obviously, the resources required involve large organizations that infinitely transcend individual effort, even the scope of the most powerful single government. This should not mean, however, that organizations become an end in themselves, preventing the independence and happiness of the persons who create them. Above all, it must not happen in the schools. Educators—and the term includes every sensitive and thoughtful adult—must constantly strive to provide the conditions in our schools without which neither individuals nor communities can be formed. For the theory of education, meanwhile, it is necessary to discover and set forth the components of a life worthy for the next generation to live.

3. INDIVIDUALITY AND HAPPINESS

IF A CENTRAL PURPOSE of American education today is to develop individuality in community, we must inquire in this and succeeding chapters about the qualities of this individual we are seeking to educate. Is he likely to gain happiness, at least more happiness than in societies where other educational goals are dominant? Our immediate reply is: we certainly hope so, for who of us would seek to be individuals, if we were convinced that individuality led to ultimate unhappiness? Though happiness can hardly be a purpose of education, it should be one of the principal fruits. To the youth who asks: "why should I individualize myself, or why educate myself to the greatest possible extent," no answer is ultimately convincing which does not take the pursuit of happiness into account.

There is something final, as Aristotle saw, about happiness as a goal of life itself beyond the purposes of education. One cannot sensibly ask a person why he wishes to be happy, for we human creatures are by nature directed toward it. Hence it is important to ask what the connection is between this purpose of education, both formal and informal, and that which all of us seek as a kind of elemental assurance that our existence has been worthwhile.

The moment we begin to reflect, doubt arises. Is not individuality a dangerous goal in an age like ours? Are not those who run with the crowd or those who hold aloof from community on safer roads? There can hardly be any assurance that the most sensitive individual will find the greatest happiness in our society. In an age that cherishes technical manipulation and specialized competence more than it does practical wisdom, are young people sanely advised to pursue that which is unique and distinctive within them? An answer is not easy to find.

Before attempting one, let us look briefly at the origins of our common conception that education and happiness have an intimate relation to each other. Like most of our academic language itself, this connection arose in the ancient Greek world. In summing up the wisdom of this small, short-lived, but glorious civilization, Aristotle pointed to the union of self-realization and happiness. For him self-realization was a matter of a lifetime, not of the springtime of youth alone. And happiness was sharply distinguished from pleasure or the gratifications of sense, since human beings, unlike other animals, cannot be satiated with sense pleasures alone. Happiness must involve the rational principle in man, his one distinctive quality. Hence, it is not incompatible with sorrow and pain as inevitable aspects of the human situation.

More important still, Aristotle recognized that happiness, in contrast to pleasures, is an achievement. It is an activity, not something that happens to you but something which you have to win for yourself and in your own way. While asleep, happy and unhappy people are indistinguishable. Happiness involves, therefore, the full development of one's potentialities and their active exercise in communities, in productive work with the instruments and institutions of culture, and in communion with the natural environment. It is a distinctively human use of intellectual powers, however varied in extent they are from one person to another; also a conscious participation of the whole being in actions that are meaningful. We can experience pleasure in one part of ourselves, over a brief period, and remain passive. On the other hand, happiness is pervasive, involving our active and total being. As one swallow does not make a summer, Aristotle remarks, neither does a year of happiness make a happy life. One must look at the full course of a career and beneath the surface to the disposition or character.

This Hellenic conception of happiness can be sharpened by contrast with its opposite, immortalized by classic figures of unhappiness in Greek culture. We think of such figures as Tantalus, immersed in water to his neck yet unable to quench his frightful thirst, clutching for fruit to quiet his hunger yet having it dangle forever slightly out of reach. Or Sisyphus, rolling his rock up the mountain only to have it come crashing down again. Or the Danaid women attempting to carry water in buckets whose bottoms were sieves. The formula for unhappiness in that society, as increasingly in ours, was frustration of natural desires and inherent potentialities. Happiness was the progressive realization of distinctive powers, of the body and mind, material and intellectual, and their harmonious functioning in a human and natural milieu.

This, then, is one source of our American belief in the belonging together of education and happiness. A more immediate origin, however, is in the optimistic assumptions of the Age of Enlightenment. Our career as a nation was launched in that era under the banners of liberty, equality, and the pursuit of happiness. Influential thinkers of the eighteenth century were sure that man's miseries were largely attributable to false dogmas of a corrupt human nature or to evil social institutions or to remediable ignorance. Dogmatism in religion, absolutism in government, and widespread ignorance of nature and human nature were, they believed, chief hindrances to progress and to the attainment of what they liked to call felicity, their favorite synonym for happiness.

The German philosopher, Immanuel Kant, in his famous little essay, "What Is Enlightenment?" summed up the convictions of this epoch by proposing the Latin slogan: *Aude sapere!* (Dare to know!) For Kant Enlightenment signified that man leaves behind "his self-caused immaturity," an immaturity which was a product of laziness and cowardice, fostered by autocratic state power and a priestly tribe who clung to power by frightening ignorant subjects. Kant put his trust instead in representative government, in the moral autonomy of every individual, and in an eventual world order at peace. It is evident that his confidence in such a world was guided by his faith in education.

"It is delightful to realize," he wrote in another essay, "that through education human nature will be continually improved, and brought to such a condition as is worthy of the nature of man. This opens out to us the prospect of a happier human race in the future."

Such a statement can stand for dozens that any student of history could cull from European and American literature of this period regarding the promise of happiness through education. In a real sense these writers were reasserting the classic humanistic ideal of self-realization. Their optimism initiated free, compulsory, universal schooling in America during the nineteenth century, implying a steadily increasing confidence in the educability of everyone. Our own philosophers of education have not been numerous, but in John Dewey we find an important culmination of the eighteenth century vision of self-realization and happiness through education. In his refusal to believe in the tragic character of human life, in his commitment to the trinity of science, education, and democracy, John Dewey expressed, on American soil, the hopes and dreams of his Enlightenment predecessors.

If we try to look at our situation in America today with as much detachment as possible, we find a curious paradox. Most of the expectations of the eighteenth century founders of our educational theory have been realized beyond their expectations. We middle class Americans, a large majority of the whole population, have what they merely dreamed of. Ours looks like a golden age of literacy, leisure, and plenty. Our youth have been freed from the necessity of earning a livelihood long enough to enrich their minds with the lore, if not the love, of learning. We have maintained our democratic institutions, our science has rushed forward in giant strides, schools have multiplied, and the comforts and amenities of civilization abound.

Yet restlessness and discontent are everywhere apparent. Insecurity and care make so many of us spiritually unwell. Even when its conditions seem to be within our grasp, the self-fulfillment at which we aim remains elusive, a will-o'-the-wisp. The possibility of education for happiness has come to seem so dubious a matter that one hesitates even to discuss it. Knowledge is power, we know, and learning commands prestige and status as never before. But their capacity to contribute to gaiety of mood and the serene mind are very far from being unquestioned.

How can this be possible? Any full answer would have to take into account large social factors and forces which have little to do with schooling and education directly. Our inquiry, accordingly, must necessarily be limited in scope and focused largely on youth in relation to schooling. Within this focus let us ask the following question: Which forces in contemporary education promote and which impede the goal of self-realization and happiness?

We may well start with the problem of growing up in our American society today. Its goal is the achievement of what is called maturity, though no one is entirely clear about everything implied by that ambiguous term. This involves schooling for nearly every youngster. If we ask the simple reason for this, the answer must be that schools are society's attempt to transform the natural creature entering upon life into a being who is distinctively human. All of us are an amalgam of biological needs and desires with the acquired habits and learned responses of our society. The natural and the cultural are already so intermixed in the child of tender years that no one can say with any certainty what is purely natural and what the effect of learning. Still it is certain that one of the things we mean by maturity is a human being who has made part of himself some of the wisdom of the race without losing the spontaneity and freedom of the natural. Understood in this perspective, education is a balancing of the claims of nature and culture so that the individual is liberated from the limitations of the animal without being estranged from the biological bases of so many satisfactions. Maturity is the acquiring of a "second nature," as it were.

But the perils of growing up lie in the possibility that this synthesis of nature and culture may never take place. Learning involves the postponement of immediate pleasures in the interest of longer range and presumably deeper satisfactions. And something profound in us resists this process. Future joys are never as real as present ones in the eyes of youth. The pleasure principle, as Freud dubbed it, comes into conflict inevitably with the prin-

ciple of happiness. It lies behind the dislike of youngsters for
school, which is surely as old as the institution of schooling itself.
Whatever the practical and immediate explanations for this
phenomenon may be—poor teaching, physical confinement, etc.—
the more ultimate one is the burden of culture itself, the sacrifice
of immediate satisfactions.

However joyfully many of us entered upon schooling in
kindergarten or the first grade, few of us indeed can deny the
reluctance we experienced at later stages to the acquiring of
knowledge. Our literature is full of the theme: "He who increaseth knowledge increaseth sorrow," or, as a poet expressed it:
"Knowledge is but sorrow's spy." It is as though the youth is
subconsciously aware that the more books he reads or academic
hurdles he leaps, the further he is pushed away from the spontaneous joys of living in the present and for the moment.

Our contemporary culture reinforces this natural reluctance.
We have become more and more a youth-centered society. Forgetting Aristotle's wisdom about one swallow not making a summer, we have also tended to identify happiness with pleasure, or,
in our current idiom with fun. The more fun a young person has,
the happier he is conceived to be. Such fun or pleasure is identified by the mass media and in the popular mind generally with
the fifteen or twenty years of adolescence and early adulthood,
during which certain prescribed social goals such as sexual fulfillment, marriage, children, financial security, and the like, are supposed to be achieved.

This initial conflict between living and knowing is one of the
most enduring in the history of our Western civilization. Few of
us can rid ourselves entirely of the suspicion that there is an
inherent connection between ignorance and bliss. More exactly,
we are likely to feel that childhood and happiness have an affinity
for each other that adulthood can hardly duplicate. Idealizing of
child nature is an inheritance from the Christian religion which
has been furthered by some influential educational philosophers.
Romantic poets of the last century drew on such sources for
their fervent persuasion that "Heaven lies about us in our in-

fancy." We seem unable to rid ourselves of the nostalgia for the immediate and unreflective before the advent of self-consciousness separates us from the rest of creation. The thinking man, in Rousseau's striking phrase, is an animal who has become sick. And Freudians are only the latest of a long line who speak of the burden of culture in its demands on the postponement of immediate joys and the sublimation of many imperious demands of our animal natures.

These are the perennial perils of growing up, a process that never has been easy where a society advances beyond the level of the primitive. For reflection is born when a youth learns that he is not the center of existence, that the world does not circle around his little life. The birth of self-awareness represents nearly always a great threat to happiness, for it isolates us in the first instance from others. Often as this slow awakening to the full human condition has been described in literature, each of us experiences it in slightly different fashion. Still the sense of being almost unbearably limited and mortal must be widely shared by youth. Reflection does not proceed far before we realize that we are not necessary, that we might well not have been, and that dying is as much a part of existence as being born.

The phenomenon of death, of a friend or parent or even of strangers described or pictured in news media, provides a series of shocks to the growing youth that only his overflowing vitality and egoism can counter. "No young man believes he shall ever die," wrote William Hazlitt. But though many succeed in deluding the self to the point of feeling that death is something which happens only to others or at most, will happen to them in some unimaginably distant future, nevertheless the possibility of a violent end obtrudes itself, in adolescence particularly, at the most unpredictable moments. Today with the threat of nuclear extinction hanging over all of us, it is not only adults who are chiefly aware of the contingency of their individual lives.

One evening while saying goodnight to my ten-year-old daughter, I made the mistake of reminding her that she would never again live the day she had just passed. It was a fairly thoughtless remark, for I had little idea that she was old enough to take seriously the fact of her own mortality. But my wife told me reproachfully the next morning that the child had cried a lot about this reflection and that she had the greatest difficulty in getting her to sleep. Most parents rarely realize that the puzzling, often profound questions their youngsters raise are half-conscious attempts to discover some ultimate rationality in life that their elders have themselves been unable to decipher.

The process of growing up, insofar as it is also a process of education and not merely biological growth, can be characterized as a constant departing from one protected resting place after another with no assurance that the new one will be as secure as the last. It may be likened to mounting a spiral staircase where each new stair is narrower than the one below and the danger of dizziness increases all the time. The greater the reflection, in quality and amount, the more hazardous becomes the ascent. Though adults may strongly believe that reflection will finally lead to a new closeness to nature and fellows, there is really no assurance that a youth will not lose himself in the process, and miss his chances for happiness again and again.

For the greatest threat to happiness is, after all, the threat of meaninglessness, and education understood in its full philosophic sense is a search for the meaning and purpose of individual and collective existence. However little most young people realize this, I am convinced that the discovery of purpose and direction in their lives is the source of their deepest and most confused yearning. No parent or teacher can assure them of the outcome of their search, and all reflective adults realize at some level of their being that this search is life-long and beset with all sorts of accidents and chances. *Growing Up Absurd* is the title. of a recent book and the title is the most significant aspect of the book. For the prospect of absurdity, the contemporary term for the meaningless, is always a real possibility for the growing youth.

We are perhaps obsessed with absurdity in our generation. It has become a fashionable word in the Existentialist movement in philosophy and has invaded the theatre and the other arts. A young person who is exposed to current literature in his Humanities courses learns to confront it in books before he has felt its full force in life itself. But it is a serious mistake to believe that our age has any monopoly on the despair that ensues from a loss of faith in the meaning of human existence. The most poignant expression of meaninglessness our English literature knows was written by a poet who lived in a more hopeful age than ours. It comes from the pen of William Shakespeare, who remains at the very pinnacle of dramatic achievement, and who wrote that life

> *is a tale*
> *Told by an idiot, full of sound and fury,*
> *Signifying nothing.*

Though my readers may protest that most American youth are not really troubled by this disease of meaninglessness, that at the very most it constitutes a threat to a minority of the college generation only, I must answer that at the fully conscious level the readers are undoubtedly right. Yet beneath the surface a far greater number of high school and college youth as well as those not in school struggle with this problem, as their predecessors have done in all past ages. It haunts their minds at intervals and because they are more exposed at an earlier age to the larger world through travel and the mass media, the consciousness of absurdity probably afflicts more of them more frequently than in any previous age. I am not suggesting that such a threat is the most immediate or even the most frequent, for after all our society has many safeguards against the birth and growth of reflection. What is true is that absurdity remains as the longest term and deepest-rooted threat to the attainment of happiness, not only among adults but more especially in youth who seek to anticipate where their fulfillment lies.

If we attempt to determine some of the less perennial and more contemporary perils to self-realization, those that American youth confront in our time, one of the more obvious but most difficult to describe is the loss of authority in our social and moral structures. Over one hundred and thirty years ago, Alexis de Tocqueville noted in his famous book, *Democracy in America*, the difficulty which a democratic people have with the principle of authority. He wrote:

> In democratic ages enjoyments are more intense than in the ages of aristocracy, and especially the number of those who partake in them is larger; but, on the other hand, it must be admitted that man's hopes and his desires are oftener blasted, the soul is more stricken and perturbed, and care itself more keen.

Tocqueville attributed this fact to the revolution of equality, then most advanced in our country. In contrast to a class structured society, equality, he felt, separated and isolated individuals from each other. The conditions of life in America seemed to throw everyone on his own resources at a very early age, and to weaken traditional bonds which earlier had tied men in associations of caring for and cherishing the weak by the strong in economic, social, intellectual, and religious groups. This meant for him a decline of the authority that manners and morals had once exercised over most of mankind. It signified the embarking on an untried way of life for future generations.

He closed his remarkable book on the character of this country with sentences which have a haunting force today:

> Although the revolution that is taking place in the social conditions, the laws, the opinions, and the feelings of men is still very far from being terminated, yet its results admit of no comparison with anything that the world has ever before witnessed. I go back from age to age up to the remotest antiquity, but I find no parallel to what is occurring before my eyes: as the past has ceased to throw its light upon the future, the mind of man wanders in obscurity.

Perhaps we have gotten used to the equality that so deeply confounded this visitor from an aristocratic Europe, but we have today a new kind of revolution to separate men from one another and further deteriorate organic roots of human union. The scientific revolution, as everyone knows, has steadily yet swiftly through its technology so altered the pattern of our lives that the experience of one generation is no longer very relevant to the next. If in the nineteenth century equality served to weaken the natural bonds among men, in the twentieth the very speed of social change has been even more effective.

For the young person this decline of authority takes a very concrete form. For many youth parental authority at an early age tends to be shared, sometimes replaced, by the peer group and this grows into what is now called the sub-culture of the teen-agers. This denotes not so much a vanishing of authority, since youngsters need a model for conduct almost as badly as they need food, as it denotes a shift in the source of authority. But the peer group standards are constantly ambivalent and unstable, lacking as they do the weight of experience and reflection. They seem to be drawn from the more articulate and popular leaders of various social groups and diffused by the mass media. Many of the entertainment and sports figures, so prominent a part of the youthful image of reality today, act as opinion shapers and form-ers. Parents and teachers feel frequently quite impotent to reach the disposition of their children who are under the spell of these peer leaders and public personalities from the entertainment and athletic worlds.

As a teacher I have had more than a few perplexed parents confess to me that they had "lost" their offspring somewhere in the process of growing up and were unable to communicate with them any longer. And for everyone who confesses it, there must be many more who do not admit it, and still more who do not even realize it. Relatively few of the teachers of such youth, I would guess, step into the place of parents to influence deeply the formation of their character. At the most formative stages of their lives such young people are left without effective authority except from their peers. This is a hallmark of our age and the cost in unhappiness is usually painfully large.

The accelerating revolution in scientific technology has like-wise helped to produce a still deeper tear in the fabric of our tradition which may be simply, if inadequately, called a loss of hold on our natural environment. The world in which our youth grow to manhood today is increasingly man-made and machine-manufactured. Time is required, I believe, for the human psyche to invest such implements and structures with human warmth and feeling. Such time is not being given us, for the face and form of our civilization are being constantly altered. Consequently, many of us live and move among the standardized products of our over-populating society without gaining relationships of depth to them. They are like the furniture of a hotel room in which we spend one night. Everything once familiar because unchanged becomes new and strange, and we move about, in Rilke's phrase, in "unpersuaded landscapes."

Something in youth, of course, likes this constant novelty and variety in contemporary life. This something in them finds excitement in the shifting scenes, the most recent fads, the newest consumer products. At the same time these constant alterations prevent their forming deeper attachments to places and things, inhibits the growth of roots and often results in the sense that everything is expendable and replaceable. And below the surface, our youth become easily bored. For at bottom there is not variety enough; a dreadful sameness underlies the superficial change. The reason for this is not far to seek. For genuine difference and creative novelty must be sought in the familiar and the homelike. This is as true perhaps for things as for persons. How the forming of dispositions of closeness to nature and to the products of culture can be attained in a prefabricated environment is not yet clear to even the most perceptive of social thinkers.

The relationship to nature and to the products which man makes from its materials is an infinitely diverse and subtle one. It is not simply explainable by the fact that our cities increasingly remove more of us from direct contact with trees and sky and soil. Nor is it merely that standardized products from clothes to automobiles to furniture render it more difficult for us to feel any satisfaction in their craftsmanship. Ultimately more important is the fact that we cannot project ourselves easily into their nature; failing that, we lose our sense of belonging to the world about us. Our relationships to things become abstract. The useful and the esthetic, the formal and the functional, the emotional and the intellectual tend to get separated from each other. And with none of these in separation can we penetrate into things very far.

Technology's threat to happiness is being recognized more and more by sensitive scientists in our time. Harrison Brown in *The Challenge of Man's Future* has put this estrangement from nature in the following sentences:

> The machine has divorced man from the world of nature to which he belongs, and in the process he has lost in large measure the powers of contemplation with which he was endowed. A pre-requisite for the preservation of the canons of humanism is a re-establishment of organic roots with our natural environment and, related to it, the evolution of ways of life which encourage contemplation and the search for truth and knowledge.

If we agree that forces like these are chief obstacles to happiness in our generation, we may now turn to the resources that exist at present or which are coming into being for overcoming them. Perhaps it requires a certain boldness to assert that despite the perils of this anxious time it is still possible for individuals to lead a full and fulfilling life. But if we believe that the pursuit of happiness is a dependable urge of our species, we can expect that for every obstacle new possibilities for its conquest will in time reveal themselves.

I have suggested that the inner and more general hindrances to the achievement of individuality within the communities of men and nature are the tendencies toward the isolation of man from man and of man from nature, the temptation each of us experiences at the onset of reflection to feel that we are insignificant, impotent creatures of change and of the moment. Such feelings are perennial but in a highly industrialized and unstable environment they are likely to take possession of millions who have not even reached the age of reflection and so become a social *malaise*. Nevertheless, in the realm of education are to be found today as never before possibilities for the combatting of these feelings as well as a margin of time for overcoming them.

Today it is clear as it has not been in earlier epochs that liberal education is a key that unlocks many doors to the uniting of what has been artificially separated in the past. So long as schooling in this country had to be largely devoted to acquiring vocational skills there was neither time nor opportunity to use it for the kind of knowing that unites the practical and the theoretical, the esthetic and the utilitarian, the particular and the general. Knowledge had to be largely directed toward mastery of single, hence abstract, segments of any subject matter. Now in America we are in a situation where education can be truly liberal, where it can be used not only to make us free but to make us generous. Generosity in its philosophical sense is the capacity to participate imaginatively in others' experiences, to explore freely many worlds, and to give ourselves to them for their own sake without calculation of returns. Generosity implies that disposition of mind which generates intimate attachments not only to other persons but also to objects of beauty and use in nature and in culture.[1]

There are today in the conjunction of a generous education and leisure, I am convinced, untapped resources to point the way to "the evolution of new ways of life" and possibly to "the re-establishment of organic roots with our natural environment." The clue lies in interpreting this education in a more concrete and specific way than is commonly done. As I have suggested, its promise lies in uniting each of us to the multifarious aspects of our culture, past, present, and future, without divorcing us from the uniqueness and spontaneity of our own being. Liberal education aims at what philosophers like to call the concrete universal,

[1] John Dewey pointed out several years ago that the term liberal means both to be free and to be generous. Since the phrase 'liberal education' has become in the endless quarrels about education somewhat tarnished and ambiguous in meaning, I prefer to use in appropriate contexts throughout the following pages the phrase 'generous education.'

that is, the revelation of the individual's relationships to the numerous communities which form his total being. It insists on concrete reflection in the context of our own unique situation within these communities in the effort to call forth wholeness of response. In the struggle every one of us constantly makes to order the flood of impressions that pour in upon us hourly and daily, this kind of education enables us to seek the principles which unify and explain the otherwise chaotic and unrelated data of consciousness. The genius of liberal education is that it helps us to achieve this understanding by calling upon emotional, intellectual, intuitive, analytic, and physical powers, not in isolation but, as far as may be, in intimate conjunction.

It is sometimes thought that liberal education excludes the realm of manual skills and bodily excellences, being concerned solely with the ideal products of the arts and sciences. Nothing could be farther from the truth. For unless the educated man learns to use his hands, unless he acquires the feel of an instrument exquisitely fitted for its function, he runs a danger of missing a whole area of his relation to the world. The acquiring and use of physical powers are surely as integral a part of liberal education as is intellectual understanding. For that reason, as often remarked, there are few subjects in any school that are not capable of being taught in a liberal fashion, if only the teacher is educated. It is likewise true that of all forms of education, liberal education is least dependent on formal instruction. It can be pursued in the kitchen, the workshop, on the ranch or farm, in the casual acquaintanceships of every day as from the rarer friendships where we learn wholeness in response to others.

At its inception in Greek society this kind of education involved, as everyone knows, gymnastics and "music," the harmonious development of body and mind with the end of happiness for individual and city-state clearly in view. Nothing that has happened since then seems to me to have changed the basic truth that if education is to promote happiness either in the individual or his society it must devote itself to an all-round development. Any unequal growth either of the mind or body or of certain powers of either over others risks derangement of adaptation to our individual situations as well as derangement of relations of local communities to the larger society.

If earlier in America the chief threat to a generous education was the need to prepare for jobs, since we had a continent to civilize and too much physical work to do to take time for a many-sided development, the danger today is likely to be a misguided professionalism. The argument runs that the expansion of knowledge has been so enormous as to make impossible any grasp of more than a tiny segment of it. If a student wants to reach the frontiers of any discipline, he must begin to specialize very early and continue to master the literature of his field in the hope that he may contribute his tiny bit to the vast amount already amassed. Or if he is to be a practitioner of a profession, he must work early and late to keep up with the new discoveries of his field in order to be useful to his clients and to the larger society. There is now little time for a liberal education, not because our society is any longer a raw and undeveloped wilderness, but because it has reached a degree of complexity and sophistication that, to be effective, the individual has to be one-sided.

It is surely true in some sense that the demands of one's society at any stage are likely to be in conflict with the individual's desire for happiness. The need for specialization in the fields of learning as in vocations is unquestionable today; the very survival of our technological, industrialized society depends upon it. And that this creates a problem for the proponents of liberal education is self-evident. In the more thoughtful circles of our society, there is a growing sense of the sheer bulk of knowledge. A scholar may work as hard as he will and yet never be abreast of the latest developments in his field. The flood of new discoveries grows in volume year by year, new disciplines proliferate, and new generations of school children are required to learn more, stay in school longer, and leave ever less prepared for the revolutions in new knowledge that will make what they acquired outdated within a short time. We are given to lamenting this explosion of knowledge as demographers do our uncontrolled growth of population. Seldom do we take time for the reflection, which should be self-evident, that knowledge in whatever amount is a blessing to mankind, the best promise of a new golden age.

Specialization in the sense of concentration on a limited subject matter is not in itself destructive of a generous education or of the promise of happiness. Just as it is not the amount of information or knowledge which makes the educated man, so it is not the subject matter known which makes the happy man. Rather it is the quality and completeness of response on the part of the knower which distinguishes the generous from the ungenerous education as it distinguishes the happy from the unhappy man.

Striking testimony to this fact comes from a variety of voices in our past. John Stuart Mill was a broadly educated man in the sense of subjects mastered; his father saw to that. His *Autobiography* recounts the story of one of the most unusual minds in our history, systematically trained and guided from earliest childhood under an exacting tutor. But in the early twenties, when he was already an author of some renown as well as an accomplished scholar, he suddenly lost all interest in and enjoyment of life. This was all the more ironical because he belonged to the Utilitarian movement whose major tenet held that the happiness of the greatest number was the sole end of individual and social life. In his depressed state he was forced to admit that even the full realization of everything he had hoped and previously worked for would bring him no satisfaction whatever. His later explanation of this serious and prolonged crisis of his youth is highly significant: the habit of analytic thinking which wears away the feelings. His father's teaching had totally neglected to develop the powers of sensibility by which all the color and tone are added to existence. Instead he had become a kind of intellectual automaton, a research machine. Love and tenderness, the intimacy of childhood association with his peers, openness to beauty and the expressiveness of art, the indulgence in idleness where one accepts one's present condition without question—all this had been denied him. The only cure that he finally found reasonably effective was the reading of poetry, particularly that of Wordsworth. Only then did he discover that he could feel emotions begin to surge within him, that he could shed tears for the first time, gain refreshment in sunshine and sky and with every-day association with his fellows.

Mill puts the blame on analytic habits of thought, but it seems to me that this was too narrow an explanation for an experience that has been attested to again and again by great scholars like Kant and Darwin. Scholarship may be ever so broad in scope, and intelligence of the highest quality exercised upon it, without producing any real change in the scholar in the sense of his involvement or sense of well-being. The real villain, I think, is the habit of abstraction which tears us away from the context of concrete particulars among which as natural beings we constantly move. It is so easy to become absorbed in one facet of our being to the exclusion of others, so easy to forget that we are attached to the world in a thousand ways and cannot afford this forgetfulness if we are to be truly educated and happy.

John Dewey puts this well in a passage in *Experience and Nature* in tones eloquent for him:

> To waste of time and energy, to disillusionment with life that attends every deviation from concrete experience must be added the tragic failure to realize the value that intelligent search could reveal and mature among the things of ordinary experience. I cannot calculate how much of current cynicism, indifference and pessimism is due to these causes in the deflection of intelligence they have brought about. It has even become in many circles a sign of lack of sophistication to imagine that life is or can be a fountain of cheer and happiness . . . The transcendental philosopher has probably done more than the professed sensualist and materialist to obscure the potentialities of daily experience for joy and for self-regulation. (pp. 38-39)

The piercing truth of these lines can well be pondered by all of us who believe that education, properly conceived, aids in uniting us with nature and our fellows. The danger of analytic and abstract thinking of all kinds is that, if pursued exclusively, it separates us from our natural and human environment. And it can do this only because it first divorces us from our own dispositions at the level where intellect and emotions fuse. Specialization is an enemy to liberal education, not because of the subject matter studied, as so often thought, but because of the isolation of one facet of our beings from the others. For the goal of all knowing is to effect relations between knower and the known, to bridge the chasm that opens up when we first as youngsters become conscious of our differentness.

Analysis is a necessary and indispensable attribute of the way human creatures relate themselves to their world. But without the powers of feeling and the mirroring of past experience in memory which we call reflection, it can detach us and cause us to be "lost." Imaginative and intuitive knowing enables us to participate in the world outside ourselves, to penetrate its foreignness, and to involve our beings in its preservation and development. The various skills of abstraction can make us capable men, able to function effectively in a technical society. But to gain communication in depth with this world, our feelings must be cultivated constantly, sensitized and exercised as fully as the powers of intellect. Only thus can our sundered selves be made integral; only thus can a profound sense of kinship with the objects of daily experience evoke gaiety and a serene mind.

Perhaps a personal illustration will be useful. For several years my daughter and I have been riding horseback two or three times a week on the plains immediately adjacent to Pikes Peak. As we ride down the deep gulches and climb the eroded slopes, we are all too frequently without any relationship to this landscape, at once splendid and barren. So often the scurrying rabbit, the frightened deer, the early crocus, the towering mountains seem to be simply there, objects and creatures without any essential meaning or relationship to us. Absorbed in private thoughts of what happened at school or future plans, we ride in silence, even our horses no more than utilitarian objects to carry us from here to there, hardly other in kind from the automobile that takes us to the ranch.

I should speak for myself, for I have no real idea of what goes on in the mind of my daughter. Only rarely do I possess the sky, the sun, the air, and the panorama of the earth. But when I reflect what this landscape would mean to an alert poet, a Wordsworth, Shelley, or Robert Frost, I become painfully aware that being in its vicinity is different from being near to it. For them these single objects and creatures would be suffused with individuality and feeling; they would be conscious of the rippling muscles of the horses, the subtle changes in weeds and flowers from one day to another, the ever-varying face of the Peak. They would understand how to commemorate these things and be lifted out of the monotony of inner repetitions, the causes of which I falsely attribute to that outer world. Both more active and more passive than I am, more practical and artistic, they would enter into this landscape. It would stimulate them to song and help to reconcile them and others to the transiency of individual existence. They would not be oppressed, as I often am, by the seeming deadness of this physical universe. Intuitive knowledge would rescue them from the alienation that is induced by the merely intellectual recognition that the inanimate is the womb of all the living.

I envy not only the poets at times on these rides, but the scientists also. How much a keen-eyed geologist could discover in these eroded hills and valleys; what exciting clues to the history of the earth he could point out to his daughter! A botanist would distinguish varieties of plants, the names of which I hardly know; a zoologist would understand the lore of the animals we see, and know how to explain their complicated interrelationships with the soil they leap upon. Such possibilities for entering into this landscape are unlimited. In these situations I realize with special keenness the power and potentialities of a generous education for the fuller enjoyment of living.

For liberal education insists on the belonging together of the scientific and poetic aspects of human beings. It stands for the principle that scientists should be able to participate in the richness of artistic perception and learning as it emphasizes that humanists must know a good deal about the sciences, if either are to explore the best possibilities of their own disciplines. And both groups should be conversant with the social sciences which can bridge the gaps between knowledge of man and knowledge of nature. Such an education is more concerned with avocations than with vocations, for it acknowledges that man's happiness is often found in the number of things he does well rather than in specialized excellence in one field. And because its essential emphasis is not on learning as such but on learning how to learn, liberal education makes schooling an incident and impetus only to the pursuit of knowing and enjoying.

Since it is an elemental truth that the stages of life from childhood to old age require different activities for their fulfillment, the importance of learning how to learn is transparent. At the crisis period of middle age so many find that the things that hitherto provided satisfaction and serenity lose their savor. Unless they are able to re-orient their activities along new paths, the promise of happiness will fail. Without the variety of interests and abilities a generous education alone can provide, the second half of our life span is all too likely to be spent in repetitions, increasingly meaningless, of the first. As more of our population can anticipate living into old age, with more years of retirement than any previous generation enjoyed or suffered, attention to the kind of education one pursues becomes ever more significant.

Perhaps the greatest error of our youth-centered society is just this failure to realize the necessity in the happy life for variety in activities and enjoyments. Few students are sufficiently aware that the relatively narrow avenues to satisfactions in the teens and twenties must be gradually and greatly increased if they are to gain the same or deeper enjoyments in the forties and fifties. Repetition and routine are fearful hindrances to happiness, especially in a society where earning a livelihood necessarily demands them. The job that was fascinating once can become after a time a gradual and, finally, a deadly bore. Unless the mind has been prepared for other kinds of fulfillment than the vocational, unless we learn how to keep our experiences refreshed with new viewpoints, even the most creative employments can bring this curse.

Charles Darwin has recorded vivid testimony to this fact. He wrote to his friend Hooker:

> It is a horrid bore, to feel, as I constantly do, a withered leaf for every subject except science. It sometimes makes me hate science. The loss of these tastes for music, poetry, and painting is a loss of happiness and may possibly be injurious to the intellect, and more probably to the moral character.

Liberal education cultivates the amateur spirit in every field as opposed to the professional. There are those who argue that the keener joys are reserved for people who have achieved complete mastery of one field, whether that be in the arts or sciences or in sports, carpentry, cookery, or any of the vocations or professions whatever. They maintain that the professional skier, tennis player, gardener, botanist, writer, politician, or painter can know, and only they can know, fullness of happiness implicit in performing such activities excellently. The amateur can have only a foretaste of what the professional experiences in its perfection. Such an argument is surely wrong. Though it is undeniable that increasing mastery of almost any discipline brings increased enjoyment, there is a fairly definite limit to this principle. The limit is discovered when one no longer practices any skill for its own sake. The more activities we can practice for their own sake, the happier we are likely to be. The professional gets involved in competition with others all too often and finds quite quickly the satisfaction ebbing out of his work. On the other hand, the amateur spirit, to which liberal education is devoted, insists not on winning but on enjoying the game, whether the game be play or work. Furthermore, such a spirit is a relentless opponent of the idea that most men are fitted for one thing only, that activity must be concentrated and specialized to be excellent.

It is, however, necessary to point out that the amateur is not at all the same as the dilettante. There exists unfortunately a type of mind that prefers to know a little about everything and balks at the labor of learning the principles of any subject matter or skill. Such minds are at the opposite extreme from the narrow specialist as both are distant from the truly educated. For dilettantism never reaches the level of either skill or knowledge in art or science, hence misses the joys of competence. It, too, is involved in activities which are not for their own sake. Such persons are enabled to talk with an appearance of knowledge and enjoy the transient and superficial pleasures of approval by other dilettantes.

It is sadly true that what passes for liberal education in many of our American schools and colleges is little better than dabbling in the information of many areas with little attention either to the principles or the wisdom that underlie and unite these subject matters. Hence the frequent antagonism of many scholars, who rightly conclude that specialization is better than a smattering of many things with no real knowledge about any. But the perversions of liberal education should not be used to evaluate it.

Yet even those who grant the virtues of a generous education I claim for it are likely to reply that with the vast floodtide of knowledge in the modern world, it is increasingly difficult to attain amateur competence in more than one or two fields, at least for those in our society who pursue the professions. At an earlier time, they point out, it was easily possible for a good scientist to spare the time to be conversant with the field of music or a physician to explore the domains of literature. Nowadays, with the best will in the world, dilettantism is likely to be the result of any endeavor to be broadly educated.

There is an undeniable, if superficial, rightness to this criticism. I recall the remark of the aged Goethe in his *Conversations with Eckermann* to the effect that when he was a young man it was still possible by working hard to get a fair survey of the whole realm of human knowledge. But even in his lifetime the increase in all fields of learning had been so enormous, that it was beyond the powers of any single person to compass more than a fraction. Goethe died more than a hundred and thirty years ago. Everyone knows what has happened to the rate of increase since then!

Nevertheless, it must be repeated that the amount of knowledge possessed can make neither the educated nor the happy man. If I am right at all, happiness is related most closely to activity and to that kind of activity which understands how to relate the head to the hand, theory to practice, feelings to reason, and the individual to community. And for this kind of knowing, we have nowadays, thanks to the spectacular advances in productivity and of automation of routine work, an unprecedented amount of leisure. Amateur competence in a number of fields may not be possible to acquire in adolescence, given the vast increase in learning. But we no longer need to limit education to formal schooling; it is manifestly becoming a matter for a lifetime in our land.

At the origin of our civilization in ancient Greece, liberal education was intimately tied to leisure. The Greek word for leisure was *scholē* and the essence of both education and leisure was a life spent in "living and doing well." In practice this meant that the more time one could devote to activities performed for their own sake, the greater the happiness one could achieve. That life had the best chance of being lived well which was the least burdened with tasks mechanically performed for the sake of gain or making a livelihood. The realist Aristotle recognized that for such a good life human slaves were necessary, to provide the margin of freedom required from menial tasks and assure time for genuine cultivation of intrinsically valuable activities.

Today we have in our country an unprecedented freedom from onerous labor, an incredibly rich culture and society, as well as a nature that offers diversity and possibilities for undiscovered delights. In so many ways our American tradition is fortunate, for we cherish pluralism as a cultural value and openness to creative novelty. As a people we have held fast to the principle, in theory at least, that each must seek and find happiness in his own way.

On the face of it the promise of happiness has never been greater than in the United States at this moment of history. The restless discontent, the threat of meaninglessness, the anxiety about annihilation, the loss of depth in relations with our fellows and with nature can be combatted if we learn how to take advantage of our new leisure. The task of education is to cultivate that kind of individuality which rejects the conformity making for standardized behavior in vocations and avocations, in manners and mores, in recreations and in tastes. The genius of a generous education is its intent to aid each person to become what he alone can be. Its perversion is the production of specialists and dilettantes who withdraw from or surrender to their fellows.

It is commonly asserted that Americans are peculiarly unfitted for what is now called the Age of Leisure. We are a work-oriented people because of our past and our Puritan values. This signifies that we are accustomed to regard leisure as either vaguely sinful or equate it with amusement and recreation, and not with the pursuit of intrinsically satisfying activities and individually appropriate interests. We have been, as Tocqueville noted well, a people given to rush and to tumult, to joining organizations and to flight from solitude and reflection. All of these characteristics are undoubtedly inimical to the gifts of leisure and liberal education, hence to happiness itself.

Still, we are no longer, as we were in an earlier time, a raw, youthful people with a continent to conquer, where schools and universities were so minor an aspect of society that even Tocqueville could overlook them. On the contrary, education is rapidly becoming the dominant force and factor in our land. And if it is to be a liberal education that is to prevail, we have grounds for hope that the forces threatening happiness in America may be balanced, even outweighed, by the promises of a more sanely conceived notion of a whole life devoted to living and doing well. Not only may enjoyments continue to be more intense and include more people in our democratic society, but also we may be able to meliorate the blasting of hopes and desires, the stricken and perturbed souls that Tocqueville believed to be inseparable from this democratic life of ours.

However, it is unwise to conclude without reminding ourselves once more that education even broadly conceived is by no means all that counts in achieving happiness. There is something finally mysterious, indeed unfathomable about the secret of being happy. Reflection about it and experience in living will convince us that happiness is in some sense a gift of the gods, being dependent to some degree on inherited factors such as good health, a sunny disposition, a degree of intelligence, and the semi-accidents of a full span of years, a fortunate marriage, and other things. Though these are not sufficient conditions of living and doing well, they may indeed be necessary ones. There is no likelihood that anyone will enumerate all the ways and means to the end of the good life. For the purposes of education, however, what is important is continued reflection on the contributions of knowledge and wisdom to the infinitely diverse ways in which we human creatures seek fulfillment.

4. ARTISTRY IN CONDUCT

The wise and fool, the artist and unread.

—Shakespeare

IF THE CONJUNCTION of education and happiness cannot be taken for granted, what of the relation of education and moral character? By educators nothing is more commonly accepted than the notion that education, both formal and formative, aims at improving the character. Currently the least challenged of educational goals is that learning is supposed to lead to the forming of good habits and reflective attitudes in personal life and greater responsibility for social and political improvement. The educated man is simply expected to be a more moral person than one who is without learning.

In the popular mind, on the other hand, there continues to exist an age-old doubt and suspicion about this equation. One's character is believed to have little to do with the amount of learning one possesses. It is possible to be a good man with little or no formal education and in comparative innocence of reflective learning. Conversely, it is possible for a man to be a learned scoundrel; the most morally despicable of human beings indeed being sometimes the best educated. Even where anti-intellectualism does not enter into this popular judgment, there is considerable evidence to support the common view that virtue cannot be taught or that increase in knowledge is not closely consonant with improvement in character.

This is, to be sure, an ancient dispute. Plato's dialogue, *Protagoras*, contains one of the most suggestive discussions of the problem ever written. In some sense nearly all Greek moral theory centers about the teachability of virtue. Socrates is father of the doctrine that if we know what is right and good, we will seek to do them. Vice was for him identified with ignorance and virtue with knowledge. On this view education became the pathway to moral character and knowledge the prerequisite for wisdom in conduct. The Christian faith, however, arose to challenge this assumption. For the early Christians goodness was a quality of the will, not the intellect. Faith, hope, and charity or love as the pre-eminent Christian virtues did not presuppose much knowledge or learning in contrast to the Greek cardinal virtues, temperance, courage, justice, and wisdom. For the Christians good conduct was not dependent on what one knew about the good. Love for God and neighbor could not be learned in any academy. It required a turning about of the natural impulses and appetites, a conversion of the heart or soul to produce a "second nature," a religious nature. Henceforth, the true Christian, by the grace of God, could draw the strength and guidance to form a good character from the model of Christ and from an ethic of love and faith, rather than of learning or wisdom.

Much of the history of Western moral theory can be read as recurring attempts to synthesize Christian and Greek virtues. Because they stem from opposed interpretations of man's origin and destiny, no synthesis is very durable. Some ages and peoples have put primary emphasis on religion as the only secure basis for morality; others place their hopes on education. Individuals in every period have shifted from a religious to an educational base, sometimes back again to the religious foundation, and sought to unite the two continually. This desire to fuse Greek and Christian teachings, tried by countless moralists, is as hard to resist as it is difficult to carry through in a thoroughly convincing fashion.

In response to revolutions in other spheres, contemporary American society appears to be changing significantly its earlier convictions about the nature of the moral ideal as well as the origin of moral values. A host of sociologists keep informing us constantly that our values and ideals are undergoing profound alteration. Earlier Puritan virtues, such as thrift, sexual restraint, self-denial, and belief in hard work as the prerequisite for worldly success are being gradually replaced by a morality whose dominant virtues are pleasure, affability, tolerance, and peace of mind. Whereas nineteenth century Americans were willing to sacrifice present satisfactions for future accomplishments, we in the twentieth century are oriented toward immediate happiness, distrustful of a future that is immeasurably insecure. An earlier generation found in the conscience an absolute guide for conduct; the present generation tends to believe that what the group considers moral is the guide. The arts of sociability, getting along with others with minimal friction, have replaced the Puritan emphasis on personal integrity, which was based on Biblical imperatives and prohibitions. The sense of shame, socially determined, has largely driven out the former sense of sin and guilt, God-instilled. Tolerance for deviant conduct marks another change from previous condemnation and strictness of judgment. Whereas our grandfathers were convinced that right and wrong could be fixed once and for all by reference to divine imperatives, we are increasingly persuaded that right and wrong are determined by the spirit of an age, social needs, and by the level of cultural attainment.

All of us are familiar with these analyses and descriptions and with the deep-seated cultural changes which are responsible. Many of the Protestant virtues which served us well in the building of our country are rapidly becoming irrelevant. It is plain that the virtue of industriousness, for example, has already lost a lot of its force in an economy rapidly becoming automated, with ever-shortening work week, persistent problems of unemployment, earlier retirement, and increasing longevity. Such a change has led David Riesman in *The Lonely Crowd* to assert that American character is now other-directed, no longer inner-directed, that we have shifted from a producer- to a consumer-oriented ethic, from a Bible-centered morality to a hedonistic one.

Though no one is able to deny the evidence upon which they are based, many of us wonder at times how lasting these changes really are, how widely they extend in our population, and how profoundly they alter the springs of individual conduct. It seems more true to say that millions of Americans are confused and drifting in their efforts to discover the right and the good. Religion still occupies an important place in our society; it is a common error to underestimate its indispensable function as a rudder in the revolutionary winds of change. Nevertheless, its former role in furnishing the basis of moral character is surely diminishing. Moral values claim an independence of religious faith that they did not possess for most of our grandparents. Hence, the search for a different source and ground for morality is one of the great new tasks of the present generation. This search is undertaken by those involved Americans who discover that many of our most urgent dilemmas of conduct remain unresolved by traditional religious faith.

The tremendous growth in influence of liberal education in recent decades has, as I have already indicated, done much to promote the search for a standard of behavior that is more secular than religious. If one looks beyond the sociological descriptions of our conduct to their philosophical base, I think the change is best understood as the groping for an artistic criterion of conduct as opposed to either a religious or a purely rational one. Such a criterion places primary emphasis on individual achievement in coping with the complex and various relationships of private and public existence.

What does it mean to speak of an artistic basis for moral conduct? The term *artist* has a narrow denotation at present, but it still retains a wider connotation stemming from an age that did not distinguish art from science nor the fine arts from the practical. "The earliest and the abiding implication of *artist*," according to Webster's Dictionary, "is skill or proficiency; it was in Shakespeare's time, and later, applied to anyone who made or did things requiring learning and skill; thus a teacher, a philosopher, a physician, a scientist, an alchemist, or a craftsman was then called an *artist*."

It is my conviction that skill or learned proficiency in the conduct of life is assuming ever greater importance as our society grows more confusing and tense. This in turn implies a shift in the model of moral character which the rising generations seek to imitate. The person most admired is one who can achieve significantly in whatever field, not only in a vocation but also in private leisure and in public service. Under the influence of Christian ethics we Americans were formerly inclined to separate sharply the inner intention from the external act. What a man thought in his heart was the measure of his moral stature. We accorded ready recognition to outstanding accomplishment, but withheld moral approval for worldly success when it was not accompanied by professed adherence to the traditional moral code. A man might be great and not good, that is, a master of himself and his situation, but inwardly impure and without humility. Or he might be good and unsuccessful, that is ineffective in personal relations and social graces yet saintly of mind and will.

Now we are increasingly coming to regard accomplishment in a more comprehensive sense. We do not admire the single-minded doer who concentrates his energies on amassing great wealth and is uninteresting and monotone in other spheres. Nor do we care for the person who seeks private advancement in egotistic disregard of the claims of community and service. We withhold admiration, too, from one who manages to accomplish greatly in the public sphere, but fails to lead a private existence that is rich in emotional rewards and capable of running a household, holding a wife or husband and rearing children successfully. In short, we tend to reserve the title of good man and woman to those who achieve in the varied realms of competence in vocational and cultural, social and recreational, private and public spheres.

Such a development means that the moral is inseparable from other aspects of the whole personality. A man's vision of himself as well as his social and political views are as much and no more a part of his moral character as is his effectiveness in his vocation and in his family relations. The most important effect of educational sophistication in America is this widening of moral evaluation to include areas of behavior formerly not considered. As one of my students remarked in class recently, a teacher who frequently comes to class unprepared and is unable to communicate his subject matter to students is behaving immorally, regardless of how well intentioned he is and how highly esteemed in the community. More and more of us are perceiving, even if dimly, that conduct of this kind has more relevance to morality than private irregularities in sexual behavior or occasional aberrations of temper or mood. Though many people are, of course, still judged harshly in terms of isolated standards, willingness to assess character by reference to the larger personality is steadily becoming more dominant.

This ideal of artistry in conduct is hardly a novel development. The ancient Greek ideal of *aretē*, virtue in the meaning of skill in the art of good living, is reasserting itself once again. In classical times the good man was he who best worked up the materials available into an existence that was harmonious, rounded, and complete. Virtue was then synonymous with skill and skill was the application of intelligence to all relationships one shared with men and nature. The making of a good life was analogous to the construction of a good piece of sculpture, a workable constitution for the city-state, a sea-worthy ship, or an effective drama or epic. Indeed, virtue included for them excellence of function in non-human creatures and implements; the *aretē* of an ax was its perfection of cutting edge as the *aretē* of a horse was his spirited performance as a steed. The virtue of a human being correspondingly was his capacity to respond with proficiency and flair to the variety of situations which daily life presented. The man who was insensitive to the esthetic dimensions of nature and art was as lacking in *aretē* as he who was incurious about their knowledge components. For both esthetic and scientific elements were considered means to the skillful use of available materials in molding a satisfying and satisfactory individual career.

An example will make clear what the Greeks understood by *aretē* in practice and what we Americans, I think, are coming to accept as excellence in the widest sense. The figure of Socrates served as a vivid model of moral aspiration for the thoughtful minority in that society as he increasingly does for ours. In the *Symposium* of Plato we have an unforgettable image of the man as a thinker and actor on the stage of everyday life. And the highpoint of that dramatic dialogue is not Socrates' speech on the nature of love, though it is still in the opinion of many the best that has ever been written on the theme of *erōs*. The climax is the description of Socrates on the battlefield, the marketplace, and the private bedroom, given by the drunken Alcibiades in an utterly frank and shameless confession induced by wine. Alcibiades gives us the portrait of a man who can not only out-talk all his compatriots but also act in public and private in superior fashion as well. On the occasion of a disastrous defeat for Athenian arms, Socrates by his coolness and courage, saved his (Alcibiades') life as well as those of others and then later insisted on medals being distributed to those he had rescued. When Alcibiades becomes infatuated with Socrates, he confesses how Socrates repels with infinite tact his illicit advances while patiently seeking to improve the quality of Alcibiades' love. In these few pages of Plato we gain a vision of a man who embodies *aretē*, not simply as the power to think well and communicate his ideas in fascinating style, but to act well in the trials of existence, a far more difficult excellence. Yet Socrates refuses to accept the mask of hero; he remains ironical and playful to the end. The *Symposium* closes with his drinking his companions under the table and arguing them into acceptance of the view that the genius of tragedy and comedy are essentially the same, after which he rises from the party at dawn and proceeds to spend the day as usual.

Perceptive observers of the American scene have already pointed out how closely our recent emphasis on excellence parallels the ancient Athenian ideal of virtue.[1] Of course, many of us are still inclined to think of excellence as hardly more than acquiring academic skills, the ability to excel in mastering school curricula. This results from an understandable reaction to a psychology of adjustment and a biologistic theory of education, and

[1] See John Conway's fine article, "Standards of Excellence," in *Daedalus*, Fall, 1961.

like all reactions is in danger of turning into the opposite extreme,
namely a narrow, intellectualistic notion of excellence. Nevertheless, the prevalence and popularity of this concept points, I think,
to an important development of the American ethos. With good
fortune we can expect the idea of excellence to spread to wider
areas of culture and to become a pervasively moral as well as an
academic ideal. Our traditions ought to save us from uncritical
worship of sheer intellectualism just as the emerging ethic of
artistic proficiency can rescue us from our earlier tendency to
overrate exuberant activism.

Nonetheless, educated skill in the conduct of life is not a standard of the good and the right. Rather, it presupposes one. What is
the standard that is assumed by this new way of thinking? Di-
vested of a religious and absolute warrant for behavior, artistic
morality turns to the more individual notions of the appropriate,
the fitting, or the congruous as a standard. The artist in life is one
who is able to grasp, rationally and intuitively, what is proper for
him and appropriate to the great variety of situations in which he
moves. The fool and unread, on the contrary, commit acts which
are inappropriate and incongruous. When one asks at once: appropriate to what or congruous with what? the only answer that
can be given is: with or to the person's conception of himself and
his present situation. As character develops and understanding
matures, there is or should be a corresponding expansion of
horizon, enabling us to view our situation in its more universal
aspects and our character in terms of the ideally human.

It is an old idea that the poets are the teachers of mankind. If
we use poetry in the generic sense of imaginative literature, our
novelists and other serious writers help the student today to form
his conception of the fitting and congruous, much as the Bible
served this function for previous generations of Americans. Because of easy availability of books, recordings, and the visual arts
this tradition of literature extends for the youth in search of an
education back to Homer and beyond, and is as contemporary as

the latest poem, play or film of his favorite artist. Naturally, no one can be exposed to more than a tiny fraction of this tradition. In the first instance, the teachers of humanistic subjects have the task of selecting from this store the portions they wish to transmit to the next generation. If they are at all successful, the awakening youth will soon seek out for himself the writers who "speak" to him. And he will continue his search for such "poets," changing them as he develops, far beyond the direction of any teacher, hopefully as long as life lasts. For the standard of the appropriate cannot be fixed once and for all, but requires to be expanded and deepened as insight and responsibility enlarge. There will always be areas in which the appropriate in conduct and attitude remains for anyone clouded and unsure.

Equally important in forming such a standard are the immediate relations each of us gains and suffers in the process of growing up. Goethe once remarked that "a talent is formed in solitude, but a character in the torrent of the world." Below the level of the books he reads and the lectures and discussions in school, the notion of the fitting is developed in many a youth by what he sees those in authority over him actually doing and what he guesses are their motives. If virtue can be taught at all, there is general agreement that it must be done by indirection and by more subtle arts and methods than most of us parents and teachers ever consciously know. The current preoccupation with the genuine and deeply honest in attitude and behavior, so popular in our literature and with our students, testifies to increasing dissatisfaction with the gulf between what the adult world professes and what it really believes. The new standard of morality, it seems clear, will be formed in explicit rejection of what it perceives to be spurious and phony about behavior in previous generations.

There are certainly great dangers in the pursuit of excellence in conduct, using a standard of the appropriate as a guide. One of them is the inevitable tendency to confuse the subjective and personal with the relative, individualism with individuality. In an age where organic community is hard to achieve, our youth are exposed to the temptation to identify the appropriate with what they immediately desire. It requires a modicum of experience and of reflection to detect the wide gulf separating those who act as they please from those who act in response to the fitting and the congruous. Without experience of community, it is hard for youth to realize that character is not formed in isolation and that rights imply duties; privileges, responsibilities. The isolated individualist can only follow impulse, and impulse can be egotistic and destructive as often as it is creative and considerate. The individual, on the contrary, learns to follow educated sensibility and intelligent intuition. The difference amounts to that between the barbarian and the civilized man. For it is the mark of community among human beings that restraint is put upon primitive desires, and impulses are directed by some conception of the common good. Those who act only from motives of egotistic pleasure or fear of painful consequences tend to have neither character nor understanding; they can be controlled only by harsh external authorities. In an age like this, the hazards of moral anarchy are patent and deeply troubling.

The opposite danger of confusion between the appropriate and the conventional is hardly less obvious. In the insecurity attendant upon the development of moral character, there is always the tendency to fall back upon the socially accepted habits of one's immediate environment. In such cases the appropriate becomes merely another name for what is commonly done, hence no standard of conduct at all. The tendency to over-conform, particularly at certain stages of life, has become a serious moral problem in our time. For every teenager who is in open rebellion and completely alienated from the conventional standards of his community, there must be dozens whose growth in moral freedom is inhibited by too great identification with current mores.

The distinction between the appropriate and the conventional is not always easy to make, even for the mature individual. Consequently, teachers and school systems have clear responsibilities in this regard. Most conventions are strongly negative in import, in the sense that they set the limits of acceptable behavior, rather than prescribing what should be done. When a local community is reasonably tolerant and appreciative of diversity, it is usually possible for a youth seeking artistry in conduct to behave within the confines of the permissible. He will come to recognize the general wisdom of socially acceptable behavior and use it to promote his own growth in morality. If his private justifications for his conduct are frequently different from those of his less reflective associates, they need not necessarily concern anyone but himself. Within the confines of social convention there is usually room for the play of individuality and personal interpretation of the mores. In a period of ferment like our own it is even possible for a single individual, through cautious advance, to change substantially by his own example these conventional standards.

But in a social order that has failed to change, where conformity has become a compulsive force and personal freedom is threatened, the individual has no choice but openly to oppose the ruling powers. His sense of the fitting would be in conscious opposition to conventional standards. In the last analysis, the interests of individual integrity always precede the claims of social order. Artistry in conduct cannot reconcile itself to dictation from without, whether it be religious, political, or simply the imagined requirements of a socially dominant majority. In short, the conventional and the appropriate may travel parallel roads and often intersect, but they rarely coincide for long.

These opposing dangers to the development of a standard of the appropriate in attitude and conduct have a common root; they do not recognize the necessity for continuous evolution in the moral sphere, both in the individual and in society. Morality is relative, as our more thoughtful minority have recognized, in the need to take full account of novelty and uniqueness in individual and culture. Conduct, for example, that once was appropriate in pioneer America no longer fits our situation. And what is congruous with adolescent stages of understanding and behavior can be grossly inappropriate, even bizarre, when indulged in by adults. Variety of situation requires of us a corresponding variety of response. He would be a fool or a dunce who would not alter his behavior in a sports arena, at a high tea, or in a committee meeting. The person who obeys rigid rules of conduct and attempts to apply them indiscriminately to the enormous variety of circumstances and personalities he confronts is moralistic rather than moral. Such absolutism has earned the poor name it enjoys among the sensitive and genuinely sophisticated. The fact that many Americans do act like adolescents when adult, or pattern their conduct on the model of pioneers, or refuse to take account of diversity in persons and places simply testifies to the lack of artistic skill in the conduct of life.

If artistry in conduct is becoming ever more important in our future as a goal of education, it is necessary to inquire what its ingredients are. How relevant is knowledge, and what kind of knowledge must it be? Since morality is increasingly conceived to be a quality of nearly all conduct, rather than a separate sphere, what role can schooling and education play in the formation of moral character?

The first requirement of such a moral ideal is fairly clear. It demands knowledge of oneself and of the world much more than do external systems of ethics. And this sort of knowledge is, of course, not two kinds of knowledge but one. The term self-knowledge is frequently misunderstood; it suggests to many people an amount of introspection that is unrealistic. Actually, however, knowledge of oneself depends upon experience of the world, particularly of other people, which only close observation and habits of reflection can bring. The difficulty with self-knowledge is that young people need time in order to acquire a self to know. Because they have not yet a conception of their powers and limitations, hence no stable character as a center for experience, youth stumble into incongruous behavior and overlook essential elements of their situation. Nor is this difficulty peculiar to young persons only. Since most of us are in process of becoming what we are, the goal of self-knowledge is never complete. More fragmentary still is our acquaintance with our setting, social and natural, all the more so in a time like ours when most of us change our residence so frequently that even the familiar becomes strange. Furthermore, the knowledge that moral skill demands is direct and first-hand. Our schools must necessarily deal in vicarious experience, and our homes, eager to shield children from unpleasant mistakes, tend to keep life at one remove as long as possible. Our mass media make us observers of others' behavior, actual and make-believe, and foster the illusion that we know, when we do not know. "Knowledge by acquaintance" is separated from "knowledge about" by as wide a gap as it ever was. The plain fact is that no one can know himself and his world without a generous amount of exposure to the hazards of uncontrolled experience. This includes experience of the extremes of human conduct, for few of us can know in advance how we will react to the crises of violence, falling in love, unemployment, the death of a close friend, loneliness, mob behavior, or any of the other boundary situations that confront our career in time. Inwardly we stand amazed at our own actions in such encounters and discover dimensions of the self we never suspected. To gain knowledge of use in moral artistry, then, it is necessary to know the world in at least some of its raw and unpredictable aspects. And this requires escape on occasion, even frequently, from the security of wealth and comfort, fond guardians, and the protective environment of pedagogues and books.

Yet heterogeneous experience is not sufficient, no matter how direct and intensely lived. Unless one learns to reflect on these experiences, the peculiar kind of self-knowledge required for moral skill will fail. Reflection is the process of mirroring the outer world to the self, a continuous process in which that world is caught at one remove. The ideal is not detachment, however, but precisely its opposite. For the reflection that is a mirroring teaches us how intimately our little psyches are entangled with those of friends, chance acquaintances, and a host of those we never expect to meet. Such reflection also enables us to grasp in some measure the complex ties our existence sustains to the non-

human creatures and objects of our natural setting. It is a kind of
thinking that has little in common with the logical sharpness and
facility so much in vogue at present in our schools and in certain
philosophical movements. Nor is it closely allied with the kind of
contemplation so beloved by mystics and devotees of hidden
ways to salvation. Reflection is not introspection, though it includes introspection. What characterizes moral reflection best of
all is its growing awareness of the substantial relations between
the private world of desire, aspiration, and secret longings, and
the objective world of cooperative projects, social conflicts, and
endless striving for communal fulfillment. Practical wisdom consists in the ability to act in a way that will keep these two worlds
in mutually productive development.

Though it is hardly possible to overstate the importance of
knowledge in shaping the good life under modern conditions,
knowledge is after all only one condition, a necessary but insufficient prerequisite of artistic morality. There is, in the second
place, the requirement of order or structure which involves discipline of will. To know the right and good is not enough to carry
through their accomplishment, however tempting Socrates' case
may appear in dialectical argument. In our chaotic present, to
triumph even partially over distraction and haphazard choices
involves a powerful effort of will in addition to intelligence. We
moderns realize with particular pathos the centrifugal forces that
dissipate the energy and resolutions of our attempts to direct our
lives. Anyone who tries to create anything superb becomes aware
that he must exert the utmost concentration of will as well as skill
in order to succeed. And the individual career that resembles
even vaguely a work of art reminds us of the tremendous concentration of effort that has made it possible.

Nothing is more disastrous to this accomplishment than an
inadequate sense of form in the moral life. Our days appear to
tend naturally to the formless and chaotic. In earlier times when
the necessity for work dominated everything, form was often
imposed from without on the majority of the waking hours.
Now idleness can become a threat, even a calamity, without the

self-control that imposes form on experience. We fall into the practice of awaiting simply what will happen. The temptation to be passive spectators has surely never been greater in a period when so much from without impinges on our consciousness.

The feeling for form, and the strength to impose it on experience is perhaps above all a sense for the right time. It is difficult to escape the impression that much moral failure comes from wanting too much too soon. It is surely as great a failure as wanting too much too late. Our youth are notably impatient to taste fruits whose flavor and quality can only be appreciated by mature people. The terrible sense of insecurity that afflicts all of us nowadays certainly contributes to this *malaise*. But Americans have always been in a hurry and the rush appears to have actually increased as the need for hurry has decreased. Rich and variegated as American culture is, it is sorely deficient in guidance for the young. As a result there is too little conception of the climaxes and the level plains of experience, no proper appreciation that there is a time for storing and a time for the expenditure of vital energy We seem unable to plan for longer stretches of existence, not to speak of conceiving our lives as a totality. All of this is deeply inimical to the ethic of artistic skill.

But timing is not everything in the feeling for form. There is also the interplay of the spontaneous and the controlled. Certainly form can become a tyrant, and vitality can seep out of the over-designed career; there are people who seek to escape formlessness by regulating their behavior to the point of excluding the chances for growth. They lose the notion of the appropriate by banishing the whole sphere of the impulsive and spontaneous. Self-consciously anticipating every eventuality, they discover that experience is "stale, flat, and unprofitable." Such lives have none of the richness of meaning of a work of art. For the secret of form is its coexistence with the vast realm of possibility. Skill in morality as in art consists in the recognition that one must yield on occasion to the demands of the material and refrain from interfering with the inevitable. It is the capacity to let alone as well as the power to shape one's will. The wisdom to yield and permit oneself to be carried away is not impotence, however much it may appear so. It is an important aspect of the feeling for structure.

Scarcely less important than spontaneity in the feeling for structure is the capacity to carry the essential responsibilities of morality without evident strain. It is the recognition that the good life is never limited to essentials nor bound to the practical in the narrow meaning of that term. Moralism is always neglectful of the all-important details which add color and vividness to the necessary. For too many generations morality has been conceived by too many earnest men as a burden, an affair of duty in opposition to all natural inclinations. For such as these, pleasure and gaiety represented a moral holiday, an escape from the serious business of right behavior. Such a conception of a holiday from morality is simply absurd. It can be held only by those who fix their eyes on remote and illusory goals, disregarding the journey with all its diversions and delights. Moral actions are not separated from the chance joys of work and play, beauty, and the quiet satisfactions of family life; on the contrary they are inseparable from all these things. Goethe meant this when he wrote in his masterpiece, *Faust*, that we take our life from the colorful reflection of it. *Am farbigen Abglanz haben wir das Leben.* This is the triumph of moral artistry, to discover in the journey a justification for the goal as much as in the goal itself. Such loving attention to the incidental conditions of existence does not, to be sure, make discipline unnecessary or reduce the need for knowledge. But it does serve to conceal the inner structure of the moral act and render externally attractive the most burdensome of duties.

This suggests a third feature of artistry in morality, a requirement which distinguishes it most sharply from the traditional. I mean the achievement of moral style. Style in reference to behavior has become of late a fashionable word, though careful analyses of what is meant by it are much rarer. The word derives, of course, from the arts, both fine and practical, and its current popularity in wider contexts evidences how our artistic and moral values approach one another.

Because the concept of style is a highly individual one, it is anything but easy to characterize it. Negatively, one can say that the absence of style in living testifies simply to the absence of imagination. Morality without imagination is humorless, dull, and all too likely to produce immorality in those closely associated with it. Uninteresting people are sure to place total stress on things moral conceived as a series of universal rules without reference to individual uniqueness and usually as a sum of prohibitions. In contrast to such moral plodders wicked and hypocritical persons are almost always more appealing to us. For the unimaginative are unable to conceive any other ways of interpreting experience than the ones they have adopted or, more frequently, have had imposed upon them. They have never made the distinction which Nietzsche insisted upon between the solemn and the serious, never suspected that a person may be light-hearted and yet highly in earnest about the right and the good. It is difficult to condemn their way of life; too often it is the only path they are able to tread. They do the good, as we say, according to their lights. But their examples are peculiarly graceless and the only escape from their stifling environment is to depart from it. "The harm that good men do" is a phrase that applies to them with peculiar force.

Perhaps the conventionally pious are a prime example of the absence of style in behavior. They seek to ground all conduct in a single principle or interpretation of behavior which makes no allowance for personal uniqueness and freedom. The requirements of the immediate situation are held to be inconsequential. Because the variety of personalities and the diversity of situations are difficult to disregard, the pious are constantly subject to charges of hypocrisy, that is, of behaving in contradiction to proclaimed principles. When, in rare instances, a man or woman may be so permeated with religious truth that his or her actions achieve a distinctiveness that is wholly natural, piety can become a style of life all its own. Such an example can be a sublime one, though essentially inimitable as a model. But in the majority piety tends toward rigidity of conduct, degenerating into complacency and sanctimoniousness against which we moderns rebel in disgust.

If we seek now to define moral style in a positive fashion, a first step will be to distinguish between what is done and how it is done. The same deed may be highly moral or deeply immoral, depending on the manner of its accomplishment. The most familiar example, almost hackneyed, is that of the social worker. One who is sensitive and skilled may bring baskets of groceries to an unfortunate family without humiliation, indeed, with a gesture which makes it unmistakably clear that all men are in need of charity. Her unimaginative colleague, with the best will in the world, can make the same action odious in the extreme. One banker may refuse a loan to a customer in such a way that the would-be borrower feels understood and appreciated even in his disappointment; the second banker conveys the impression of a greedy money lender. Two men may make love to their wives in such a fashion that one feels violated, the other ineffably flattered.

Such examples are endless and the point easily grasped. More subtle are those involving relations between individuals separated by long-standing ethnic or religious differences. It took me a long time to understand why sensitive Jews despise the philo-Semite among Gentiles only slightly less than they hate the anti-Semite. Or why the Negro sometimes prefers the conventionally prejudiced Southern white man to the over-friendly Northerner. All of us want to be liked or disliked, of course, in terms of our unique personality and not by reference to our derivations. The accident of color or nationality or religion or even of sex, we feel, should make no difference in comparison with that which is distinctive in us as personality. Hence attention to the manner in which a deed is done as opposed to the substance of behavior inevitably reveals the presence of style. It marks individuality as truly as the style of a writer or a painter proclaims the work to be his in the absence of a signature.

Nevertheless, style is more than manner; it roots as well in the very springs of moral behavior. The artist in morality conveys the impression of a fullness of life which makes all acts infinitely less significant than their source. The good person towers above his deeds; they are the product of his superfluity, as it were. Like a skilled builder or the master of an intricate machine, his works look effortless and carry us in admiration from the deed to the doer. The person whose behavior is predictable entirely even to his closest friends is doubtless lacking in the finer sensibilities. The moral artist is governed by subtler perceptions and more flexible attitudes than is the conventional moralist. His hallmark is the open mind, the search for wider perspectives, the unfettered imagination. Such a person is never completely known or knowable for the simple reason that he is in process of becoming, under way, not at the end of development. The fascination of a rich personality is one of the few inexhaustible phenomena in all experience. Again like a work of art, every time we return to it, new facets are revealed.

The possessor of style in moral behavior is blessed with the gift of perspective on the situations of daily experience. Because he recognizes the impossibility of knowing the future consequences of any action, his mood is one of gentle irony, restraint, a freedom from dogmatic assurance. This does not suggest detachment, however, if detachment be interpreted in the common sense as freedom from emotional involvement. Perspective, on the contrary, permits us to be engaged emotionally, to sympathize and share in the current struggles for social, religious, and international justice. It requires not merely sensitivity of conscience, but willingness to act skillfully and accept compromise. What perspective prohibits is commitment in the fashionable modern sense of going "all out" for a single cause or particular person, of becoming a partisan for a religious or political credo. Such commitment blinds its followers to other possible interpretations of the right and the good and causes them to forget that the moral is only one, if an all-pervasive, element in every situation. Folly consists in the inability to transcend the local scene; wisdom, in the possession of reserves which carry one beyond the partial view.

Moral style, at its very best, is a kind of de-moralizing of the moral. It does not call attention to itself. The good man acts

without specific regard to his virtues, for they have been blended
into a pattern of living that is all his own. Others may disagree
with his interpretations and may even dislike his total style. This
is inevitable because artistic skill involves a high degree of individuality in relationships with others, with the realm of nature,
and with the many facets of our own being. But if these others
are honest, they will respect his decisions to do or let alone because they recognize that such decisions do not spring from mere
willfulness; on the contrary, they are the expression of a freely
chosen and entire structure of experience.

Such are a few of the requisites of artistry in conduct, an
artistry that the new demands and responsibilities of our complex
society require of the student in search of an education. The
major values embodied in this ideal of character are hardly new;
they are rather a rearrangement of tradition as all, or nearly all,
central values are likely to be. But the shift in the seat of authority for these values, from a religious to a secular base, represents a
considerable revolution in a crucial area of our national life.

The requirement of artistry in moral conduct, as opposed to
obedience to Biblical imperatives, puts a heavier burden on education, formal and formative, than it has ever had to bear, particularly in our land. As a more individual ideal, artistry requires a
kind of instruction that takes full account of diversity in temperaments and variety of endowments. As a more relativistic ideal, it
requires a kind of instruction that will serve to bind the developing individual to his fellows and to nature in freely willed
relationships. Artistry in conduct implies more attention to
knowledge of the kind that really affects the will and forms the
character. To insist on self-knowledge, self-discipline, and personal style in the moral life is to make generous assumptions about
the capacity for imagination, reflection, and radical openness to
new experience in the rising generations.

Though little more than a beginning can be made in the
schools in the actualizing of this educational goal, the be-

ginning is of primary importance. There is widespread agreement that these virtues of which we have been speaking are incapable of being taught in the manner that traditional subject matter is capable of being taught. Still, many things which are not teachable are nevertheless able to be learned. In the process of developing a moral character, all of us are dependent on models to an extent that is difficult to exaggerate. If the new seriousness about formal education in America should succeed to the point of attracting to the teaching profession a much larger proportion of the most able and dedicated of our people, the effect would be incalculable.

In that event our teachers might well become admired models of great numbers of their pupils in the most formative years of character building. Real advance in moral insight and action has, after all, always been the work of a small minority, whom others have imitated with more or less reluctance. A few teachers in every generation have exerted, in this most precarious area of education, an influence out of all proportion to their numbers. In this day of vastly improved communication, opinion leaders are able to be more effective than ever before. Hence, the conclusion suggests itself that the realization of this educational goal depends to a considerable extent upon the artistry of American teachers at every level of schooling.

In the past our universal, free, and compulsory school system has been put in the service of creating from a heterogeneous population, a tolerably unified national consciousness. It has helped to make us into Americans rather than English, Italians, and Germans. In this moral purpose our schools have achieved a large measure of success. But now it is evident that the schools should turn to the task of helping to build a wider common basis of values, in which the accident of nationality is put in its proper place. We Americans like to think of ourselves as a self-made people and of our culture as the product of a distinctive vision of individuality and freedom. The notion of the fitting or the appropriate in behavior is very much in line with our specifically American inheritance. As a moral ideal it is eminently capable of becoming an educational ideal. Guided by the analogy of the artist in molding his materials and goaded by the concept of excellence in living style, these ideals can be bolstered by our own American past, by that which may be said to have been implicit in our national consciousness from the beginning.

Part III

PHILOSOPHICAL PROBLEMS OF PRACTICE

The genuine teacher is only superior to the students in that he has far more to learn than they, namely, to let learning occur. The teacher must be capable of being more teachable than his students. The teacher is far less sure of his task than the students are of theirs. Hence in the relationship of teacher and learner, if this relationship is a genuine one, it is never a question of the authority of the great knower or the dominating influence of the instructor. Therefore, it is a great thing to become a teacher, something quite different than to be a famous professor.

—Martin Heidegger

The Question of Leadership

5. THE EQUAL AND THE ABLE

AT A COCKTAIL PARTY not long ago a high school teacher, slightly under the influence, told me in no uncertain terms her opinion of the majority of the students she taught. "I couldn't care less about the average and below who are going to be the taxi drivers, little business men, and unskilled workers of this country. The only ones that interest me are the future leaders in politics, education, the sciences and the arts. The others," she yelled to make herself heard above the chatter, "are simply bodies, so many ciphers who take up space in my classes."

With a certain uneasiness I wondered how many teachers are coming to conclusions like these as a consequence of our widely advertised pursuit of academic excellence, called the great talent hunt. Not many years ago sentiments like hers would have been regarded as highly offensive, if not downright subversive of our American theory of universal education. Then the average student was the main concern of our schoolmen; the gifted one could take care of himself. Teachers were advised to pitch the level of their teaching to the majority of their students and were judged successful in most school systems if they improved the competence of the lower ranking students in their classes. To prefer the talented over the average was widely regarded as being undemocratic; even casual reading of educational literature in earlier decades of this century affords convincing evidence of this.

Just when we are finally growing serious about ending separation in our schools on the basis of color, we are insisting on introducing it again on the basis of intellect. Those who once believed that all youngsters should be schooled in the same classrooms, regardless of ability, are now witnessing the rapid growth of a multi-track system in the public schools, an increasing segregation of the highly talented from the superior, the superior from the average, and the average from the "exceptional." This eagerness for homogeneous grouping in the public schools is paralleled by the demand that the "best" students go to the "best" universities and colleges in order that they may occupy key positions of leadership in future society. Good reasons are adduced by the proponents of this revolutionary shift from emphasis on equality to emphasis on academic excellence. An old phrase of Jefferson's about "raking the geniuses from the rubbish" as the purpose of public education has been resurrected nowadays. Everywhere we are warned that unless we give primary attention to our most brilliant youth, our kind of society is doomed.

For those with even slight historical memory, it is difficult to avoid a certain cynicism at this most recent swing of the educational pendulum. But it is much more instructive to become reflective, to ask the simple question: How did we get this way? Why this sudden passion for academic excellence? Reading the mountainous literature that is accumulating may well confuse us unless we engage in the labor of thought.

The yearning for and belief in equality is historically very deep in Americans. Our immigrant forefathers came to these shores to escape old Europe's inequalities. They rejected the aristocratic ideals in government, social affairs, and education that they had inherited there. Though the leaders among them were for the most part themselves aristocrats, intellectually they were profoundly affected by the equalitarian impulses that were gaining the upper hand in the growth of democratic thought. Consequently, they helped to organize a society in our country based not only on individual freedom and individual rights but on social and legal equality as well. The advance of the idea that all men are born equal as well as free was a striking and fundamental fact of the first century and a half of our national existence.

Alexis de Tocqueville, who visited our country in the 1830's, convinced himself that the principle of equality was the most pervasive and powerful one of this new society. The real struggle in our land he conceived to be that between the principles of equality and liberty. The brilliant Frenchman concluded that the love of, indeed the passion for, equality was our first and most deeply rooted love, whereas the taste for liberty was of a different sort and much less potent. Because he was objective and believed himself to be observing an irresistible force of history, Tocqueville was able to see and say things about this passion for equality in America better and more profoundly than had been seen or said before—and perhaps since. Though he found much to praise in this new country with its passion for equality, his strictures were reserved for the tendency to repress individuality, to impose uniformity of opinion, and to keep from high office distinguished and independent minds. Tocqueville feared that the love of well-being, which he called "virtuous materialism" and which seemed to be inseparable from this passion for equality, would gradually sap the love of liberty which was to him the other wellspring of democratic life. Far from believing that liberty and equality are brothers, he was convinced that they are in tension and conflict; though related, they require quite different forces and safeguards for their co-existence and preservation.

The renewed popularity of Tocqueville's book in our day is doubtless due to our awakening consciousness that equality and freedom are in danger of destroying each other. Twentieth century totalitarianisms represent in some sense the triumph of equality over liberty and are clear evidence of the strife of these principles. But the situation is hardly simple. The English, who love liberty as much as we, have never possessed our preoccupation with equality and hence have maintained a class system of education and an early division of the intellectually able from the average. They and many other free peoples have been reluctant to follow our early example of compulsory, universal, and free public education with its tendency toward a single-track system in the schools.

The core of their objection to equality as a principle of educational practice is that it leads to neglect of quality and produces mediocrities. Europeans have not been slow to remind Americans of our tendency to interpret equal as meaning the same. The seemingly easy way of assuring equality in our schools, they pointed out, was to provide the same education for all. This often led to the view that every child was entitled to the same amount of education as well as the same kind. If college education becomes necessary for success, everyone should be "given" a college education. When the material is too difficult for the slower student, it should be simplified and rendered easier of comprehension. From this standpoint it is always the school system which fails, not the student. The solution is to pass weak students up the educational ladder until such time as they "catch on" and learn from classmates. If they do not excel in subject matter, they will at least acquire the skills of adjustment and groupmindedness, which are, in any case, more important. Such were some of the extremes to which our educational theory was seduced in the not too distant past.

Democratic and undemocratic Europeans alike remained unimpressed with such thinking. With Aristotle they insisted that it is as unjust to treat unequals equally as it is to treat equals unequally. Hence they clung fast—and still do in the main—to their two-track systems of schooling whereby the intellectually promising are separated at an early age from the majority and given subject matter that leads to university entrance and later professions. All others are provided with various training in trade and specialist schools designed to fit them for early wage earning in the less demanding occupations and jobs. Though European nations vary greatly, of course, in the kinds of schooling provided, they agree in principle that the intellectually gifted should be separated and that this separation should take place at the beginning of secondary schooling.

Until very recently we Americans have been hard to persuade that there is anything wrong with our reliance on a single-track system. The virtues of our formal education lay on the surface. The schools served to weld our diverse immigrant population into a desirable unity; with great speed they made children into young Americans. If the schooling they provided did not pro-

duce many superlatively educated adults, they did at least raise
the general level of literacy in our people above that of most
other nations. And the single-track system also prevented the
elitist feelings which we most disliked in our European cousins.

But the Second World War, and the Korean conflict, perhaps
especially, revealed weaknesses in our educational system. And
the startling success of Russian technology, which resulted in the
first Sputnik in 1957, began to cause great doubt in many minds
about this aspect of our theory of education. The resultant debate about theory and practice in the past few years has been
conducted in a highly charged emotional atmosphere of crisis,
sometimes approaching hysteria. Our old assurance that American schools are the best in the world has vanished under storms of
criticism and comparison, predominantly invidious. The clearest
change in practice thus far has been a shift of emphasis to education of the gifted, for the excellent rather than the average, to the
point where the term *excellence* has already become a banal
slogan in American education.

Hard as it is to think clearly amongst the clamor of voices, for
the student of educational theory nothing is more important. On
this question of the proper claims of talent and ability over our
traditional belief in equality and faith in the average man, large
decisions are being taken nowadays with all too little thought. It
is easier in certain circles to take the side of those who condemn
our equalitarian heritage and proclaim that "education for all is
education for none," decrying in bitter tones "the worship of
commonness" in contemporary society. In other circles it can be
fashionable to set one's face stubbornly against current demands
for excellence and oppose homogeneous grouping and the so-
called upgrading of our school system. Easiest of all is to remain
confused and indecisive, aware of the pros and cons on both
sides, and expecting soon another swing of the educational pendulum. Far more appropriate is the attempt to probe to the philosophical roots of the differences between the average and the able
student and the kind of education suitable for each in a society
that cherishes both liberty and equality.

The first question we should ask ourselves is: who are the truly able among our youth? Seemingly so easy, this is in reality a most difficult question to answer. Our first reply is likely to be: the able are the very intelligent, those with good memories, quickness of apprehension, abstracting powers, and the other traits associated with native aptitude. Yet most of our recent experience confirms the impression that it is impossible to distinguish native endowment from environmental influences. Even if we could, native ability would still be an inadequate measure of the gifted. There is something passive and merely potential about intelligence, whereas educational accomplishment is something active and actual. There is a stubborn sense in which ability must be established in the tests of practice, for the exercise of intelligence is not identical with its alleged possession. Deeply understood, intelligence is even identical with its use; it is not a thing, a quantum, but an activity and a quality. Just as there is no virtue in mere willing, so there is no intelligence that is not exercised. Though we continue to think of intelligence as a sheer "given" and will not give up our search for it as a separate entity, we reveal thereby the ineradicable tendency of the human mind to rest in abstractions.

Those of us who teach, however, are quick to identify intelligence when it is combined with what we variously call the desire to accomplish, love of hard work, persistence, staying power, and the like. The truly able, we like to say, are those youngsters who do not necessarily have the highest Intelligence Quotient but who have strong motivation to perform outstandingly, who make full use of their native endowment, whatever that may mean, and who consistently tower above their classmates by virtue of the effort they display. Though such students rank high or above average, as a rule, on aptitude and intelligence tests, they are by no means always at the top in such tests. If it is quite clear that certain students because of low ability will never become great physicists, engineers, or writers, it is the reverse of clear that students with average endowments cannot become so, *if* they possess sufficient drive.

A chief difficulty with this combined criterion of the truly able is that it is restricted to *academic* ability and aptitude; the underlying assumption is that those who perform well in school will also accomplish outstandingly as future adults. Though we are increasingly able at relatively early ages to predict success in the academic world, there has been little advance in our capacity to foretell who among our youth will excel in the art of effective and productive life beyond the school. Everyone knows that there are special aptitudes for music, art, athletics, political leadership, and the like, most of which elude our academic testing and grading procedures. Students who possess them are truly gifted, but by no means always academically talented. The schools are at a loss to know what to do with the lack of interest and indifferent performances of such students in the regular disciplines. Our devotion to the ideal of the well rounded man requires us to expect of them at least minimal competence in the knowledge of citizenship, mathematics, and the arts of language and history, difficult and unappealing as these may be. In the rapidly growing demand for better academic performance and increasing preoccupation with standardized measurements, such specially gifted ones find the going ever harder and must often wonder whether their gifts are not a curse in a society that equates, more and more, future success with academic performance.

This problem is, of course, a universal and timeless one. A large factor in genuine ability is the gift of originality. If individuality is, as we have said, a comprehensive goal of education, its constituent is precisely that which is unique and unmeasurable in the youth. And schooling in contrast with education must of necessity be primarily devoted to that which is held in common by the group. Every able student is able in his own peculiar fashion. His originality, at least, requires to be brought forth and made real by highly personal skills on the part of the teacher. Quite apart from this, however, schools have great trouble, as do other organizations, in dealing with originality. By definition it is a highly troublesome, if exceedingly precious quality. Though it is undeniable that many students imagine they possess it who do not and revolt against the inflexibility of teachers who demand conformity of them, it is just as undeniable, if less frequent, that genuine originality is rigorously suppressed by such teachers who fail to recognize or refuse to believe in its presence.

Our grading system is frequently a chief offender in this respect. How often do all of us as teachers give the highest grades to students whom we are reasonably certain are far from the best in the class! On the other hand, we give average grades to those we suspect are genuinely original. The former have done what we asked of them, worked hard, and reproduced in tolerable English the wisdom we have dispensed. The latter have been too impatient to take the trouble, but have shown here and there powers of penetration and thought when their whole interest has been aroused. These cases are, of course, not the rule. Yet it is hardly sentimentality to believe that the most original minds are frequently not those who leave school with the highest grades on their transcripts or score best on national tests. This is no one's fault in a sense, nor can it be easily corrected. Sensitive teachers, who usually have a bad conscience about grades, are likely to retort that their grades must be based on accomplishment in mastery of the material, not on originality or on flash performances. And the standardized tests are set up for widely recognized abilities, not for the exceptional talent.

There is also "the late bloomer," the student who for one reason or another does not come to himself until late adolescence and then by his stellar performance amazes all of his teachers who have long since written him off as hopeless. After considerable experience every reflective teacher comes to the realization of how little he knows about these dormant powers that enable many indifferent students of his to excel in the world beyond academia. He is equally in the dark about the opposite phenomenon, dubbed "the morning glories," of whom he predicted great things but who gradually reveal that their talents were solely academic. Studies are recently being made of this latter group in an effort to determine why they suddenly stop growing and fail to realize their early promise even in academic pursuits. In the scientific field especially, according to current literature, this phenomenon has reached disquieting proportions. There are too many students who have given every evidence that they will become creative scientists—and hence have been aided in every way to the doctorate and beyond—who turn out to be sad and tragic disappointments to themselves and to their mentors. The old Greek fable of the tortoise and the hare and the Biblical reminder that "the race is not to the swift nor the battle to the strong" appear to be as applicable to our day as they ever were.

It is naturally protested that statistically these cases are not significant and that to dwell on them permits the uninformed to rationalize and the unsuccessful to become sentimental. Those who are engaged in testing and "sorting out" the able point with justifiable pride to the improvement in testing procedures; they insist that for nearly the first time such tests permit us as a nation to discount the effects of material privilege and to develop sheer ability in whatever stratum of society it is found. Some of our prestige universities take a percentage of these socially disadvantaged students and publicize freely their successes in overcoming unfavorable early environments. They admit that all predictive procedures are unreliable as yet, but stress the considerable recent improvements and look forward confidently to their perfecting. If one looks at the larger picture, they tell us, it is clear that we are increasingly able to discover the gifted earlier than ever and through proper education to assure their maximum contribution.

Still, a cautious scepticism is very much in place. That we are making progress in discovering the academically talented is clear. But whether these are the youth best fitted for leadership in the multifarious fields in the world beyond the schools is another question. Even if that world selects the top academic performers for its future leaders, as seems likely, there will still be the large problem whether or not these are the ones society should choose for leadership posts. We may well become a society that overrates a narrow conception of intellectual ability. We may confuse, as we have often before tended to do, prominence with distinction and success with merit. If intelligence in any limited sense is put in the first rank of our order of values, we may discover at a future date that intellectual effectiveness is not the quality that guarantees survival. Or perhaps survival may be guaranteed by such choices without the richness, diversity, and opportunities for fulfillment that make survival worthwhile. In short, reflection requires us to raise the question whether the truly able do not possess qualities over and above those we call natural aptitudes and superior desire to work hard in order to actualize these aptitudes.

There is a little noticed phrase in Plato's *Republic* which seems highly significant in any discussion of discovering the gifted. After stressing the importance of natural aptitude, after adding to this inherent ability the requirements of testing for physical vigor, love of learning, memory, intellectual endurance, and the like, Socrates puts one other indispensable quality in first rank which able children must have if they are to be desirable leaders of an ideal state. It is "a sense for the whole." Socrates is sure that this disposition manifests itself early in life and hence counsels long, and unobtrusive, observation of children to detect those comparatively few youngsters who display such a sense for the whole. It is, of course, true that in his educational masterpiece Plato is primarily concerned with political leaders and their proper education. It might well be doubted whether artists, scientists, or business executives, and other kinds of future contributors would possess such a sense. Nevertheless, we need to remind ourselves that the philosopher-kings of Plato's imagined state were thought of by him primarily as educators, not statesmen or politicians in the modern sense. Hence, the possession and careful education of such a sense was as relevant for the poet as for the politician; for the scientist as for the general.

In contemporary language, this quality in a youngster might well be called a sense of responsibility, in the primary meaning of willingness to respond to the demands of his time and situation. The youth with a sense for the whole is not simply gregarious nor is he possessed of an executive type of personality. On the contrary, he is one capable of caring passionately, of concern for others' welfare, and an intuitive sympathy for their differences from him and need for distinctive educational experiences. He is quick to recognize that education implies mutuality and that his own self-realization can take place only in a focus of community. Individuality is the end of his striving and neither individualism nor conformist collectivism can tempt him long from the path of his true interests. Conduct he soon learns to conceive neither as a matter of rules nor a yielding to immediate impulse, but a careful choice of what fits his situation and does justice to the sensitivities of those affected by it. In a word, a sense for the whole implies caring greatly for the distinctiveness of others, their right to develop in their own way, but also in relation to him in the context of community. This is a capacity to recognize that he who would find himself must first lose himself, a phrase as appropriate to education as it is to religious salvation.

The real danger in our present preoccupation with quality, in reaction from our traditional passion for equality, is forgetfulness of this third and perhaps most important ingredient of giftedness. Our prevailing insecurity as individuals and as a culture, induced by too rapid social changes, tempts us into too external ways of interpreting genuine ability in the rising generation. Our love of competition, of material success, of status seeking, and pride of power are traditions that contribute to this peril. Superior intelligence, however difficult it is to define, is a quality widely distributed in any population, and we ought to have learned by now that it can be put as readily into the service of self-seeking as of constructive purposes. Fewer have the drive to work hard and to persist until their natural talents are fully developed, yet strong motivation is also of itself no sign of election to the truly able. All too many young people with drive and determination are out for themselves alone, are on the way to becoming individualists but hardly individuals. Unless there is some indication of a concern for the whole, some early evidence of potential excellence of character as well as of intellect and of will, there is little reason for considering any youth really gifted, with claims on special attention in our public school system.

Though our traditional love of equality in this country has many failings, particularly when it becomes a passion, one of its real virtues has always been that it sought to judge a man in terms of what he *is*, rather than what he *has*, even when those possessions were intelligence and determination. In other words, we have, though with numerous lapses, tended to put character in its proper place at the top of our structure of values. Our durable heroes in this land of equality have all possessed a sense of their public responsibility, a vision of their role in advancing the ideals of our common humanity. It will require both clear heads and vigorous speaking in this new day of specialization and worship of short-range efficiency, if we are to hold fast to the good in that tradition while trying to expunge the bad.

Even if we are agreed that the truly able among our youth are those who possess this capacity for caring as well as native intelligence and willingness to work hard and long, it is still doubtful whether we have any means to discover these abilities in the schools. Is potential superiority of character determinable in advance even to the degree that intelligence and the will to persevere are measurable? Certainly we are far from any standards at present and will remain so as long as we seek to deal with children in large classes and pay comparatively little attention to individual counseling. To discover the truly able in character requires that a teacher know his students in depth, that he gain their confidence and trust, which means spending much time with them. Most of us who teach are unfortunately not trained observers in this realm. Though educational theorists since Plato have stressed close observation of children at play in order to find out the natural bent, and though "the play way" in education has been adopted to greater or lesser extent in our schools, few of us use our powers of observation to advantage. Nor have we adopted any organized method of recording and passing along observations on the growth of character traits in children. Every school year is a new beginning in a bad sense for the developing child; the new teacher is expected to learn afresh what kind of person he has before him. Many teachers prefer it this way. They want to form their own impressions of character, even though they are eager to study intelligence and aptitude scores.

As a consequence many of us mistake amiable mediocrities for rare characters. We are prone to be overly fond of those students who respond well to our personalities and flatter, wittingly or not, our egos. We justify this deficiency by scornful references to the inevitability of "subjective" judgments in the area of character development and student values. By and large our emphasis is still on the averagely good in character. We are too likely to believe that most of our students have good enough characters to fit the organizations in adult life in which they are destined to labor. "The good guy and the good girl" are still standard American types, despite the recent accent on excellence, and as always are rated too high in a school system that values adjustment and conformity. Superlative gifts in character are more easily overlooked and doubtless rarer than superlative intellects and a passion for outstanding performance.

Yet a few exist in nearly every school and in most American communities, the leaven that gives our bread its flavor. He or she will possess that quality of sensitivity, the capacity for reflection and self-knowledge in his relations to others and to the larger world that sets him apart. He will be the unforgettable student who knows gratitude for what he has been given, who experiences deeply and passionately the ideas and events that are real for him, the student who cherishes growth in the inner life as a supreme value in learning, who has capacity for human tragedy far beyond the imaginative range of others. Such a student is destined to be a life-long seeker for practical wisdom, for the life that is proper for man to live.

These are, as Nietzsche once called them, "the rare, strange, and privileged." Their fellow students may more easily sense their presence than can their teachers, with that intuitiveness which adults commonly lose. Yet the young person who will perform greatly in the future may, as things are at present, slip through our schools all but unknown to teachers and students alike. He may be incredibly shy, reluctant to reveal his inner nature to a teacher or fellow student because he lacks confidence that they will respond in kind. Often such students take longer to mature, to find the relationships which are alone fruitful for their development. There is a late bloomer in this sphere too, requiring occasions of crisis or a once-in-a-lifetime friendship to bring out reserves of character. Whether these youngsters ever come into positions of leadership in American life is largely a matter of accident. They may well be ahead of their times and only sway the minds of men long after they have passed from the scene. We are still largely led in ways that matter by men and women who belong to earlier periods of history, some of them martyred by their contemporaries. Who can deny that a Socrates, a Jesus, a St. Francis, a Comenius, a John Adams, to name only a few, is not at least as influential in the present as in his own times? The true leaders of a people are as likely as not to be remote from the influential posts and positions of their day; they carry on their work frequently in neglect and solitude, serving their age far better than the prominent and the outwardly successful.

Viewed from this perspective, it is quite certain that we in the schools are unable to identify with any assurance those who have potential for providing our future with the necessary guidance to keep our culture not merely in existence but worthy to survive. Nevertheless, this is no argument against the obligation, indeed urgent duty, we have in the schools to seek out and offer the best education we can for the promising. There is certainly no rule that the academically able and the strongly motivated will later disappoint us in the quality of their contribution to the larger society. Since this is so, we need to inquire by what right those youngsters we presume to be able are entitled to special attention, time, and money in our public schools. Can we justify the current tendency to segregate them in small classes, provide better teachers, and public financial support for them through college and graduate schools? What philosophical basis is there for homogeneous grouping, when we have no assurance that we are at present able to identify those who will some day perform outstanding service to our society or to the world?

The first claim that talent of any kind imposes on us is that of individual justice. Though Aristotle was concerned with the equitable distribution of political power in enunciating his famous principle that "it is as unjust to treat unequals equally as it is to treat equals unequally," the principle applies with the like force to education as well. There is an elemental injustice in holding the bright and industrious youth to the pace of his more numerous classmates. Surely there is something perverse and even stupid about insisting that democratic equality implies sameness. The age-old doctrine that every child has the right to full development of his potentialities should take precedence over the demands of strict impartiality and mechanical distribution of educational resources.

Nor does the old utilitarian slogan of the greatest good for the greatest number, with its corollary that "every one should count for one and nobody for more than one," satisfy the claims of individual justice. It used to be said that the brighter children could help themselves in school and the teacher's main duty was to minister to the average and dull. His presentations must be pitched at the level of the more numerous students in his classes, since only by so doing could he serve the majoritarian goal of democracy. Were it true that able children need teaching less than the average, this corollary of utilitarian philosophy would have at least practical cogency. But considerable evidence has been adduced by psychologists to suggest its falsity. Superior talents appear to have no greater tendency in the earlier years to develop independently than any others, and indeed are likely to suffer more from neglect than average ones. Excruciating boredom is only possible for the child who has great capacity for absorption in the process of discovery. In an atmosphere that is routine and undemanding, the gifted youngster tends to protect himself in any number of ways—from day-dreaming to active mischief-making. His undeveloped capacities can become worse than useless, for they allow him avenues to evil practices that those of more moderate abilities never divine.

One of the most sobering facts turned up by the recent efforts to reform public education is the number of highly intelligent youths who drop out of school at the first opportunity and display no interest in higher education. The aspect of this phenomenon that is due to economic factors we are making notable efforts to correct by providing state and national, as well as private foundational, subsidies; also the growth of local junior colleges and extension branches of state universities is helping to equalize educational opportunities for the more isolated fraction of our population. But the part that is due to insufficient challenge in the public schools is much more troublesome. Far too many of the able, in the sense of the intellectually brilliant, are simply not stimulated enough to want as much schooling as our wealthy country is able to provide them. Surely this is due in great part to their experience in uninspired classrooms, filled with students of average interest and abilities, with inadequate teachers, and an atmosphere of dullness and distraction. No escape from this situation appears feasible except the separation of the able, even with our present insufficient measures for determining who they are, and providing instruction for them of a high order with the ablest teachers we can recruit. This seems to be, in the first instance, the requirement of elemental justice to the individual.

In the second place, the needs of our society at the present juncture of history require special attention to the most able of our youth. We may well decry current taste in referring to these youth as "our greatest natural resource" after the analogy of timber, minerals, and water power; the minds of children are hardly resources to be used by society as means to its ends. But it cannot be denied that in present conditions of world instability, failure to develop the best talents we possess is likely to be fatal, even quickly fatal. For the values of democratic individuality are under attack today as they have hardly been in several centuries; as a result of world wars, overpopulation, and the impact of technologies our problems of freedom and order have become simply staggering. They demand a kind of leadership and creative thinking that only the best schooling can hope to prepare, if even then it will be sufficient. Hence, the imperative of reform of our educational system takes on a categorical form: Develop the best talents in your nation that you possess! Otherwise you will perish and with you many inherited democratic values. Leading democratic states can no longer afford the imputations fastened upon them, that they foster mediocrity, grow hostile to outstanding personalities and keep their best men and women from positions of leadership.

The crisis atmosphere of these times is naturally perilous to the cause of true progress in education. It tempts us to think of training for survival, of education as a weapon and as collective indoctrination. The major task of education can never be the identification of gifted youngsters for the purpose of rapid training in the natural sciences as front line troops in the battle against Communism. On the contrary, education of the most able must be in the interests of demonstrating to ourselves and to the so-called uncommitted peoples of the world a superior quality of life and efficiency of action, sufficient to triumph over the values of collectivism and a regimented society. To accomplish this we must cherish and develop our best talents, not only for themselves, but for the rest of us as well. Democratic leadership, always in too short supply, is certainly one of the indispensable keys to this struggle; and for this reason the genuinely gifted have superior claims to the best schooling our nation can provide.

Nevertheless, superior claims imply greater duties. If the able have a just claim to better schooling, those concerned with their education must endeavor to teach them their responsibilities to justify the considerable sacrifices our society has made to assure them of it. To whom much has been given, of him much will be expected, in accordance with the parable of the talents.

Many reflective observers fear homogeneous grouping, our

rapid change to the "track" system, because it will foster inevitable superiority feelings and an elitist mentality. These fears are soundly based in large measure. For a society as complex as ours where the unskilled and unendowed are becoming more and more superfluous in an occupational sense and where those of superior ability and training are more and more in demand, it will be difficult enough to retain the best features of our equalitarian heritage. Unless we can instill in the talented a sense of gratitude for their gifts and an unforced desire to return to society the benefits received, we shall forfeit the real advantages of ability grouping. If we foolishly insist that ability consists alone in sheer brain power and ambition to succeed, something like this is nearly bound to happen.

No pride is so insidiously dangerous to a democratic society as intellectual pride. At the founding of our nation our leaders were most zealous to guard against pride of birth that accrues to titles of nobility. Since then we have become accustomed to pride of wealth and have learned in a measure how to control it and render it less than fearsome. But intellectual pride is more divisive in its effects and harder to eradicate in its possessors. For it creates resentment in the soul of man, a much underestimated vice that acts like an acid to destroy the sense of community among people. Perhaps we are especially susceptible nowadays, we Americans, for we are conscious of the baneful effects of anti-intellectualism and can think of little worse than popular distrust of the "egghead," so frequent in our recent past. The thing that is worse is the over-estimation of intellect divorced from social responsibility and a feeling of common humanity with average human beings. When gifts of intellect are joined with those of character, there is always a proper humility. The power and responsibility which we are increasingly forced to entrust to the intellectually able and superlatively trained are frightening. If it were true that the brilliant are the responsible, that intellectual superiority implied selflessness, the separation of the able from the average in schooling would be self-evidently desirable. But nothing is less ambiguous than the evidence that intellectual bril-

liance can and does co-exist with egotism, selfishness, and indifference to the common good.

Therefore, it is imperative that, along with our endeavor to be
just to the able, we keep firmly in mind a second great principle
that Aristotle was one of the first to propose. Though the few
brilliant, he held, are best fitted to initiate policy, and should
hence be in executive positions in a society, the many average are
the best judges of policy. Translated into educational terms, this
principle means that the major task of education among a people
resolved to be free is the strengthening of the powers of the
average student, particularly his powers of judgment. Faith in the
democratic process is quickly lost once one begins to doubt the
capacities for judgment of the ungifted majority. There is, of
course, no inherent superiority of judgment in the average man.
Aristotle's point was simply that collective judgment of average
people is likely to be wiser than that of the few brilliant because
they bring greater experience to bear. Not only that, but also
when they pool that experience through discussion and information, the results of such collective judgment are usually far above
that of anyone singly or of small aristocratic committees.

There is nothing mysterious or romantic about this principle,
no claim that the voice of the people is the voice of God. The
majority of men when they take counsel of one another and are
reasonably free of passion and narrow self-interest are less likely
to make irremediable mistakes than any smaller group, however
brilliant. Since they have indisputably more at stake in the common good than any minority, they are more likely to be the best
guardians of it. To be sure, there is a faith in the average man
involved in this principle, a faith in his capacities for judging
wisely policies he could not have initiated. Creative powers are
not coincident with those of weighing properly and coming to
decisions, the latter being much more widely distributed than the
former. If this faith be false or if it has become outmoded because
of the technical nature of decisions in modern society, then democratic individuality is doomed in any case.

But so long as our people believe in the democratic principle that the majority have the right and duty to decide who shall rule, so long as we believe that the ultimate power of decision belongs in principle to the average person, then it follows that our primary task of public education is with the many and not the few. Our best resource against intellectual pride and an elitist mentality is to keep uppermost in the minds of the presumed future leaders their dependence on their ungifted fellows, a dependence based upon no democratic mystique but upon the principle that an informed average judgment in contact with others has been found to be wiser for a people to follow than any other. More important still will be our determination to improve the schooling of the average student at least as much as we are currently seeking to provide special education for the gifted.

What kind of instruction is appropriate for the academically gifted? To this question no easy answer has been found as yet. Far too much depends on the nature of talent and the kind of temperament of the individual child. Classes that are homogeneously grouped to include only the academically talented show nearly as wide a spread of differences as many heterogeneous ones. Even within a single subject matter talents are greatly diverse. Some academically gifted youngsters reveal great capacity in one or two directions; others demonstrate an all-round aptitude for most academic disciplines. There appears to be also a very uneven development of both interests and abilities in youth of great potential. Teachers of such classes report that they are thrilled but at least as perplexed by them as by more mixed groups. Perhaps the perplexity will lessen as we develop appropriate texts for instruction of superior youth, as we have only just begun to do.

Still a great many riddles will remain. Should the child of near-genius ability in a single field be permitted to neglect other areas of knowledge for which he has little interest or competence? How much freedom should he be allowed in school to develop his own initiative and creativity when it means slighting the school's demand for competence and accuracy in more prosaic but necessary skills? Can we afford to pass over solid grounding in physical development and the arts of communication in the interests of getting such youth quickly to the frontiers of knowledge? The claims of balance and harmonious development are frequently in conflict with those of creativity and the urgencies of rapid growth. On the one hand, some observers believe that nothing can keep a child of great powers from realizing his talent, no matter what blunders are made; on the other hand, many are certain that mistakes in instruction may utterly destroy the delicate balance of potentialities. The truth appears to be that some of the academically talented are robust enough to survive any trials and blunders in their schooling while others are easily destroyed.

In the absence of answers to most of these questions, or at least in the absence of anything approaching majority opinion, there are a few general propositions most of us can hardly doubt.

One of them is that the academically gifted require imaginative and creative teachers. As a nation we could well shift the current emphasis on the great talent hunt from children to teachers. For a generation we have read in educational circles about individual differences in children, but have heard precious little about individual differences in teachers. Yet nothing is clearer than the influence of greatness in a teacher to inspire imitation in both gifted and average youth. Since no teacher, no matter how superb, can hope to reach all talented children, exposure to as many excellent teachers as possible is self-evidently desirable. It is equally evident that those teachers who have achieved some sort of mastery of the difficult art of instruction stand the best chance of awakening the fullest response in classes of the highly talented. It may be regarded as a definition of the excellent teacher that he combines the love of learning with the skills of communicating both love and learning to the taught.

Still, there is much more to be said about the relationship of gifted teacher to gifted student, no matter how much has been written about it previously. The effective teaching of the gifted requires, I think, more directness than is customarily necessary. It involves a dialogue, even when many are present; hence the requirement that gifted classes be quite small. Yet the teacher of such children will not simply engage in talking, for there is a vast difference between talking and teaching, a difference involving the meaning of authority. Such a teacher waits for their response, either verbal or tacit, to what he says. For such dialogue involves the intimacy of community while at the same time preserving the individuality of dialogue between two people. This ability to preserve the virtues of community while insisting on personal communication is close to the crux of great teaching. It can only be possible where there is a rough equality of student capacities for comprehension and in the teacher superior force and skill in concentrating his thoughts in the process of communicating them.

The successful teacher of the gifted draws them to his subject by pulling them out of themselves. For the time being he demands that they rise to his level of understanding, as far as possible. While respecting their private worlds, he insists on joining them to his own so that an expansion may occur. In this sense, all good teaching is a lifting of the taught to higher levels of awareness. It is an ecstasy in the original meaning of the word, an abandoning of the narrow limits of the self. They are caught up in his world and made participants in his vision, compounded of enthusiasm, suffering, prejudices, limitations, and insights. They may see beyond him in this or that vista; they may well struggle for their own contrary interpretation, but they will be part of his embracing understanding. Such teaching is direct and personal; it is above all compelling while it is in progress, regardless of future reservations the taught may have. It is compelling because it relates the self to the encompassing human and natural environment.

The creative teacher manages to be compelling when he is fertile in ideas and nothing is more important in the education of the talented than a profusion of ideas. They may not all be valuable or correct. Indeed the greatest teachers of the past originated a great number of preposterous ideas, to which they were frequently as devoted as to the immensely fruitful ones. With gifted students there may well be positive value in propounding questionable notions, incautious suggestions, to provoke the exercise of their critical powers. Teaching average youth requires greater care, for they are inclined to take what the teacher says on trust and are normally unable to discriminate so sharply between wheat and chaff. Exercising the judgment of the average is in the first instance an exercise in criticism. But with the academically talented it is immensely important to provide them with a diet of ideas greater than they can assimilate at any given time. If they are to be absorbed, they must be struggling to assimilate, far from the threat of boredom which is their greatest enemy. In this sense it is true, as Whitehead has observed, that it is more important for an idea to be interesting than for it to be sound.

Such students should never be able to fathom their teacher wholly. For fertility of ideas is most valuable when they are greatly suggestive. On every theme he will manage to convey the impression of much more to be said, of avenues that are illimitable in extent, if only his students care to venture down those avenues. On a few he will show them the way, for analysis is important and can be taught, indeed must be, above all to the talented. But for every idea that he draws out to its full range he will suggest several to invite reflection and initiative by his students. For they require perspectives so long that only years will be sufficient for their exploration.

It is part of the stupidity of the very bright—a paradox that has not yet been analyzed sufficiently—that many need others to open up possibilities if the fire in them is ever to be kindled. Often, without direction and stimulus, they are the most helpless of mortals. Even Shakespeare, as everyone knows, was weak in invention, requiring the germ of a plot to stimulate his creative genius. The most successful teacher of such children will understand the peculiar inabilities of the able and will keep searching for the spark that ignites. His boundless respect for their capacities will not blind him to their weaknesses or make him less critical of their fatuous qualities.

There is another aspect of such teaching which compels gifted students and keeps them under the spell of their teacher: spontaneity. If he is to reduce to a minimum the routine of daily instruction, the teacher must be full of surprises, diversity of moods, unsuspected dimensions. The indispensability of imagination is never more apparent than in such cases. Only the teacher with an abundance of this quality can be spontaneous enough to diversify the class hour sufficiently for his restless charges. He will not be without plan and order in his teaching, or lightly diverted from his purposes. But he will not often make the mistake of ignoring the unplanned occasion, the unguessed curiosity, the naive question that may make all the difference to himself and his students. Spontaneity in him will be contagious; it will open up the minds of others and kindle enthusiasm as nothing else can do. Some trifling incident may furnish the opportunity for an absolutely memorable experience, given the spontaneity that can make the most of it. There is hardly a competent teacher who has not discovered to his amazement that some of his best teaching was totally unplanned; he hardly knew how or why that he and his students became utterly absorbed in discovery and exploration.

Of course, generalizations of this sort must take into account the age-level of instruction. That teacher who may be superb for twelve- or fourteen-year-olds will not necessarily do for those who are older or even younger. As gifted students mature, they require independence of mind in a teacher above spontaneity, fertility in ideas, and the power to compel absorption. The college teacher must be something more for them than a teacher; he must have his own projects and research in which they are invited to share as possible contributors. The professor who lives only for his students is not living sufficiently. They cannot imitate anyone in whom they do not surmise larger horizons than the pedagogical. For many of them sense the approaching end of their tutelage. Increasingly they want to explore for themselves and seek to think their own thoughts without guidance. Too much teaching, even of the superlative sort, becomes burdensome for them and they are likely to judge harshly even the professor they will later revere.

To teach such advanced adolescents is an enormously complicated affair. They still require guidance and restraints, for they are never as intellectually mature as they imagine. The effective teacher will learn to make himself dispensable, to transform himself into a counselor or tutor, and to give them maximum freedom without simply abandoning them to their own resources. Half-consciously they have come to fear his power to mold them in ways that may hinder their own individuality. What they want of him now is to be persuaded that he is master of a subject matter which they insufficiently possess; that he can demonstrate, more than teach to them, such mastery. The qualities they valued earlier in a teacher are as important as ever; now they demand more, namely, assurance that he can help them to an independence of judgment and power to originate that he himself possesses. They subject him to tests, seek to surpass him, and are impatient with even his best efforts. Often they are learning most from him when they appear to be intractable and cruel.

The etymology of the term 'tuition' is suggestive here. Before the word came to mean money for instruction, it connoted the act of instructing, and to instruct signified originally to protect or to guard. What the teacher or tutor of such gifted adolescents must attempt is to guard and protect them from the pitfalls and blind alleys that beset the course of their development. He will understand that such dangers stem both from the weaknesses in themselves and the strengths in him. His duty to lead them to independence—to lead from behind as it were—to divine when to hold on and when to let go, where to be patient and where to be imperious—this kind of tuition requires a quality of practical wisdom like no other art man has ever practiced.

There is one other generalization, perhaps not so widely accepted as the necessity for superb teachers, about the appropriate education of the really able that seems equally important. It is the requirement of privacy, the need to be left alone. Teaching is, after all, only one means to the development of a talent, and at the higher levels of schooling probably secondary in importance to self-education. In our characteristic American haste, we are in peril of forgetting the slow processes of spiritual development.

At present our methods seem designed to produce precocious geniuses who may perform outstandingly at age twenty-five but be sterile by age forty. The publicity that attends any unusual achievement today is now directed toward our gifted youth and it is difficult to believe that most will not be harmed by it. The youngster who displays an aptitude for one of the fields currently in the forefront of attention is encouraged to develop it speedily without much regard for the necessary supports of emotional stability and other inner resources needed to sustain him in disappointments and arid periods. He may even be pushed into the wrong specialty and encouraged to neglect strong natural interests that are dearer to his heart.

Everywhere the speed-up in American education is apparent, not only in the schooling of the gifted. Our youth are studying subjects in high school that were formerly taught in college; in elementary schools, former high school material. Homework compels many of them to spend nearly as many hours in the evening as they do at school. The pressure to get admitted to prestige colleges has increased the tension of school competition at every level. Much of this new seriousness about academic studies is highly beneficial, in view of our earlier slackness, and many of the complaints made in the popular press are beside the point. But the threat to privacy and leisure on the part of the academically talented is very real.

Why is privacy important for such youths? One answer is that they can only consolidate the materials to which they are exposed if they have opportunity for reflection in privacy. If teaching is creative, they need time to ponder the ideas it has given them and to follow out the suggestions it has provided. The distractions to which they are particularly liable are bound to be increased, if they are continually in the presence of others. Quiet and undisturbed hours, when memory is in full play, are a necessity if creative sparks are ever to become more than that. An even more important reason for privacy is that they can only reach those recesses of uniqueness in themselves when they are left alone. A talent is easily warped and teaching is all too likely to direct such students into momentarily appealing but finally unrewarding paths. No one can fuse for the student his interests and special abilities, which are so often at cross purposes in the early years of life. Only he can do it, and he can only do it if he is given time to "waste" in freedom from all external duties and constraints. To be left alone and even disregarded by parents and teachers is frequently the greatest boon.

Leisure is an indispensable accompaniment of privacy. Our present tendency to load down such students with heavy assignments is surely unwise, for they provide privacy without leisure. Of course, they can master materials that are far ahead of their grade levels and for a while show zest in such precocious activities. But what happens to the precious qualities of spontaneity and creativity when they are burdened with "lessons" during most of their waking hours? If they must wait until they are free of school to give their minds untrammeled leisure, their education may be fatally impeded. Everyone knows that the greatest discoveries have come when the mind is relaxed, seemingly idle and at play. If we accept at all the Toynbee principle of "withdrawal and return" as characteristic of great leadership in the past, it is time we made allowance for it in the schooling of those who have a chance of becoming future leaders.

Leisure is best designed to encourage that habit of reflection unforced and inner directed, which makes a youth many dimensional. Surely we do not want our ablest youth to be simply highly trained producers of what we have in abundance already. On the contrary, we need, above all, new ideas and new solutions for the problems that stagger our complex culture, even the imaginations of the most brilliant. Perhaps by forced feeding and speed-up methods we can attain the kind of trained competence that many fearful people think is necessary for survival. But such talents are too important to risk everything on survival. And if individuality is the goal, gifted youth have rights of their own, one of which is the opportunity for a balanced and harmonious development with some chances of happiness. Unless we learn to resist the temptation to regard our ablest youth as instruments of contemporary national politics, we may cause their talents to become a curse to them. Without greater care for their privacy and leisure we may yet produce a society that is too like the image of the political structure we dislike so much.

There is a real possibility that we *can* foster excellence and still retain our American faith in equality, as John Gardner optimistically claims in his recent book on *Excellence: Can We Be Equal and Excellent, Too?* But the real question is whether we *will* do it. In the present situation there are scant grounds for complacency. If the attitude of the teacher cited at the beginning of this chapter is widespread and increasing, there are indeed many grounds for despondency. Unless we retain our traditional faith in the averagely endowed, who, as always, remain the preponderant majority of our population, and put our main emphasis on raising their level of enlightenment and judgment, our equalitarian ideals will wither away. Unless we interpret giftedness as inclusive of excellence of character as well as brilliance and ambition, we will educate a generation of "experts" who will feel superior to "the others." These others in turn will be bitterly resentful of a class that is prominent, knowledgeable, and clever, but not really wise.

The Question of Method

6. AUTHORITY IN TEACHER
AND TAUGHT

As a practical people, we Americans are tempted to believe that the real issues of life and education concern means and not ends. Goals are thought to be easier to determine and delineate than are the ways of attaining them. Hence, problems of method are usually at the forefront of our planning and action. At times we are nearly obsessed with the urge to reduce the complexities of individual and collective life to questions of "how to do" this or that, rather than "why do it" or "what is it" I am trying to do. It would be an interesting, if idle, task for a computer to determine the number of books our presses turn out yearly that are devoted to problems of method with the interrogative How in their titles. They certainly run the gamut from *How To Be Happy Though Married, How I Made a Million on the Stock Exchange, How To Study, How To Be the Life of the Party*, to *How To Be Paul Tillich*. This faith of ours is at once naïve, even amusing, and full of pathos, attesting a boundless optimism underlying our view of the world. It expresses a kind of innocence native to youth, a confidence that the riddles of existence have a hidden handle by which they can be got hold of and resolved.

A profounder explanation for our faith in method doubtless lies in the gradual coming to dominance of modern science in Europe and America. Recognition of this powerful cultural influence can be attributed as much to philosophers as to scientists, though they were until recently hardly distinguished from each other. It was René Descartes, commonly called the father of modern philosophy, who was among the first to proclaim that most problems could be solved if only men applied the method of mathematics to every imaginable subject matter and every human concern. Since him we have become accustomed to learned discourse about methodology and to devoting inordinate amounts of energy and intelligence to the search for right methods in every field. The latest, though doubtless not the last, school of philosophy to put major emphasis on method are the language analysts, who are devoted to the proposition that most philosophical problems will disappear if and when we learn to use our language correctly.

Formal education and educators have likewise been preoccupied with method. Not long ago, students preparing to teach were under the impression that the "how" question was the primary one. At its extreme, such pedagogy asserted, in substance, that anyone could teach anything provided he had the right method. Methods courses proliferated in teachers' colleges and elsewhere until they became a scandal on the educational scene. Now, as everyone knows, we are in full retreat from this extreme, and emphasizing knowledge of subject matter as primary. As usual in such sharp reactions we are in peril of going too far, to the point of forgetting the vital, if subordinate, role that methods play in both schooling and education as a whole. The more perceptive students of educational theory clearly understand that problems of method dare not be neglected—as little in colleges and graduate schools as in elementary and high schools.

Many questions of method, however, are not mainly philosophical; they do not involve principles so much as educational psychology, sociology, and the practice of administration. For our philosophical purposes in this study the major questions of method become the kinds of relationships between teacher and student which promote the aims of education already outlined. In this relationship—and our focus will clearly be now on schooling —the teacher is primarily a means or a method. In simplest terms, the problem of method is this: how can the teacher best promote self-discipline in his students; how can he encourage them to care sufficiently for the values of individuality, artistry in conduct, and happiness to be able to realize them without him?

If it is true that individuality implies responsible freedom, it can be equally asserted that authority must be shifted from outside to within the growing youth in order to achieve this goal. Freedom and authority mutually imply each other. That individual is free who can control his impulses, discipline his desires and emotions, command himself in the pursuit of the goods his reasonable nature requires. So long as he is pushed and pulled this way and that by momentary moods and vagrant passions, he is in bondage and must be controlled from without. Unless he achieves self-discipline and learns to direct his life toward certain steady ends, he has no chance of gaining freedom. Hence the development of authority in individual life is the other pole of freedom. Without authority there can be no freedom, and so long as it stems from outside ourselves we are limited in our moral choices. So long as we are in the power of another we cannot be fully responsible. Until we learn to obey ourselves, we must obey others. Authority, as Hannah Arendt has stated it, implies obedience in which men retain their freedom.

One of the oldest educational doctrines is that the best kind of discipline is self-discipline. At every level the teacher's task is to impose order and to establish obedience in such a fashion that they gradually be transferred from the exterior forum to the interior. In the early grades this discipline is closely associated with maintaining physical order. That teacher has "good discipline," we say, whose pupils are quiet, obedient, and reasonably responsive to his or her directives. At more advanced levels discipline is grasped in more sophisticated ways. If students are mentally attentive and progressively ordering the subject matter they are studying into the pattern of their previous knowledge, their teacher is thought to possess good discipline. At a more advanced level still we sometimes feel that good discipline means "learning how to learn."

However, we commonly consider too little how much discipline is a continuity in education from first grade through graduate school. Unthinkingly we are likely to limit it to the sphere of outward behavior. The college professor may be as poor a disciplinarian as any primary teacher. His students have learned the elements of courtesy, but they may be making no advance whatever in control of impulse and attention. Morally his failure to command is far more culpable than that of one who has to impose physical restraints on the very young. If we try to think of authority in its essentials we will see it as a single problem throughout education.

That inner power to command obedience without force or violence in such a way as to transfer itself gradually from the teacher to the taught deserves the most careful reflection. For it is close to the secret of good teaching not merely of subject matter but of necessary values by which a free people live. The person who can speak with authority is a natural teacher, even though he may be a mere child. In the New Testament it is recorded of the boy Jesus that he taught in the temple "as one having authority," to the astonishment of the elders. It sometimes happens in the classroom that a student may have more actual authority than his teacher. I have observed students taking notes when one of their classmates gave his opinions and failing to do so when their teacher lectured. Though authority issues from many sources, its impact on us is likely to be single. In its absence there can be no real growth in autonomy and all teaching is in vain. The will to obey requires to be learned as truly as the will to command. Unless we discover authority in others as a compelling power to inspire our subordination of impulse, we shall assuredly never find it in ourselves.

Nothing concerns the beginning teacher in grade school and secondary education so much as his ability to keep good discipline in the classroom. Perhaps more young people turn away from teaching from fear of this inability than for any other reason. Thousands desert the profession after a few years' trial for the same, often unconfessed, failure. And those who stick it out will tell you that they find the problem of "keeping order" the chief liability of their calling. It wears them out, frays their nerves, and subtly undermines the real joys they discover in instructing the young. Thousands of American teachers are enthusiastic about their subject matter and gain incomparable fulfillment in the discovery that they can convey this enthusiasm to children and observe their growth in knowledge and understanding. But all too often they perceive little similar growth in the power of the taught to discipline themselves.

In nearly every class there are two or three "troublemakers," children who demand far more than their share of the teacher's attention, reproofs, angry expostulation and frequently punishment. Not only do they hinder the progress of their classmates, but they often infect them with the spirit of disobedience as well. In order to deal with these youngsters, a teacher finds himself adopting a harsh tone, which is frightening to the more timid spirits and likely to inhibit all the spontaneity and naturalness which the best learning situation requires. He finds it necessary to change his tone and mood a dozen times in the course of a morning, to become distracted from his main tasks, and to draw on the last reserves of his nervous energy. Because of a few students he discovers that he is turning into an image of himself that he most dislikes. The two or three students who provide him with the greatest joy of teaching are commonly balanced by a like number who sour his existence. So it is in a million classrooms over the land on every school day. Such conditions may be said to be among the most enduring features of school life in every generation. They do not always prevail, but they are the rule.

There are two kinds of problem children who need to be distinguished and treated quite separately: the disturbed or incorrigible children and those who are merely difficult. The former for one reason or another, usually discoverable to anyone who investigates their home background, have become pathological in their rejection of anyone placed in authority. Punishment of whatever kind only increases their defiance and resentment and their teacher soon realizes that he is incapable of teaching them anything of value so long as they reject the social situation entirely. Belatedly we are recognizing that such children must be taken out of the average classroom and taught in special institutions under the guidance of counselors and other experts who can often rescue them from outright delinquency and restore them to society. A few of our larger school systems have taken the lead in attempting to educate these incorrigibles separately. It is one of the tragedies of our educational organization that such children are not earlier removed in every community and given special care for their own sake as well as from consideration of the teachers they harass. While all of us recognize that no clear line can be drawn between the pathological, the borderline case, and the high-spirited child who is quick to resent authority, every teacher with experience is adept at distinguishing differences in a general way. In the following discussion of the sources of authority, we shall not be concerned with the seriously disturbed.

There are many elements of authority in the early years of school, but one of the most obvious is the status of the teacher as an adult. It was Aristotle who pointed out with the simplicity of genius that education is a process of age instructing youth. There is a natural deference which children at the pre-teen years pay to maturity. When they come from permissive homes in twentieth century America, this fact may not be obvious at first, but it is relatively easily established by a teacher with a modicum of assurance. However familiar the home environment has come to be, the youngster in school is dependent on direction and control by the adult world. He wants to be under supervision of a superior in the physical sense, an authority that is measurably different from that of his parents. The source of authority the teacher exerts by virtue of his age is not the same as that of the parents, but is easily assimilated to theirs. That is, the child transfers his habits of obedience, provided he has acquired any, from mother and father to teacher. He expects to be told and his teacher is the only one available while he is at school. The teacher has not brought him up from the condition of infant helplessness, hence school authority is derived and transmitted from parents. The important thing to notice is that it need not be won in the first instance, as must authority of other sorts.

Nevertheless, this elementary authority is very limited in its effects and particularly in modern America. In a society where the status of teachers as figures of authority is more secure, this natural deference exerts a far more powerful influence. Writers who complain constantly about the breakdown of authority in our society might well emphasize more than they have the popular image of the teacher. Problems of poor discipline stem not simply from the inadequacies of teachers, but also from our social failure to provide teachers with sufficient independence to assume authority easily. We are currently engaged in a national effort to raise teachers' salaries and to redeem the profession from the neglect into which it has fallen. But the struggle to regain the respect and dignity inherent in the position as such will not be easily gained by more adequate compensation or higher social status. These are certainly necessary prerequisites in the sense that they will attract abler people into the profession. But community attitudes toward teachers will be the decisive factor. When parents learn to regard the instructors of their offspring as professionals and not simply employees of the local school board, some of the natural authority will be rewon. And when teachers come to regard themselves as persons of key importance in the society, they will retain much longer than at present something of the respect in which the young should naturally hold them.

Not long ago a middle-aged woman introduced herself to me as "only a grade-school teacher." It represents a frequent extension of the "merely a housewife" syndrome of which we have heard so much. When youngsters are introduced to authority by mothers and teachers who think so little of themselves as this, small wonder that the problem of instilling authority into the souls of the young gets a poor start. Such teachers are in constant dread of their Principals and Superintendents, who are, in too many American communities, fearful in turn of the displeasure of two or three influential families of the school district. Though obedience is rendered by most of the young to adults in school as a natural consequence of age difference, it does not endure long when those adults reveal their servile fear of superior authority.

In the nineteenth century and lasting well into the twentieth, the problem of keeping order in the classroom was more easily solved by simple reliance on fear. Teachers were usually authority figures in a dreaded sense. Physical punishment was a commonplace and discipline was held to be a separate function, a precondition of any worthwhile instruction. A teacher's ability to "keep order" was the criterion of success and, as John Dewey somewhere remarks, too many of them did little more than this. Obedience was regarded as an absolute duty, needing to be attained in home and school by physical force. The teacher as stern taskmaster from whose slightest wish there was no recourse made school a hated experience from which the young escaped at the earliest opportunity. The notion of an inherent relation between freedom and authority even in youthful hearts was farthest from the mind in that earlier day. But the revolution against the excessive reliance on fear was not long in coming. A whole generation of writers and teachers appeared to denounce its relevance for a society seeking to become more democratic and equalitarian.

The complex movement we now loosely term progressivism—and few of us yet fully understand—was dominated by the conviction that self-discipline could never be instilled by fear. Keeping order in the classroom involved radically different methods. The teacher was enjoined to renounce his fear-inspiring authority and become a counselor, guide, and friend. School must be, above all, a happy experience where children were loved, their wishes respected, and their wills gently matured into responsibility. Teachers were failures only when they were unable to secure the enthusiastic cooperation of their charges in whatever project the class was engaged. The argument of the progressivists ran that once the interests of the children were engaged, the problem of keeping order would take care of itself. In any event, order was not the prime requisite for learning. A classroom in which the best learning was taking place would normally be one of creative confusion. The theory held that youth must achieve the precious boon of self-discipline through a liberation of their powers in school tasks which appealed to their stage of development.

Philosophically the chief difference between the old and the progressive concepts of discipline lay in the interpretation of child nature. The followers of John Dewey in education were thorough-going naturalists who thought of children in terms of the new biology and evolutionary theory of Darwin, Huxley, and others. The child's nature, they held, is not different in essence from that of any other organism; its chief activity is adaptation of itself to the environment. But the human species alone is able to adapt the environment, within limits, to its own needs by the use of intelligence and manipulation. Hence, schooling is the progressive induction of the child into the natural and social life of his time in such a fashion that his active nature may not simply adjust to the external but transform the world around him by a developing, creative intelligence. The problem of discipline is not to break the will of the child in order to subject it to adult culture, but rather to give it free rein to seek its own place and level in an organic order. Whatever is wrong with society—and the progressivists were highly critical—is not due to original human nature but to bad traditions, authoritarianism and false dualisms between man and the rest of nature, between reason and emotions, science and religion, and many others. The new pedagogy was nothing if not optimistic about child nature and looked forward confidently to a time when the scientific spirit would transform existing social institutions.

By contrast, the older view was pessimistic in doubting that the young were naturally directed toward the good. Permeated by the religious consciousness of a rebirth into a second nature as a condition of responsible maturity, the authoritarian tradition assumed an inevitable recalcitrance of youth. Goodness was an achievement in the mortal struggle with the merely animal and natural. Left to their own devices boys and girls would unfailingly seek the path of disorder and sin. How much the Christian distrust of the natural was responsible for the reliance on fear and punishment as primary aids to discipline depended on the pervasiveness of the Calvinistic persuasion. Progressivists were given to painting their opponents' view in somewhat lurid colors. Undoubtedly, the conviction that Adam's sin of disobedience would be repeated in his offspring if they were left free to pursue their natural impulses played a role in this older conception of discipline. Yet anyone who knows the history of education will discover this distrust of child nature in non-Christian cultures as well and will not too hastily conclude that Puritanism was a major ingredient. In any event, the belief that "to spare the rod was to spoil the child" and that "he who loves his child will not hesitate to reprove it" found solid Biblical support. There seems little question that before progressivism it was a widespread persuasion of the American public, whatever the origin. Such punishment and reliance on fear, it hardly needs to be added, were not inconsistent with love of children. Even the old schoolmaster of fearsome memory used sternness and the rod in the belief that these methods were best designed for the improvement of the young.

Today we are no longer so sure about the methods of discipline best designed to internalize authority. Though our society is in full retreat from the excesses of progressive education, there is little disposition to return to the nineteenth-century conception. Essentially we are looking for some kind of synthesis of the old and the new, whereby freedom and authority can be progressively related to each other as the child advances. The authoritarian teacher is regarded in more thoughtful circles to be as harmful to this enterprise as the one who has effectively lost control. We are aware that this problem is much more complex and subtle under the conditions of modern life than once it was thought to be.

Nevertheless, the dangers of extremism are very much present. Under the impact of the reform movement, there was a widespread revulsion against the harshness of the older discipline. Most American states established laws against physical punishment in the classroom. Now some are repealing these laws and there is active debate about the merits of punishment under carefully controlled conditions. A whole literature of extremism is growing up according to which progressive education is held to be responsible not only for our intellectual deficiencies in education but for moral failings as well. In the state of alarm into which we have fallen as a nation, there is danger of losing many of the great gains of the past half century. It is of the greatest importance to assess correctly the basic elements of discipline at the various stages of growth and to avoid dogmatism in a subject of the greatest difficulty where any generalization will be subject to numerous exceptions. As always, in dealing with education, it is helpful to keep in view the end toward which discipline in the teacher-student relationship is directed.

Surely we know enough about child nature by this time to reject some of the dogmas of the past. Children are born neither corrupt nor incorrupt. We cannot say with Rousseau that it is "an incontrovertible rule that the first impulses of nature are always right" and that therefore children are by nature directed toward the good, every vice being attributable to malign social influences. Nor would most of us hold that human nature is inherently corrupt in the literal sense of being predisposed to wickedness. It does not follow, of course, that children are born morally neutral, hence completely moldable to whatever experience writes on a blank tablet. We now believe that they bring to school dispositions that are still plastic, bundles of potentialities and powers that can be directed either toward constructive or destructive behavior. Some of these tendencies require suppression in the interests of giving others full play; many need nourishment and careful guidance in order to turn them in social rather than anti-social directions. In short, every youngster stands in need of authority, fitted to his own potentialities, that will enable him to achieve step by step free self-development.

What is the role of fear in establishing such creative authority? Is it at all consistent with the relationship of respect and confidence which should form the essence of authority in the early years? The answer is far from easy, given the variety in every classroom. With many children respect is easily won through confidence, friendliness, and the assurance that his teacher accepts him as an important member of the group. With others it must be established through a kind of friendly neutrality which insists on a line beyond which the child cannot go in refusing obedience to a teacher's command. With difficult children respect appears to be a subtle blending of love and fear or of trust and dread, and this blending forms the endless dilemma of the conscientious teacher. All of us have known teachers who were intent on "loving children into goodness" as well as those who did not scruple to rely on fear as a primary instrument. Both fail with many children at different stages of development. Fear does not necessarily breed hatred, as many allege. As an emotion it can be salutary not only for children but for adults as well. Soft pedagogy always undervalues its effect. The difficulty arises when fear is not mixed with other sentiments and displays itself as an arbitrary force.

Should teachers be permitted to punish troublesome children in order to induce the necessary respect for authority? Certainly every teacher must be permitted some means of correction; the question concerns only physical punishment. So long as such punishment remains within clearly defined limits there is probably little harm in it. Pupils quickly learn the limits of the teacher's power to punish in those systems where physical correction is prohibited and some take advantage of it. All depends on the way such punishment is administered as well as on the degree of severity. The wise teacher will pay great attention to the pragmatic factor. With some children such physical correction engenders resentment and further defiance, a sure sign that the teacher has failed in an important function. With others mild punishment of a corporal kind appears to work wonders. On occasion nothing clears the air, when repeated threats fail, so much as a mild but well administered spanking or slap. But the teacher who finds himself relying on such punishment as a regular measure can be very sure that he is a failure. The fear of the teacher may be the beginning of wisdom, but unless it gets transformed into deference for other qualities in his authority, it cannot produce the desired results.

The discipline acquired through fear and love should yield pre-eminence early in the school career to the discipline inherent in subject matter. Between the teacher and his students lies the material to be learned, the fundamental reason for their relationship in the first place. The teacher's ability to make relevant this objective factor in the situation determines in great part his success in imparting discipline to his charges. At first the authority of subject matter lies outside the teacher, but his skill and enthusiasm in appropriating this material and transmitting it can cause it to lose its impersonal character and become vital. Subject matter can remain, as it does for many students, something detached, external, and inert. As such it hinders the development of discipline and alienates teacher from student. But if the will of the student is made to confront this body of material, enter into it little by little and follow the structure of knowledge incorporated there, his energies are subtly if gradually transformed.

We speak glibly of the teacher's ability to make his subject interesting. There is, however, an interestingness which is external and relatively unimportant. Many a teacher gains a pseudo-authority by his capacity to dazzle students with isolated facts and facets of the material. Their attention is caught and held more by what the teacher does to the subject than what it does to him. There is a subjectivizing of material, a popularization that destroys the authority inherent in knowledge. Only as the teacher loses himself in his subject can he speak with authority about it or, more exactly, from within it. And only as the student learns that he is confronted with material that he must master, that has its own laws not dependent on his subjective will, does he begin to learn that primary lesson of self-discipline, namely, the overcoming of immediate impulse.

The teacher's authority as a knower, therefore, lies not so much in his ability to make material interesting as to make it appear relevant. For the majority of youth the vast store of human knowledge appears not only dead but irrelevant to their present concerns. They experience an initial resistance to mastering such patterns of the adult world. So much of it appears to belong to the past whereas the future is their primary interest. The teacher must impose his will by persuading them that, in the words of a recent novelist, "the past is not dead, it is not even past." He must constantly win their reluctant allegiance to lose the immediacy of the moment and so expand the narrow circle of their experience by adding to it material which yesterday lay outside their horizons.

Nothing tests a teacher's ability to utilize fully the discipline of subject matter so much as his success in absorbing students in material for which they felt a prior aversion. The required course in any curriculum frequently meets a resistance that exceeds the natural reluctance of youth to exert themselves on foreign material. Such a teacher may never succeed in interesting them greatly in such material. Yet he may nevertheless induce them to a mastery of the content of the course that exceeds all expectations. Most of us rememember courses somewhere in our school career for which we felt a positive dislike, but in which we learned uncommonly much almost in spite of ourselves. Even though we quickly forgot most of the content and confess that we hated every minute of it, we can hardly deny its beneficial effects in promoting self-mastery.

Why is this so? And what is the secret of such teaching? The answer to the first question can certainly be found in the challenge of the difficult for the young. Of first importance is the exhilaration of exerting effort on unyielding material. Youth always doubt their powers. They are especially reluctant to undertake studies in which, in Aristotle's phrase, "there is no natural sweetness," the sweetness of pleasure. But if they discover that they can succeed, even to a moderate extent, in conquering that material which holds little intrinsic interest, their sense of triumph is all the greater. The pride in mastery for its own sake causes them to boast ever after of passing such a course and the effects linger on when more popular courses have been forgotten.

It is hard to exaggerate the disciplining power of material that is difficult when it is presided over by the truly authoritative teacher. Without a word being spoken about the meaning of freedom and authority in such a course, more may be learned about their substance than in others where these concepts are part of the subject matter. It is a serious mistake on the part of some devotees of the humanities to hold that students cannot acquire moral values from the study of the exact sciences. For self-discipline is acquired precisely where the material permits no concessions to subjectivity. Such material will not contribute greatly to the student's understanding of the world. If isolated from other aspects of knowledge and from his practical concerns it may quickly be forgotten. But in its sheer factuality and emptiness of the usual attractions, it can represent something of the necessary austerity involved in all self-discipline of the advanced sort. I agree with John Stuart Mill and others who hold that every student needs to be confronted at some point in his career with material that is without any external appeal. If he chances to have a teacher who is a master, it may well turn out to be a decisive experience in the course of his moral maturity.

One of the refreshing aspects of higher education is the fact that many students do at times seek such subject matter on the reputation of the teacher whose discipline they wish to submit to. As often as not they never learn to care much for the subject matter, but they do acquire that steel in the character which all of us so badly need for a life of democratic responsibility. There is, of course, a tremendous difference in effect when students are permitted to elect such courses rather than having them forced upon them. In this discussion we are not concerned with the problem of the required versus elective curriculum. There exists sufficient evidence against introducing requirements for the sake of self-discipline alone. And the goal of educating for individuality demands that we insist on students' rights to choose their subject matter at the earliest point consistent with responsible freedom. Doubtless there are subject matters which our educational system must require as a necessity for life in the modern world. Such prescription should not be undertaken as lightly as is commonly done. For without freedom, discipline cannot be learned, whereas external discipline can be imposed years on end without much growth of freedom. Also it is foolish to deny the importance of interest as a primary motivation, above all in the early stages of education.

It was, however, an error of progressive pedagogy to over-emphasize the importance of building on already formed interests of youth. We are now coming to recognize, in Jerome Bruner's words, that new interests can be created. It is the teacher's primary concern, indeed, at nearly all levels of education to create these new interests. There is so much knowledge which all of us need to acquire for which we have no ready-made inclination. It is, in fact, startling to realize how much one needs to know in our complex civilization in order simply to escape the common dangers of life. The chasm between what many of us *want* to know and what we actually *need* to know even to lead a humdrum existence has surely never been so wide. Hence the central importance of constantly creating new interests is everywhere becoming apparent. Little can be credited to the teacher's authority when he succeeds in advancing knowledge and enthusiasm for material his students already like and for which they find immediate application. We who teach should not congratulate ourselves so much for success with students like these. They do not gain greatly in the kind of discipline freedom requires so long as they merely follow the paths of aptitude and interest in subject matter. The sensitive teacher rejoices more over the lost sheep he has rescued than in the ninety and nine already in the fold.

In creating these new interests, the level of difficulty of the material presented is a perennial issue for teachers concerned with helping students mature in self-discipline. Ideally, of course, all subject matter should be difficult enough to stretch students' abilities to their utmost without going beyond their present powers. The too easy will bore them, the too difficult discourage, and both are equally destructive of authority. Given the wide range of intelligence and diversity of previous preparation in any heterogenous class, such an ideal is rarely achieved. This fact in itself is one of the best arguments for the track system or homogenous grouping, as we have already noted in the preceding chapter. Even when everything possible is done to narrow diversity in students, there are within every academic discipline facts and concepts of widely varying degrees of sophistication. Consequently, every teacher must reconcile himself to failing to challenge his classes part of the time. No one has the right to expect that he can constantly advance the cause of authority in learning or in life. But unless we who teach are always alert to the problem of keeping students straining at the boundaries of their knowledge and abilities during a reasonable proportion of the learning period, we will miss precious opportunities. The tendency in earlier decades of this century to take it easy has given critics a ready weapon in their outcry for more rigor in learning.

The response of teachers to this criticism in the last few years has not, however, been uniformly favorable to the cause of self-discipline. Too many of late aspire to the reputation of being "tough" and fear unduly the reputation of teaching a course that is easy to pass. In many cases the young from grade school through college are being overloaded with work, with assignments that do not challenge their intellects so much as their endurance. The demand for quality is too often translated into increase in quantity. And the growing emphasis on grades is again a return to the external emphasis of an earlier discipline, which relied on fear alone. So long as the teaching profession is as insecure as at present, it will never achieve the golden mean.

There is as little to be said for the "tough" teacher as for the easy mark, for both commonly misconceive the discipline of their subject matter. The teacher who does not make allowance for inherent difficulties in what he teaches and does not recognize that students have only a limited time to devote to his course invariably undermines self-confidence. And the easy teacher who assigns too little material, and that of an elementary sort, and fails to hold students responsible for their work earns contempt. But the teacher who is reasonable in his demands on student time and comprehension will never be known as tough or easy and can congratulate himself that it rarely occurs to students to classify him in such ways.

At the more advanced levels of education the authority im-

plicit in the materials of instruction becomes ever more important. As subject matter becomes more complex and intricate, its
possibilities for discipline increase accordingly. A teacher of difficult material who aspires to influence his students in intellectual
discipline must be made of no ordinary stuff. For he must, in the
first instance, be in complete control of his material. The loss of
authority arising from ignorance on the part of the teacher is an
almost tangible thing. Most of us who teach have experienced the
deep dismay which rises to choke us when students discover that
we are unable to deal with a central concept on which knowledge
must be presupposed. There are many ways of covering up such
ignorance, but the perceptive student is not fooled by any of
them. He may accept a frank confession of not knowing where
details are concerned, but not on essentials. With startling sud-
denness student confidence is shattered and can only be rebuilt
with the greatest difficulty. If the teacher does not "know his
stuff," in student language, where the material is already of intrinsic interest, the damage may not be nearly so great. Many a
student in such situations finds refuge in the text book or the
library and allows them to share authority with his teacher. But
where material is not immediately appealing there is no help. The
teacher has failed and his discipline is imperiled in a fundamental
way. More advanced students will continue to struggle with the
material, but they will not take into their souls the value of such
effort.

Yet competence is not enough; it is a necessary but not sufficient condition. Hundreds of teachers who are "authorities" in
their fields do not succeed in being authorities for their students.
The spectacle of a teacher who is a master of his specialty yet
cannot "put it across," as students are wont to say, is an all too
common one. The scholar is, alas, by no practical definition a
teacher. He may or he may not be. What he requires where no
ready interest is available is an imaginative understanding of the
effect of this material on immature minds. He must possess the
gift for logical and psychological presentation calculated to
gather his students into the framework of his world. If he simply

forgets himself in his material, he may speak like an inspired man yet not carry his students with him. Without the intuitive understanding of youth in all its perversity and its disturbing unpredictability such a teacher is unlikely to succeed. Until he learns the art of playing upon the expectations, hopes, fears, and capacities of the youth before him, of expecting neither too much nor too little, of being patient at the right time and impatient at others, he will not induce them into assaulting the obstacle which his material represents. He must possess, in the Biblical phrase, the wisdom of the serpent, but not the harmlessness of the dove. For even at more advanced levels a teacher can rarely do without a measure of fear in his authority, at least the fear of failure.

There are cherished occasions in the classroom when material may become such a dominant force that students forget themselves completely, speak out and speak up in their eagerness to understand or to contribute. All the wonderful qualities of young minds are suddenly released upon a common problem, absorbed in it, and able to communicate with each other without self-consciousness. Time can be forgotten and with it all one's private problems for the moment. From being a collection of heterogeneous individuals the class is fused into something like complex unity. Even then the teacher must guard against forgetting his role. Though he will fear to break the spell and be unable to control all the forces let loose, he will nonetheless notice when some students get behind or get "lost" and skillfully herd such stragglers into the play of thought.

There is another kind of discipline, connected with, but separated from, that of subject matter, which inheres in the teacher's manner of dealing with students. So much has been written on this subject that one hesitates to add more, yet its importance in the growth of moral authority will limit our focus. It is a commonplace that a teacher must respect his students if he is to gain their respect. Such generalizations are not very helpful unless we analyze what it means to treat youth with respect. Doubtless the central element is how much the teacher cares about students as individuals. On this point every young person is sensitive to the last degree. His liking or disliking a teacher is governed by this factor almost alone. It can be argued that liking or disliking a teacher can be fairly irrelevant to the acquisition of subject matter. And a few students can surely acquire worthwhile values from teachers they dislike. The great majority, however, cannot, above all if their disapproval is a strong one. It remains as true as when the Greek philosophers first pointed it out that youth learn much in terms of character from imitation and we rarely imitate those we dislike. Rightly or wrongly, young people give their inner allegiance only to those teachers in whom they sense a concern for them as individuals.

This concern expresses itself differently in personal interviews and in the classroom situation, a fact too infrequently noticed. The teacher is one and the students many and it is frequently difficult for any teacher to shift in manner from teaching to conversing face to face. After a wearing class hour or day, he is all too likely to indicate in subtle ways that the student who wishes to confer with him is intruding. His caring is revealed in how carefully he listens to what the student says, for teachers fall so quickly into the habit of talking too much and listening too little. It is revealed in his way of discovering the necessary facts of the student's history that are relevant to the matter being discussed. Most of all, caring is revealed by the tone of voice, the endeavor to avoid that impersonality of manner of one in authority over the group. One teacher can say harsh things in private to a student without wounding him, where another can be patronizing and offensive in the effort to be kind. Nothing offends so much as the teacher's making light of a student's endeavor to meet him at the personal level, to break through the official mask and to discover the human being. Unless the teacher relaxes his guard in such interviews, he will miss the chance to show he cares.

In the classroom situation caring is most easily demonstrated by the seriousness with which a teacher prepares himself for his work. It is hard to avoid fierce anger at the thought of how careless teachers can be with the precious time of their students. There is sufficient waste in the educational process that is unavoidable without teachers adding to it by lack of planning and preparation. Though the young may seem infinitely careless themselves in this respect, they are quick to resent the implication of their superiors that wasted time is of no importance to them. The teacher who improvises a lecture, repeats himself, and allows digressions for anecdotes of doubtful relevance can fritter away hard-won respect. In class discussions or recitations, sensitivity to student reaction and response to questions under discussion mark all too clearly how much a teacher cares. Those who are always kindly and endlessly patient with students' fumbling are nearly as destructive as those who are brusque and feelingless. The demoralization that besets a class with a teacher who suffers fools too gladly or who permits a strong-willed student to monopolize time is irreparable.

The dominance that holds a class under tension and yet never tyrannizes is possible only to that teacher who cares passionately and without sentimentality. Toughness or softness in a teacher is in this respect all-important. The student who succeeds in pretense to knowledge or to preparation he has not made will mark the teacher who is himself without discipline. Harshness with such pretense, an unrelenting demandingness, and a no-nonsense attitude is the mark of authority. Under the stress of being singled out, a timid student will sometimes speak thoughtlessly and incur the amused laughter of his classmates. Such situations are often decisive. The teacher can either save the student from his embarrassment by turning his meaning into a reasonable one or crush him by exposing him to further ridicule. Kindliness on these repeated occasions is wholly consistent with rigor and stringency of thought. By his consideration for the feeling of that student he can not only win his gratitude but impress the rest of the class. There is as little to be said for the authority of a teacher who is all tolerance as there is for one who demands perfection from his students.

The mistake a young teacher frequently commits is to believe that he can be a friend of his students. The term is used loosely, of course, but on any strict construction the teacher-student relation is not one of friendship. Friends do not normally serve as authority to each other, since friendship in its very nature implies equality. Students are often more perceptive in this matter than are teachers. They do not want their teacher to be a friend, though they appreciate friendliness on his part. The reason is not only a difference in age and attainments, but an intuitive perception that teaching requires psychological distance. Unless the teacher receives a deference which the mind willingly gives as compared with an external politeness, he is simply not one's teacher. We may learn from such a one as we normally do learn from all manner of people, but the meaning of authority in its relation to freedom is not acquired this way. The teacher must be to a youth in some sense a superior; not only must he know more but must also stand for qualities of character the youth has not yet attained. Understood philosophically, our teacher is only he who embodies a kind of freedom we lack. We listen in an inner sense to those we admire, who embody in their whole personality a good we want, however imperfectly and vaguely we intuit it. Though a youngster has many teachers in the formal sense, only a few of them can develop that discipline which is the other side of freedom's coin.

Teachers, like students, are often insecure. Hence they cross the line and seek a camaraderie with their students in the effort to win their consent to be taught. At very advanced levels in graduate school this behavior may be successful. Certainly there are informal occasions when the teacher should relax with his students and reveal his common humanity, though he must do that, too, at every level. But he should never reach the point of familiarity where it will be difficult for him to resume his role of teacher. Human beings are capable only up to a point of changing roles. And the teacher who believes that he can be "one of the boys" on a festive evening or afternoon and enter the classroom the following morning to step into the old position is simply unwise. His students may consent to play the game, but inwardly something significant has happened. They will learn the facts of his field as before; they will hardly gain in self-discipline. He has lost status as an authority.

Though the authority inherent in possession of knowledge and in daily association with students is great, all of us are convinced there is something more. If we reflect on our experience in school, as too few of us are wont to do, we are nearly certain to discover that the authority of our best teachers lay even deeper than in their mastery of their fields and their personal relations with us. It matters little what we call this something more; there is inevitably something mysterious about it. Perhaps the term "force of character" is as good as any. Some teachers hold an interest for students year after year that has little to do with their knowledge or with anything else that is very tangible. They may not be the best teachers on a faculty or in some sense the most admirable of persons. They may not always be easy to get along with, and colleagues and administrators may find them on occasion positively difficult. Nor are they the teachers who have disciples or coteries, being much too independent for that. They are their own men or women, intent on an integrity that is inseparable from their very being. Though they may well be moody from time to time, they are incapable of playing roles, of being different human beings in the manifold relationships of life.

Such teachers have that indefinable quality called stature as persons. They escape that typing, a sort of "professional deformation," which the vocation of teaching fixes indelibly on so many of us. We may feel that they could just as easily have been business men or Congressmen or even military officers as successfully as what they are, though we would in all likelihood be mistaken, for they are born teachers. That is to say, they are natural leaders of men. If our society understood better than it does the importance of teaching, it would seek out such people and lure them into the classroom at almost any price. For they are, in any culture, the superlative formers of character in the young. They attract without willing it, yet hold themselves at a

distance. The reserves of emotional power they possess are such
that, always giving, they are rarely exhausted. Generosity understood in its deeper sense of a plenitude of spending power is what
they have in common.

It is all too easy to build up an unreal image of an individual in
the attempt to describe something called force of character. Perhaps it is not embodied in any single person so much as it is in the
leadership quality in anyone who is a genuine teacher. One is ever
tempted to repeat Whitehead's dictum when he spoke of greatness as the indispensable quality in all who teach character. But
greatness is, of course, an abstraction and what we should attempt
to do is to specify its qualities. Surely independence of mind and
generosity are two of them. A certain intensity is likewise part of
this complex of qualities. A teacher can be very quiet and yet
assertive; he can dominate without perceptible effort. His moral
reserve is such that students are unable to compass him, to find
him out. Once a teacher is no longer interesting to students as a
person, he can no longer be their moral instructor. If he himself
ceases to advance in inner reserves, his students will catch up and
surpass him. Such eventualities are inevitable, of course, the distribution of abilities being what it is. No teacher can be expected to be authoritative for students at every level. Enough if
he brings them past a stage in the long growth toward self-mastery. And the best teacher does not aspire to more, since he
recognizes himself as a means only and disdains to make the
young a carbon image of his own values. The true authority in
teaching is always intent on making itself dispensable, the master
teachers those who point us beyond themselves. We leave them
behind usually without much thanks, for such appears inappropriate. But in later vicissitudes we bless them as men or women
who have made it possible for us to hold out. The moral force
they instilled in our characters by power of example may make
all the difference as to whether we acquit ourselves like men in
the lonely hours.

In conclusion, perhaps it needs to be emphasized that such
teaching and teachers are becoming ever more important on the

American scene. To many critics it appears that authority in the wider society is rapidly eroding away. They speak of a crisis of authority in our time. The primary institution of the family as a source of authority has allegedly lessened its hold; that of the church is surely not so strong as once it was. And the political institutions that could trace their origins to the founding fathers and provide for our youth secure values, in this realm at least, are no longer compelling in the first global age. As a consequence, education has become for many a last desperate hope for a new foundation of authority that will save our society from dangerous drift. For most youth education begins with schooling and school continues to play a larger and longer role in the lives of the majority than ever before. On any calculation it is difficult to deny that schools have inherited, usually without willing it, a larger share in forming our future *ethos* than is perhaps desirable. In the absence of other authorities young people are forced to rely on teaching and teachers not merely for the knowledge they need but also for the values which will help to rescue them from confusion and inner anarchy. In short, teachers are increasingly important in a society adrift; their burden, assumed or neglected, is a heavy one. Sooner or later nearly all students of educational theory come to the conclusion that qualities in the teacher are the alpha and omega of educational method.

The Question of Method

7. INDOCTRINATION AND THE MEANING OF FREEDOM

HOWEVER NECESSARY the unforced acquisition of authority or self-discipline is to the student in search of an education, it is nevertheless preliminary only to his exercise of freedom. Authority is a basis for freedom in the individual as order is the basis for freedom of society. Freedom is a notoriously ambiguous term, as everyone knows. As children we almost instinctively think of it as absence of restraint, as freedom *from* undesired duties, irksome responsibilities in school and home. Even as adults we never slough off this connotation of the term entirely, and it is right that we hold fast to it. But reflection teaches us that freedom also means power to act, an ability to fulfill capacities and potentialities that are more rational and of longer range than the satisfaction of immediate impulse. This second meaning of freedom involves us in the social and political dimensions of the individual; it implies responsibilities and obligations toward others as well as rights and privileges for the self. We commonly speak of this as the positive sense of freedom, the freedom for or freedom *to* act as an effective citizen, family member, team player, or any other participating member in the many relationships that constitute our single lives. Since individuality is only possible within community, as we have seen, this positive definition of freedom is held to be central to the purposes of a free society.

Accordingly, the task of the teacher in democracy's schools is not only to aid in the transfer of authority from teacher to taught, but also to provide some guidance to the student in the learning and practice of this positive kind of freedom. The teaching relationship must seek to provide occasions for learners to gain practice in independence of thought and action. It must add, to the control of impulse and immediate desire which is self-discipline, a stimulus to the development of individual beliefs, convictions, and principles on which the student can act responsibly in society. A hardened criminal may well be in control of himself, be admirably self-disciplined, but our schools are hardly commissioned to promote criminality.

How can the teacher do this? How can he hope to guide students into the forming of their individual views concerning the rights and responsibilities of the free man without imposing his own convictions upon them? In other words, how does one distinguish teaching from indoctrination, especially in this realm of freedom as the power to act? The original definition of indoctrination was simply "instruction in the rudiments of learning." But its current meaning is "the attempt to inculcate a partisan or sectarian point of view by withholding of contrary evidence and repetition by emotional appeals and special pleading of the desired beliefs." If the teacher is to regard himself as a means or a method to the free development of individuality in the student, he can want nothing to do with such indoctrination, yet he will regard it as part of his duty to further the student's understanding and exercise of positive freedom.

Like so many other problems of teaching, this dilemma has taken on a new edge in our revolutionary age. The right of the individual to make up his own mind about his duties and responsibilities has long been an almost sacred credo in our American experience; it has been for many a large part of the meaning of the open society. Should an individual desire to remain uncommitted, even on the issue of whether democracy is a just form of government, this too has long been held to be within his rights. So long as his overt activities remained within the pale of the law, he was permitted to believe what he liked or believe nothing at all, if he liked. But since totalitarian systems have arisen to challenge our democratic faith, the issue has become more complex and perplexing. The older assumption that an increase in personal and collective freedom was a natural development, a manifest destiny of advanced societies, has given way in many anxious hearts to the view that unless we imbue our youth with the doctrines and ideals of our way of life as the one right form of human association, they will fall victim to the fanatical faith of our enemies.

Hence the question becomes acute. Is indoctrination at all compatible with the goals we have set up as the guides for formal schooling as well as formative education? To what extent and by what methods should our schools attempt to inculcate into children and adolescents the beliefs and attitudes approved by our society? That any school system will attempt to instill such beliefs and attitudes is beyond doubt. And the fact that within limits the schools are the instruments of the society that set them up and support them gives them the right to do so. But the question of the means employed to communicate these principles and practices is the difficult and confused one.

In a general way the distinction between teaching and indoctrinating is not too difficult to draw. Teaching is the imparting of information and skills in the effort to aid the student to knowledge and wisdom. Such teaching always implies the endeavor to provide the explanations and evidence for such knowledge, the reason why something is as it is. Indoctrination, on the other hand, is the attempt to control the actions and beliefs of others by using skills and information with an ulterior purpose. As the definition suggests, it is always selective in the information given, never the full story, and repetition is for the purpose not of learning but of exciting the emotions of the hearers and inducing them to believe something in the interests of action. Whether the indoctrinator consciously intends to do what he is doing is often difficult to know. But it is not difficult to know that he is attempting to induce acceptance of a particular point of view, his own, through persuasive argument, withholding of negative evidence, emotional appeal, and so on. He is intent on telling rather than teaching, on winning acceptance rather than inquiry, on commitment rather than truth and understanding. In the realm of politics, religion, and moral values, where such indoctrination is most commonly practiced, the clue to the teacher's intentions can usually be detected in his manner of presentation. His method of teaching is ultimately more important than his motives. This question of teaching versus indoctrination is, of course, much larger than the school; it involves equally the home and the state. In our society it is left to parents to decide when children reach an age level to acquire rights of their own, when they can be reasoned with, taught rather than told. Because we develop as children very unevenly, it is perhaps impossible to fix any limits here or establish any guide lines. But the question of when a child becomes a human being, that is, when he acquires the right to have his opinions and judgments respected, even when they oppose those of his parents, ought to be of more concern than it is to our democratic theory. Apart from the conviction that the child has claims to physical care and public schooling after the age of six, there is too little discussion of the extent and limits of parental prerogative to indoctrinate him in political, moral, and religious creeds. The assumption is implicit, one fears, that at this stage the child's mind is less important than his body. The parent is not free to neglect the latter, but the former belongs to him to do with as he wills. This situation continues in spite of the fact that psychologists have taught us for many years the crucial importance of these early years in the forming of the future disposition.

Similarly with the state, there is no agreed-upon limitation to the right of officialdom to withhold information or to slant stories of public events in the interests of holding the allegiance of the citizens. In order to protect the morals of its citizens or to promote their belief in God, most commonly in the name of military security, our state feels justified in propagandistic activities directed at adults and children alike. The problem of censorship is perennially debated with no clear lines ever drawn on the state's authority to determine what its citizens shall see, read, or hear. Nevertheless, the absence of such determination does not prevent, indeed even aids, the *de facto* interference of public officials in the presentation, interpretation, and withholding of the information our people daily consume. It follows that the youth are indoctrinated, subtly or blatantly, by both family and state before they arrive at school.

The schools in turn are greatly influenced by the practices of home and state. They receive children in the elementary grades who have been already accustomed to indoctrination from these sources, and teachers at these levels are subtly encouraged to regard themselves both *in loco parentis* and as representatives of public authority. They ordinarily respond to the widespread belief that indoctrination in the sphere of values, telling rather than teaching, is legitimate in these grades, becoming progressively less so as youngsters advance to high school and college. At the lower levels of the school system, so the popular view runs, teaching should be practically all indoctrination, at the upper levels none at all or practically none. How and when to make the transition and by what methods are questions which the layman normally leaves to the academic profession to decide.

The reason for this prevalent opinion is not far to seek. Children develop the powers of reason slowly as they mature. In the absence of experience and judgment on matters of vital import for society, the only alternative is thought to be to train them in approved habits of response. Aristotle's view that habit plays a predominant role in forming the disposition of youth and should therefore be the main emphasis in early education has long been accepted without much question. In the name of socializing the child we normally instill in him, before the age of reflection, habitual responses to the approved customs and principles of current politics, religion, and morality. Without much question we instruct our children to salute the flag and pledge allegiance long before they have any notion of the meaning and significance of what they are doing. Parents take their children to church and imbue them with religious beliefs, even when the parents themselves are practicing atheists or agnostics. School and home and state combine to guide their reading, fix their beliefs, predetermine their attitudes—all in the name of early education. Then the logic of our belief in freedom dictates that in adolescence they be taught to make up their own minds on all these questions, to doubt and to discuss the problems of democracy, of faith in God, of right and wrong in personal conduct. We wonder and worry about the ensuing crises and conflicts of adolescent youth, with the opposed reactions of conformity and withdrawal. Today there is no longer the former assurance among the thoughtful minority that this pattern of, first, indoctrination, then instruction is inevitable or just. With the whirlwind change that has overtaken our society, we are no longer sure that we can afford to bring up our children in the image of their parents or teachers. Things that seemed self-evident a generation ago no longer seem so. Patriotism, for example, has suddenly become a radically dubious value, if not to Americans fully as yet, at least to Belgians, where a jet plane cannot reach its proper altitude before it has left the country behind. In such a religiously diverse country as ours, it is no longer clear that indoctrination as opposed to instruction in the Christian religion has any real justification. The angry puzzlement of many parents and teachers about the opposition to celebrating Christmas in the schools is a significant sign of the times. Sexual standards and mores are likewise caught in the grip of change, necessarily so in this era of overpopulation and contraceptive pills. Increasingly our youth feel impatient with, even rebellious against, adult beliefs and doctrines they feel are irrelevant to their new kind of world.

If we turn now to the specific relations of teacher and student in the classrooms of our time, we may be in a position to reflect about the teacher's responsibility to further the student's exercise of freedom. We may start with a philosophical principle that would perhaps win general agreement. It seems clear that no teacher has the right to inculcate beliefs in a student that would make the achievement of adult autonomy more difficult for him to attain. This proposition may seem so general as to be harmless. But it has specific implications. One of them is that a teacher is violating the rights of his charges if he imposes on them doctrines and dogmas the reasons for which he is unable or unwilling to give. He is making the achievement of freedom more difficult if they later have to unlearn and reject things they have been taught before they were able to understand. No one has demonstrated that there is any educational value of consequence in the process of unlearning false or unevidenced views that have been presented as certain truths. The amount of time and mental struggle most of us who are adults have had to devote to rejecting doctrines early inculcated is frequently appalling. When such ideas have been effectively indoctrinated, the process of getting rid of them may never be really completed and we remain immature in crucial areas all our lives.

Examples can be cited. Frequently in the public schools our children are told that freedom and democracy are practically synonymous and that our particular form of democracy is the only one that is really compatible with a free society. They become convinced in the absence of contrary experience that unless a government provides for the separation of powers and the kind of press the American people possess, a capitalistic economy, and so on, a people cannot possibly be free. Later they must learn that many countries enjoy freedom without any or most of these American forms, and it is normally a painful reform of opinion, possible only to those with wider experience and schooling than are open to the majority. In the sphere of religion, to use another example, it is even more common to identify the Christian or the Judaic God with divinity as such. Unless a group believes in the kind of God revealed in the Old and New Testaments, its members cannot possibly be religious; their faith is thought of as paganism, to be pitied or despised. Such doctrines are not at all difficult to instill at a certain stage. Children are all too likely to believe, in their naive egoism, that our way of governing and our system of creeds are the only true and right way. Failure on the part of the teacher to mention alternatives can be sufficient for incipient indoctrination.

It should go without saying that our form of government ought to be taught first in our schools, American ideas and ideals brought early and sympathetically to the minds of elementary school children. Similarly the basic tenets of the Judaic and the Christian faiths deserve precedence over others because they are the dominant religions of our society. At the elementary level probably no useful purpose is served by contrasting them with other systems of government or world religions. At this level children are not old enough to judge the merits of ours over others; they need most of all to learn the essential facts of our country's history and political structure as well as the inherited religious tradition. Yet here too there is a difference between teaching and indoctrinating, between sympathetic communication of the facts, pleasant and ugly, and the attempt to win allegiance to the teacher's interpretation of these facts. There is a large difference between presenting American ideals sympathetically and presenting them as though they were the only true ideals, or in disregard of the cleft between these ideals and frequent American practice.

At the high school level, students should be seriously introduced to other current ways of viewing government, religion, and standards of conduct; they should be encouraged to compare and argue questions of right and wrong, of better and worse forms in our and other people's ways of conceiving experience. The only sure way of developing reflective judgment in youthful minds is to give them materials by which to compare and contrast actions and ideas. It is not a question of the teacher's neutrality on all these issues, for a reflective mind cannot be neutral. Rather his duty is to see to it that as many sides and perspectives as possible are presented, that students are allowed and urged to use their reason, and that emotional arguments and faulty logic do not go unchallenged, insofar as he is able to prevent them.

There is surely a middle way between indoctrination and an affected and colorless neutrality in both elementary and high school teaching. This middle path is neither broad nor safe; it is more like ropewalking over a chasm. Teaching as tuition, as protecting and guarding, is the attempt to present subject matter in controversial areas in such a way that students are challenged to think, to want to know more before making up their minds, to be on their guard against the pathetic human tendency to absolutize the familiar, home versions of the truth. This middle way is aware of the dangers it runs in trusting youth to find eventually a philosophical faith on which it can build. But it prefers confusion and even mental suffering to a short-term security achieved by emotional adherence to the status quo or evasion of the duty to educate in judgment. Freedom, as intellectual autonomy, is a dearly bought and hard-won achievement; it requires early cultivation of the soil.

The case against this position deserves to be heard. It will be argued that youth are incapable of objectivity in the sphere of values. They can only gain enthusiasm and emotional fervor when they experience the great issues of life as a contest. Unless the schools follow the example of home and state in seeking the allegiance of the young to current ideals, we are likely to raise up a generation of apathetic Americans unfitted for the rough-and-tumble struggles of the times. Unless children are early imbued with religious values, long before the age of reason arrives, they are certain to regard religion as an intellectual exercise only and miss its very essence, which is feeling. If we do not indoctrinate them in the virtues of "the American way of life" they are likely when grown to be poor defenders against its enemies and unable to develop the promise of its genuine values. Objectivity, it is argued, has its place, namely in the higher academies; professors and scientists are probably right in elevating it to the highest place. But the life of the marketplace and political forum is passion. History reveals to us that only those peoples who did not shrink from indoctrinating their young prevailed, that is, counted for something in world affairs.

It would be foolish to disregard these arguments and many more of their kind. There is no doubt that human history has been largely the record of passions and will continue to be. Reflection has usually been a delicate instrument, fitted more for understanding this record than for guiding it. The efforts of a few conscientious teachers to instill a love for truth in their students do not count for much in the face of the vast irrationalities which dominate public life. It may well seem like pointless and even perilous idealism to speak against indoctrination when the majority of parents and public officials will not be dissuaded from such attempts both before and after, as well as during, the period of schooling.

Nevertheless, the teaching relationship is a special one, guided by a logic and ethic that are different from those prevalent elsewhere. The teacher in our public schools is charged with the task of aiding students to become individuals through the internalizing of discipline and the exercise of freedom. He is neither the parent of the children he teaches nor in our society is he a public official. His judgment of what history "teaches" is not especially relevant to his task, which is directed toward the future of his charges. He may well be disheartened by considering how minor his influence really is in comparison with the forces in society and in his students arrayed against his faith in teaching. But this, too, affects the demands of his task not at all.

If he is reflective, he will not be easily persuaded that to fail to indoctrinate children is equivalent to starving the emotions and making them indifferent to the values of religion and of nation. The problem of teaching is the fusion of reason and emotion at the level of disposition, not their separate cultivation at any stage of instruction. And objectivity, if it be taken as the endeavor to exclude the human factor in all knowing, is not part of his mission as a teacher at all. On questions of religion and loyalty to country he will not seek neutrality, either in himself or in his students. But he will strive to infuse into these usually emotional allegiances a measure of rationality and balance that they too commonly lack.

Likewise, he will be doubtful of the common charge that unless religious faith is early instilled it will not come to us as advanced adolescents or adults. Evidence for this argument is scanty at best because nearly all societies on record have not scrupled to imbue beliefs about the divine in their children at a tender age. The teacher who cares deeply about religion is frequently distressed by the childish, rather than childlike, images of God his students retain, long past the age when such images may have been appropriate. Their frequent inability to think clearly in this area and their woeful ignorance of the fundamental facts of their own assumed faiths are not unrelated to this early indoctrination. Such a teacher is bound to wonder if it were not far preferable first to instruct youth in the history and development of religious creeds and beliefs and postpone all efforts to recruit them into the fold until they reach an age when the need for faith and the capacity to understand are equal to the demands.

As things now are, a considerable part of the later adolescence of young persons is spent in ignoring, rejecting, or at best rearranging the beliefs indoctrinated by their elders. The much discussed rebellion of adolescent youth is by no means an inevitable movement of gaining independence from parental authority; it is at least equally due to the suspicion that they have had much imposed upon them that is questionable. And their feeling of phoniness about the adult world, so much emphasized in recent literature, plagues them and leaves them adrift at a period in their growth when adults ought to be most effective. Surely the peer group mentality is not unrelated to this phenomenon of indoctrination; it divides the generations fatefully and prevents much of the continuity of tradition that we still might transmit in this revolutionary age.

It is possibly presumptuous for any teacher to be dogmatic on this matter of indoctrinating faith in God. In any event, the conscientious will recognize that they can do little to prevent it in the home and in the non-academic world about them. But many teachers are at least resolved that they will have nothing to do with such indoctrination in the schools, even if our laws did not forbid it. They are too conscious of how far they have moved from the faith of their parents and teachers, and often at what cost to troubled consciences! It is a commonplace that many deeply religious parents and teachers have not been able to impart an iota of their faith to those in their charge. But the question of effectiveness is not at issue; it is a matter of right and wrong. The sins committed against the young are, at least in Christian teaching, said to be the most heinous of all. Yet these are the sins many adults appear to bear most easily. At all events the sensitive teacher will prefer on this issue to sin, if it is a sin, by omission rather than by commission.

The situation may be somewhat different on the matter of instilling loyalty to country and to the institutions of democracy. Nevertheless, some of us who teach can confess to a long standing uneasiness about the universal practice at PTA meetings and school assemblies of having children salute the flag and pledge allegiance. Adults usually smile when children patter memorized formulas they do not understand and everyone has at least one amusing version of such pledging. The young are so pathetically eager to ape adult ritual and so blissfully unaware of what is involved. I remember the amusement of American tourists in Nazi Germany when children of four or five would salute them when we were passing through a village and chirp *Heil Hitler!* In truth it is not amusing at all when children go through the forms of a ceremony, the symbolism of which they cannot grasp to any extent. At best there is an artificiality about it that embarrasses, at worst a separation of the organic connection of emotion and intellect that can later cause grave mischief.

In any event there is always a more effective way to teach a legitimate pride in country and loyalty to its essential principles. Youth are ever responsive to pageantry; celebration of the great occasions of our history can do far more than ritual can to arouse pride and loyalty, without its dangers. If our schools would devote more time to the biographies of our greatest men and women, teach their achievements and their speeches, without exaggeration and without sentimentality, we would attain the kind of patriotic attachment that would not require later modification. There is no necessity, in this kind of teaching even of the very young, to fear fanaticism or the separation of feeling and reason. The means we use are here all-important, not only in their effectiveness but also in their moral legitimacy.

Nevertheless, we have discussed so far only the negative

aspects of the teaching relationship concerning freedom. It is important to ask what positive steps can be taken to promote independence of judgment and the acquisition of values by which freedom can be sustained. Every teacher worthy of the name desires to aid his students in the forming of their own interpretations of experience. The question of how to do so remains perplexing. Central to the answer is the problem of the right time. There is a time when youth can participate with profit in discussions of controversial topics which would overwhelm them if introduced too early, or leave them indifferent if too late. The concept of readiness, so much discussed in reference to various kinds of academic material, has even more relevance to questions of forming ideals. There are books which can destroy half-formed convictions if read too soon, yet they can be enormously creative and beneficent if they appear at the right time. All of us can remember chance events of our childhood that were decisive for our later development in both good and evil ways. The teacher who will exert the important influence in the development of freedom is he who has an intuitive sense of the right time for the introduction of this or that idea in classroom discussion, this or that book, play, or film to recommend.

Much of the best teaching in the formation of values is by indirection. At a certain age youth are given to listening unobtrusively to teachers talking with each other and observing unguarded behavior, then making up their own minds in secret about what to believe and what to reject. The overheard conversation is frequently most fateful of all. It can teach a young person, as few things can, to distinguish between appearance and reality in the realm of ideals. At the right time he wants to discover for himself and passionately resists being told. There is an essential privacy about growth in responsible freedom. No one at this stage wants to be deceived; all of us desire to make up our own minds without the persuasiveness of someone who is older and more experienced. We are persuaded best at the right time by the actions of the teacher who is not trying to persuade at all.

The issue of censorship in our schools is such a controverted one that a simple principle appears impossible to extract from it. When has the right time come to permit the growing youth to decide for himself what he should read, see, or do? No adult is wise enough to know the answer to such a practical question. Given the diversity of the young and the different rates of maturity, probably no answer is possible or ever will be, even when child psychology is more fully developed than it is at present. The conscientious teacher, however, who knows a good deal about child development in general and about the children before him in particular, will normally be in a better position to answer the question of the right time than the rest of us. He will follow the simple principle that the young have the right to be exposed to good books, good films and TV programs at every age. He cannot prevent their contact with the unsavory, the ugly, and even the perverse, and perhaps would not if he could. Like Plato he recognizes the desirability of their association with the lovely, the true, and the gracious at this impressionable age, but unlike Plato he would not ban the false and unlovely. He will try in every legitimate way to provide an overbalance of what he considers to be the healthy, beneficent books, music, and film programs, but will also safeguard his students' right to learn about their opposites. The question of the right time will govern his more deliberate acts of student exposure to the ugly and the evil.

To practical, unreflective people this principle of exposing youth as much as possible to the good will seem to be no censorship at all. Yet, in our present state of knowledge at least, it seems to be the only kind that is consistent with the rights of children and the goals of democratic freedom. Parents and the larger society will doubtless continue to exercise a much more restrictive kind of censorship. But the conscientious teacher will feel impelled to take the inevitable risks attendant upon advancing the cause of freedom.

How much should a teacher reveal his own convictions on
controversial topics involving religion, politics, and morals? A
general answer is difficult to give. Too much depends on the age
of his students, the particular subject matter being treated, and
his own certainty of his judgment. Yet in the interests of fur-
thering autonomy of students, the question deserves the most
careful reflection. Two extremes seem clearly objectionable. On
the one hand, there is the teacher who likes to keep students
guessing "what teacher really believes." He will half conceal and
half reveal his opinions, tantalize them by chance remarks that
point to opposed views, and if challenged will frequently urge
them to make up their own minds. Insofar as this is a technique to
provoke thought and independent judgment it may not be an
extreme at all; in a preliminary way it may be a desirable method
of teaching. But too often it amounts to an evasion of responsibility, a failure of seriousness on his part and sometimes outright
cowardice. Such a teacher either fears to subject his own views to
student criticism and debate or else he regards students as too
immature to understand his superior standpoint and to enter seriously into the "subtleties" of his reasoning.

On the other hand, there is the teacher who is forever intruding his own opinions at every opportunity regardless of their
relevance. He considers the classroom a kind of forum for the
dissemination of his views, and students become victims of the
prejudices and limited perspectives of their instructor. Unable to
separate the subject matter of his course from his private reactions to it, he is constantly giving a course in his own world-
view, permitting the students no opportunity to make up their
minds after reflection or to remain primarily devoted to the
text and to the developing material of the discipline. In this
situation serious students have no alternative but to close their
ears to the teacher's opinions or to agree to play the game with
their mentor until the hour is over.

Between these extremes lies a broad middle path in which a
principle of much generality is hard to discover. If a teacher is
conscious of bias on a certain controversial issue, he should be

wary of giving his opinions to students. His very itch to do so should be regarded by him as a danger signal. When he has a closed mind in an area where no certainty is possible, he can hardly further the cause of freedom by discussion with a captive audience. In the opposite case, when he is genuinely undecided about the rights and wrongs of a controversy, he should be more willing than usual to discuss his own doubts and hesitations. Many a teacher has been able to reach a position of his own through listening to the unencumbered opinions of youthful minds in free debate and by attempting to point out for them the one-sided and emotion-clouded nature of this or that argument. More important, the students themselves are able to learn more in a discussion where they sense that their instructor is struggling, too, and genuinely listening to their arguments.

Aside from these two cases, the sensitive teacher must be guided more by his intuitive sense of the right time than by any firm principle. There is a time for him to speak up and a time to be silent. When students express a desire for his own opinion on an issue he should normally be willing to give it, making very clear to them that it is his opinion and not necessarily the truth. On many occasions students need a clearly stated opinion to which they can react and from which they can begin to form their own judgments. On other occasions they dread to hear what the teacher thinks, fearing that an issue will be foreclosed for them while they are still in the process of coming to a conclusion of their own. Good method in this area can only gradually be acquired by the teacher who is both experienced and deeply intuitive of the direction in which group discussion is tending.

The really difficult case is the teacher who exerts such a fascination over students that he habitually wins disciples and can mold them for the time being at least pretty much as he wills. When such a teacher is sensitive to the hold he has and genuinely desires student autonomy, he can of course mitigate the danger involved. Unfortunately, few can resist the intoxication of power for long. Under such circumstances the teacher becomes easily convinced of the truth of his own viewpoints to the extent that others become not simply untrue but unreal. Try as he may, his own convictions come through in nearly every subject matter, and students are subtly and sometimes not so subtly wooed to this persuasion. Occasionally his interpretations are so biased that he drives the better students into opposition. But if he is determined, however unconsciously, to win disciples, he is usually acute enough psychologically to avoid an obvious imposition. He can make full use of his greater knowledge and superior position to gain the confidence and unreflective loyalty of student followers.

Those of us who have been subject to teachers of this kind in our own youth know quite well what a disruption they caused in our own progress toward freedom. So long as their control lasted, we were not really open to other influences. We tended to look at other youth who were outside the truth either as prospects to be worked on or as hopeless idiots. No neutrality was possible, no attempt made to listen to them in order to learn the possible validity of their opinions. To the natural intolerance of youth we added the intolerance of an externally acquired gospel. Though our schooling continued, education as growth ceased, at least until we gained some new perspective on ourselves and the teacher who had converted us. When that perspective came, if it did at all, we were in danger of becoming cynical and impervious to any standpoint at all for a considerable period. The delayed effects of indoctrination are notoriously as detrimental to moral health as the process itself.

There is a temptation nowadays not to take this capture by ideology very seriously. Our students are too likely to drift without some allegiance, many will say, and it is better to be captive for a while than to run into the danger of meaninglessness and futility. So long as a teacher captures students by doctrines his colleagues and parents approve, the tendency is to shout: "More power to him!" But if he promulgates convictions in the realm of a fundamentalist religion, a materialist philosophy or psychology, a permissive sexual ethic, or a Socialist economic theory, then the response is drastically different. But philosophically these cases are the same. What too few people are able to see is that indoctrination in approved democratic convictions is not different in kind from indoctrination in Communist ones. The issue for a free society is not the nature of the ideas taught, but the crucial distinction within the teacher-student relationship between teaching and indoctrinating.

Americans are generally agreed that there is no "right" to teach, in the public schools at least. Teaching is a privilege and one that ought not to be abused. Nevertheless, it does not follow that teachers who are either unable or unwilling to give up indoctrinating students should be dismissed or not employed. So long as their effect can be countered by genuinely free colleagues, they ought to be given the opportunity to continue, even when the harm they do is potentially immense. There is always a chance that they will come to see the error of their ways. Our free society is strong enough to expose itself even to this form of perversion of its central faith. Just possibly many students are actually strengthened by such exposure to uncritical discipleship, once they have thrown it off; in adult life they will be confronted with similar attempts again and again. The proper strategy is to surround these teachers with genuinely free minds who will enable their students constantly to choose an alternative path. It is close to the crux of our faith in freedom that we tolerate many things which we utterly despise, that we take many risks and run many dangers in the interests of free individuality.

There is a more frequent and much less clearly definable situation in any teaching which endeavors to aid youth to become what they are. It arises when a teacher finds himself in opposition to the institution which employs him and to the predominant views of the community in which he works. What are the limits of his right to oppose administrative policies and to teach his students opinions that run counter to those with which they are familiar? Let us suppose he is in a religious school and is expected to uphold not only the position of the administration in a general

way but also to support required religious services. Or he finds
himself in opposition to local policy involving an athletic program, an honor system, student government, the teachers' union,
or a colleague's dismissal. The number of such cases where a
conscientious teacher can be on the unpopular side is legion.
Though they vary greatly in degree of importance and sometimes questions of principle are only vaguely involved, they
present him with a dilemma concerning his own dignity as well as
his duty to his students. When they ask him, as they frequently
will, where he stands on a particular issue of passionate concern
for them, what is he to do? Should he refuse to be drawn into the
controversy, should he respond to them as a private individual
and reveal his disagreement with his institution, or should he
defend official policy and suppress his own convictions? The
course he takes is likely to be important in any hope he cherishes
of promoting the cause of freedom in his students.

In any event it is his duty to distinguish in such a situation
between his role as a teacher, that is, his institutional role, and his
role as a private human being. His freedom to oppose regnant
opinion is much wider in the latter role than it can be in the
classroom. This elementary difference between the right of dis-
sent open to a man as a citizen and as a faculty member of an
institution is not always clear to students, and even the teacher
may forget it in the heat of anger or fear. In his public capacity
he clearly does not enjoy the right to propagate opinions that are
contrary to the will of the institution. The classroom should
never be made a forum for the teacher's case against local school
authorities, no matter how much his students importune him to
take sides. If they should be hostile to his opinions and sympathetic with majority opinion, they are very likely to suspect his
silence or find double meanings in illustrations he did not intend.
But in either case, that of agreement or disagreement with their
teacher, his duty is clearly to keep the classroom free of personal
quarrels, however appropriate and necessary it be to discuss there
questions of principle and general right.

Though this general principle is helpful and inviolable at every teaching level, it is not in itself sufficient. In these situations most teachers have wrestled with the problem of duty to themselves, to their profession, to their employers, and to the public or community in which they teach. It is one thing to stay with generalities and to avoid the personal reference; but most students need specific examples if principles are to be made concrete and vivid. And those which lie closest to hand are calculated to have the greatest effect on their efforts at reflection.

There is, however, a power in candor that is disarming. Students are quick to observe when a teacher is seeking to be fair to all parties concerned and wrestling with the moral issues at stake. Though they have no right to know in the formal classroom situation when the teacher is at odds with the authorities above him, he may well risk a discussion of his position with them outside the classroom, if they press him. There are always risks involved in teaching, and the chances of promoting students' growth in freedom are usually greatly enhanced when risks are taken. If the teacher makes crystal clear the sources of his disagreement and refrains from imputing bad faith to his superiors, the students can learn a great deal of the meaning of disagreement in principle as opposed to the clash of personalities. Even when they are unsympathetic to the teacher's standpoint, his candor in explaining himself and his willingness to allow them to disagree with him openly and frankly can be of tremendous value. If the bond between teacher and student has already been cultivated and mutual trust engendered, the possibilities of complete frankness are nearly unlimited. The strength of our society, as sensitive Europeans have pointed out again and again, lies in this agreement to tolerate opposed opinions on important matters without rancor. This strength does not grow by itself; it must be constantly fostered in the schools, and in situations like these lie the real opportunities.

The teacher's silence in acute and embittered disagreements is a delicate and disputed matter. Sometimes it is more eloquent than any words, yet the danger of misinterpretation is great. Youth are quick to suspect cowardice in such a case, particularly in our society at present where teachers are not noted for boldness and courage. Recent controversies about the Fifth Amendment indicate all too clearly that the majority of our people interpret silence as something less than admirable. Liberals may rage against this interpretation as much as they like; many of us have, but we have not been very successful in persuading others that a high principle is being guarded by it. If to speak out endangers the teacher's employment in a given school system, this may well be the best course open to him, however costly it may prove to be. Unjust dismissals of courageous teachers have been known to awaken students, as nothing else can, to the price of freedom and its inestimable value. In the opposite case, where a teacher subordinates principle in the interests of retaining his job, he provides material for moral cynicism of equal range and depth in his students.

There is, of course, a question of relevance involved in classroom discussions of controversial issues, either local or national. Many teachers avoid such discussions on the grounds of irrelevance to the material they are teaching. Students sometimes use such issues to distract their teacher from continuing with his material which they have inadequately prepared. On this matter every teacher should be allowed to steer his own course. The problem of relevance is always important and frequently troubling. The conscientious teacher will often ask himself: should I take time to discuss this problem that is bothering my students or is it extraneous to my purposes? At the time of the quiz show scandals a few years back, for example, many of us were asked for our opinions concerning the actions of Charles Van Doren. In an ethics course, evasion of such a request would surely be highly suspect; in a course in chemistry, however, a teacher might legitimately decide that it had no place. Yet, if he were wise, he would hardly refuse to state his position after class to any or all the students who wished to know it, and to defend his opinions, too, against their objections.

But if the individual teacher should be allowed to determine which controversial issues are relevant for discussion in his classroom; if he should retain the right to choose the occasion when he will give his own opinions and clearly distinguish when he is speaking as a private citizen and when as a professional teacher, then he has a clear duty to speak in unmistakable tones on questions of responsible freedom. Nothing said previously about the evils of indoctrination should be interpreted to mean that caution should be his watchword. For every teacher at the high school and college level who inhibits growth in student freedom through indoctrination, there must be dozens who fail to make any significant mark on students' understanding or practice of positive freedom. These teachers may be successful in transmitting subject matter, perhaps in stimulating advance of knowledge in their fields, but they are ineffective in the arts of teaching free individuality.

Indeed, it is hard to exaggerate the numerous failures of our high schools and colleges in this area. How many millions of our youth have passed through all their classes without ever gaining understanding of the few basic principles upon which our society rests! Only when they later become taxpayers, enter military service, join civic organizations, and enter on the duties of full citizenship do they become conscious of the many disagreements and dilemmas that divide our people. Only then, if ever, do they realize how little grasp of the important issues their formal education has given them. When newspapers daily reveal to us who teach how little success we have had in persuading our former students of the principles we cherish, many of us take refuge in rationalization. When the American Legion or some civic club attacks with venom some student or teacher who has spoken out on a controversial point, we teachers are given to railing against a narrow-minded public which totally misconceives the nature of democracy. Few of us take seriously enough the fact that this public has earlier sat in our classes, that we have failed to make clear to them what freedom means.

The only correction for this situation is to make our schools, both public and private, infinitely more exciting and involved with controversial issues than they are at present. The abiding sin of teachers and administrators in our age is spinelessness or timidity. When a school administration refuses to allow its student government to make mistakes, which amounts to denying them responsible freedom, it can hardly be surprised when its alumni clamor for restriction on free speech for the faculty. When a school newspaper is censored by a faculty sponsor before every issue appears in order to strike out criticism displeasing to any authorities in the institution, can we wonder that our citizenry demonstrate so little understanding of free speech? When teachers refuse to permit student criticism of their methods of teaching or their favorite doctrines, should they be surprised when these students, later graduated onto school boards, refuse to recognize teachers' professional rights?

There is quite obviously a limit to the freedom immature youth should have in expressing their ill-informed views. A high school newspaper must have somewhat closer faculty supervision than a college publication. Our youth need protection from the consequences of their rash angers and enthusiasms. No one can make the transition, so crucial for us as a people, from license to liberty without the tuition of those who have already made this transition. But he who imagines that this is a magical process, occurring at some abstract period called maturity, a coming of age at twenty-one perhaps, is surely devoid of understanding. We do not educate our youth without constantly risking much more than the counsels of caution dictate. It is not enough to protect the young against indoctrination. We must push them against the limits of their capacities for responsible freedom at the earliest possible age. Only teachers and administrators who expose them to the perils of free opinion and of independent action deserve to be considered true means or methods of their education.

The means by which we attempt to transfer discipline or authority from teacher to students is not the same as the means of transferring freedom, but they are closely analogous. The primary place of example is alike in both. As we have tried to show, self-discipline must precede the genuine exercise of freedom. Yet the two are intertwined in numerous respects. Students learn, through the freedom to make mistakes, the imperative need of discipline. In many areas they can learn it no other way. The growth in positive freedom is normally correlative with the advance in self-discipline. If the one precedes the other in time, the communication of freedom depends at every step upon the student's growth in capacity to assume authority. But to detail the intimate relationships of these two great concerns of philosophical method in schooling would carry us beyond the limits of this chapter.

Part IV

THE CURRICULUM

But how can we measure the good and the bad we have derived from educational influences? Every man with imagination and ambition is convinced that his education, however good, has deprived him of a still better education. He gauges the possible against the impossible, and the existent against a utopia. If he has learned languages, he deplores his ignorance in the natural sciences; but how can he judge what he would have become without the languages and more science instead?

—Robert Ulich

8. WHAT SHOULD WE TEACH?

THE WORD "CURRICULUM" has an interesting and suggestive history. Originally the word was the name of a race course, deriving from a verb meaning "to run." Later it changed meaning and came to denote a two-wheeled chaise, drawn by two horses on the race track. Sometimes it meant the actual race itself. In modern usage the course of studies, which we call the curriculum, still has something of the odor of the race track. Students compete with each other in a struggle for the goal: high grades, academic rewards, diplomas and degrees. Of course, many will say that the whole of life is a race, in which case the curriculum becomes the vehicle on which we move from the cradle to the grave.

Word meanings aside, the question of what to teach in the schools has always been a difficult one. For the question involves judgments not only of what has been important in the history of one's people and civilization itself, but also of what will be important in the proximate future. These judgments have both a social and an individual relevance. A society must determine what portions of the past it will emphasize and what pressing new needs lie on the future horizon. An individual, who cannot possibly study everything, must also choose what he is going to elect.

At the personal level most of us have felt the poignancy of this choice at some time in our lives. Once we have completed the elementary curriculum as youngsters, we are increasingly faced with decisions of courses and subject matters to nominate. Adults begin to press us with the question: What do you want to *be?* They do not want the sensible answer—an educated man or woman, but rather an answer involving our vocational ambitions. When we turn to our advisors for help, they are usually

baffled by the task of matching unknown student capacities and
interests with course materials and teacher capabilities and
temperaments.

The result often is that most adults feel their formal education was fundamentally deficient in one way or another. Most of
us are plagued with vain regrets that we did not choose to study
this or that field, select another major emphasis, even enter a
different profession from the one we are pursuing. How many
people in mid career realize that they are in the wrong field, and
bitterly reflect that choices were made at too early an age, that
another turning would have meant a more effective or a happier
life! Even though realistic observation should take into account a
full measure of self-delusion in these regrets—since we never do
know in advance what pitfalls may lie in the road we did not
take—there can be no doubt that a huge number of people have
made the wrong choices in high school and college, as many
perhaps as later make the wrong marriages. Much of the pathos
and tragedy of human life results from this; so many choices and
decisions are irreversible.

On the national level it is equally true that a people may miss
golden opportunities by choosing to teach the wrong things to its
future citizens, either by clinging to an outmoded kind of knowledge or predicting falsely looming needs and directions. By and
large, schools are conservative institutions; schoolmasters and
administrators are timid and devoted to the past. Because their
clientele, so to speak, are underage and without great power, the
pressure to change the courses of study is rarely overwhelming.
Impatient liberals in our day have coined the unlovely analogy
that it is more difficult to change the curriculum than it is to
move a graveyard. Conservatives respond with the taunt that
progressives like "to tinker with the curriculum" and the term
"to tinker" is, of course, an epithet, not a description.

Though fair-minded people would agree, I think, that societies
of the past have erred as a rule in being too slow to change the
courses and materials of study taught in their schools, the opposite error of too rapid and radical change has been occasionally

committed. One thinks, for example, of the Japanese nation in the last century, whose leaders consciously resolved to abandon their own past and to copy Western culture in the hope of quickly overtaking what they judged to be a superior mode of life. Many observers trace the twentieth century rootlessness of Japanese life and society to this forced change of direction. It can be more dangerous to disregard organic tradition in an effort to cope with presumed future needs than to rest in that tradition and conclude that what was good enough for parents and grandparents is good enough for sons and daughters. Both extremes, of course, are likely to be destructive of the requirement for continuity within change.

The problem of selectivity in what to teach seems, like all other problems of education, to be magnified today because of the increased speed of change. Though this theme of bewilderingly rapid cultural transformation has been discussed to the point of satiety, its importance *is* hard to overestimate. Perhaps we are obsessed with the rapid tempo of change, but obsession is hard to avoid when technological inventions alter the patterns of our American lives every decade and our news media continually predict even more drastic revolutions to come. The future seems to be, even on cool and objective appraisal, more of a riddle than ever before. Once, the schools could at least prepare youth for trades and skills that promised to be stable through their adult working life. Today, with the advent of automation, whole segments of industry and economic life may be so transformed as to make such preparation superfluous before half a single life span is passed.

Even when the schools renounce the task of specific job preparation and turn that aspect of training over to industry itself, as we are increasingly tending to do, the problem of selectivity is still staggering. For ours is the age of the floodtide of new knowledge. Entire new fields of study appear from one decade to the next; specialists find the task of keeping abreast of discoveries within their own narrow field increasingly impossible. Those working on the frontiers of many disciplines find it impossible to catch up if they take time out for a few years to perform useful tasks of government service or to explain to the lay public what has already been discovered. Textbooks are constantly becoming obsolete and can only usefully be revised by those who are close to the creators in their various disciplines. Teachers who are splendidly prepared at the outset of their teaching careers may quickly fall behind unless they keep in close touch with the latest publications. Even in the relatively slow moving field of philosophy, to use a personal example, I find myself teaching a course the materials of which I never heard of in graduate school. A course in Shakespeare can hardly be adequately taught unless the teacher knows much of the twentieth century critical writing on this matchless but mysterious genius.

This floodtide of knowledge makes the question of selectivity in material urgent and troubling for every teacher today. It bothers every committee on curriculum from local schools through state departments of instruction to the national bodies that deal with curriculum. If it does not, it certainly should. For the problem of what to teach is one of the most crucial of all our problems. As every teacher must daily decide what to emphasize and what to omit in subject matter too detailed and capacious for coverage, so the administrators of our school system at every level should continually seek to determine those materials that can be lopped off or pushed to the periphery of the curriculum and those new materials that should be moved toward the center. As everyone knows, we are currently making a national effort to reform and "modernize" curricula from elementary school through graduate offerings. Whether our efforts will prove to be on great enough scale and be sustained over the years, no one can at present predict.

The philosophical question in curricular reform is that of the criterion or criteria used in determining what to include and what to leave out in the materials of instruction. And the answer can only be in terms of the goals of education already decided upon. It is clear that if practical wisdom is our aim, and that encompasses free individuality, happiness, and artistry in conduct, then the subjects of study, as well as the teachers of them, should be chosen in accordance with these aims. They will provide at least a general guide to what to teach. But the difficulty is that these aims are too general in many cases, and there are, furthermore, conflicting theories of the ends of education. We do not have—and our people do not want—an educational czar who will fix such ends, because we are convinced that no single end has any absolute validity. Hence, as is usual in problems of educational policy, we are left without any universally accepted guides. Curricular choices, as at present, must be left to the discretion partly of the single individual, partly to the local school authorities and partly to the state departments of instruction. Nevertheless, the reflective student of educational theory will be able to analyze the practical problems of what to teach into a number of concrete issues.

One of these is the greatly disputed relation of general studies to specialization in subject matter. At the beginning of our national history, the curriculum tended to be general. We inherited from Europe the classical organization of courses of study which followed closely the medieval trivium and quadrivium. The education of scholars and clergy was a primary aim and education was conceived to be guided by the desire to understand and to transmit inherited tradition. But early in our development, our practical bent as a people and our indisputable needs for vocationally trained manpower and universal literacy dictated a different course for our school system. In the nineteenth century, the urge to conceive education as a means of control and an avenue to financial success became increasingly dominant. It coincided with the rise to influence of the natural sciences, especially the applied sciences, and these led to the introduction into our school systems of greater and greater specialization. By the beginning of our century the passion for specialization and for education as vocational preparation had reached the level where jesters defined the educated man as "one who knows more and more about less and less."

In the ensuing decades thoughtful educators became greatly

concerned with the vanishing of any common core of knowledge among the learned, which prevented effective communication with each other. The counter movement to specialization led to the introduction of so-called core courses, which were usually conceived as broad surveys of various fields of knowledge. It was believed that by requiring all students in high school or college to pass through these courses, the fragmenting effect of specialization could be overcome and something like the earlier community among scholars of different disciplines could be rewon. Proponents of this movement, which came to be called general education, held that the main purpose of learning was to liberate the minds of the rising generation. This could be done only by acquainting them with the best that has been thought and written in the past. Education is first and foremost for understanding, only secondarily for pragmatic and vocational purposes. Specialization, they held, is necessary both as preparation for the demanding technical positions in our complex society and for working to push back the boundaries of knowledge in the various disciplines. But these purposes should not be allowed to obscure the time-tested goal of learning as liberation of the mind for responsible citizenship and the good life.

The history of this struggle need not concern us here more than incidentally. It is the present conflict of claims that deserves analysis. On the one hand, there is no doubt that to keep our society in being a tremendous number of specialists is required, both technologists and those devoted to pure research. To keep it moving forward requires even more. On the other hand, to prevent these specialists from being isolated and unable to communicate with the larger society, requires a broad liberal education for both specialists and laymen alike. If learned men are to be effective citizens of a democratic state, able at once to speak intelligibly to their own non-specialized countrymen and to converse with scholars of other lands, they must be more than experts in their own disciplines, yet they must also be that. Both special and general education seem clearly demanded by our present situation. It is one of life's ironies in our times that so many of us require more knowledge, even to find our way home, than we really care to have. The passion to know is not so deeply inherent as the absolute need to know in order to keep ourselves and our society in being.

This dilemma of how to educate both for understanding and technical effectiveness, both liberally and specially, as many Americans as can profit from it and as we require, is not a neat logical dilemma at all. Yet the only escape from being gored by one or the other of the horns of the dilemma is for us individually and collectively to seize both horns and seek to slip between them. It is transparently clear that we need specialization today about as badly as the individual organism needs oxygen--unless we revert after a nuclear war to an agrarian society once more. On the other hand, we need general education in order to make life rich and supportable and to attempt to solve vast social problems. The larger human problems are not technical at all, but general. They require practical wisdom, not technical know-how, concerned as they are with the ends of human existence, not its means. Hence the question is critical: in the age of the floodtide of knowledge and limited human capacities and desires, how do we get both?

It is presumptuous to assume that anyone has the answer to this momentous problem. But in this time of danger, we are learning some of the elements of educational salvation. First, our schools and scholars are learning to understand general education differently than was common a few decades ago. It is not the accumulation of information in many fields and the attempt to forcefeed it to young minds. Rather, general education is the search for principles at the base of diverse disciplines and their correlation and synthesis. It is the understanding of these principles and their application to practice that can bring understanding and possible wisdom in conduct. Seen in this light there is a vast difference between a survey course that piles together mountains of information, insufficiently assimilated by students and quickly forgotten, and a general course that fastens on a few principles and attempts to render them concrete by selective examples and more universal by relating them to other fields. In such a general course there is no real opposition to a specialization that aims at new knowledge. General and special are instead complementary.

For specialization is, in the first instance, not so much a concentration on a narrow subject matter as it is a state of mind. Too frequently we think of it as pertaining to the natural sciences, whereas in fact some of the greatest specialization is found in English courses and in music. As we emphasized earlier in this study, specialization occurs when a subject matter is viewed in isolation or abstraction from its concrete context in experience. And general education aims always at the concrete, at the concrete universal. As teachers come to understand better these simple facts about the essence of specialization and general education, at least some of their present opposition and conflict will be overcome.

Nevertheless, a large part of the problem remains. Competence in any field still requires a large investment of time and energy in mastering a multitude of facts and skills. After all, principles are stubbornly different for different disciplines and at this stage of knowledge at least, methods and techniques of approach vary widely from one field to another. There is no blinking the fact that information and knowledge in these fields are accumulating at an exponential rate. A chemist or a mathematician, if he is to stay abreast of these developments, must devote the major portion of his time and effort to one tiny part of the enterprise of learning, however much he may long to know what is going on in other disciplines. If he is sufficiently advanced and skillful, he may well teach the basic principles of his subject matter to novices, but this will not make them chemists, mathematicians, historians, or literary critics.

In short, there is in every developed field a vast amount of material to digest and to transform into knowledge before one can claim mastery. Much of it is routine and highly technical, in isolation not meaningful or educative to the uninitiated, but fraught with exciting possibilities to the specialist. Since the number of these fields is multiplying today, the burden of learning in its sheer bulk weighs on the student the farther he advances through the schools. A kind of Faustian mood of futility can settle on him in library or laboratory as early as high school and not lift through the doctorate of philosophy and beyond. To be sure, there are promising signs that this burden of learning may be lightened by the development of machines, such as computers, which will increasingly take over routine tasks, even those not so routine, to free the specialist's time and mind from preoccupation with facts and techniques. Robert Morison has recently suggested exciting possibilities of this development for education. He writes:

> It will not be easy for most of us to relinquish to the machine the arts and techniques which have taken us decades to master, and to concentrate on the even more demanding tasks of generalization, synthesis, and judgment which only man can carry out. Perhaps the greatest demands for ingenuity will fall upon the field of education, once it is decided to hand over to other means the mere memorization of information, the computing of sums, and such other routine intellectual tasks as may be found appropriate. It will be an excellent teacher indeed who shows us how to program our school and college experience so as to maximize the capacity to grasp general principles, detect relevance where none was seen before, and create new conceptual schemes. When that day comes, all education will in a sense be general education, since the technical problems which now divide the specialties will in large part be handed over to the computers, and we will have taught ourselves a language we can all use in common.[1]

But until the day comes when all education becomes general education—and I suspect that Mr. Morison would agree that it will not be tomorrow—the schools must attempt to communicate both specialized and general knowledge to all students, except perhaps to those whom, in Comenius' phrase, "God has denied intelligence." We are also coming to realize in this country that these two kinds of courses belong together throughout the pro-

---

[1] Robert S. Morison, "New Types of Excellence," pp. 770-771, *Daedalus*, Fall 1961.

cess of formal schooling, indeed throughout the course of formative education as a whole. As we can only hope to be equal to this era of the floodtide of knowledge by starting our education early and continuing it through life, so our schools must juxtapose the more general courses with the specialized at every level. Formerly it was believed that general education belonged early in the school career. Specialization should gradually come to dominance in later high school and college work, and in graduate school it should monopolize the student's time. Though such practices are still all too common, they are surely misguided. For some, specialization belongs at the high school level, college courses should embody as complete a union of the two as possible, and some general courses should continue through graduate school.

The reasons for this intimate conjunction of courses both general and specialized are many. Here we may list only a few of them. Diverse interests are certain to assert themselves very early in life. Often a youngster may become alive in junior or senior high school, if he is allowed to pursue a genuine but specialized talent much further than is usual for his age. Discovery of certain principles in his field of interest may well lead him to see the validity and importance of other disciplines of study when forced presentation of material he does not "like" will only stultify his perceptions. In any event the psychology of learning suggests that many of us can only come to appreciate the general through immersion in the particular.

The usual survey course in American history, for example, in high school fails very often to awaken student interest in one or another phase of that development, whereas a more detailed study of one aspect might well lead to later passion for the larger picture. Similarly, the ubiquitous Western Civilization course for college freshmen could more profitably be given in many cases to seniors, after more particularized knowledge of this or that aspect of our culture is achieved. Furthermore, there is an invidious value judgment involved in putting general courses first in formal education and specialized courses later, a subtle indication not missed by students, that the latter are most valued by adult society. But more important than any of these considerations is the fact that specialized and general knowledge belong together in our lives from first to last. The tension between them can only be minimized if they are acquired at the same time—where possible, in the same course—and enabled to interpenetrate and supplement each other.

The antagonism between these ways of knowing has been sharpened in recent decades by the division of the curriculum into natural sciences, social sciences, and humanities. The artificialities of this division become apparent to anyone who reflects upon principles at all. Yet students are given to imitating the attitudes and prejudices of their mentors, so that this arrangement of convenience becomes too frequently a wall of separation for the schools. It is, to be sure, undeniable that differences in method, in precision, approach, and desired results do exist among the separate disciplines. In a general way the natural sciences have as their subject matter for investigation our natural habitat; the humanities, our human, largely individual, ways of experiencing nature and man's relations to it; whereas the social sciences deal with man's collective experience and the interaction of the social and the natural. These differences of focus and emphasis dictate variations in ways of investigating, in the use of formal or empirical methods, in acquiring of data and search for generalizations, even in the kind of knowledge, theoretical or practical, desired. There is also no doubt that youth have interests and talents that predispose them toward one or another of these general divisions, even particular segments within these fields of knowledge. The great principle of division of labor has as much validity within the academic realm as it has in all other phases of an advanced culture.

But for philosophical theory of education which endeavors to see things whole, these divisions are largely unfortunate, often pernicious. The human being is not apart from the world he inhabits, his nature is not knowable in separation, just as it does not exist in a separable realm. The study of nature must be intimately linked with the study of man, the individual with the gen-

eral, the formal with the empirical, the practical with the theoretical. The process of creativity, it is generally agreed, is the
same process in all these fields. And the goal of pushing back the
limited horizons of our knowledge, of achieving more truth
about the mysterious and infinitely complex world we inhabit in
common and about which we still know so little, cannot vary
from one discipline to another. Natural science is still natural
philosophy, its generic name everywhere until very recently.
Likewise the social and the humanistic sciences are differentiated
from this love of wisdom by their attributes only, not their substance. Those who have worked through the specialties and stand
at the pinnacles of achievement in one or the other of these fields
of knowledge are commonly of one voice in perceiving the unity
of knowledge, in decrying the futile warring of disciplines. Creative scientists have usually no difficulty in sensing their kinship
with poets, economists with philosophers, or historians with
geologists.

One of the indispensable functions of general courses in the
schools is to keep uppermost in the minds of students this equal
dignity of various subject matters. Teachers today have a clear
duty, more than in the past, not to denigrate other disciplines nor
to yield to students' biased opinions that the sciences deal only
"with nuts and bolts" or the humanities are "subjective opinion,"
and the like. In large part, the determination of attitudes toward
the arts and sciences is the crucial issue and this is overwhelmingly the responsibility of formal education. There exists alas an
academic "pecking order" among disciplines that is all too easily
transmitted to students. Of late the natural sciences enjoy great
prestige, some of them more than others, and humanists feel
threatened and defensive. But in other lands and even in certain
schools in the United States the humanities still hold supremacy
and scientists are regarded as grubby artisans, powerful but not
quite respectable. Frequently both natural scientists and humanists join forces to derogate the rising influence of the social sciences by imputing inchoateness of subject matter and uncritical
methods of inquiry. The sad strife of competing teachers and

disciplines is waged to win students who are as yet too young and inexperienced to know where their own interests and talents lie or to glimpse the possible principles that could unify their bewildering courses of study.

It is at present beyond debate that the educated man must have knowledge of both the arts and the sciences. Assuredly he cannot hope to be an expert in many fields, but he can by diligent effort become informed about the basic principles of subject matters other than his own specialty. Our society is increasingly recognizing that the literary intellectual who knows nothing of the natural sciences is woefully one-sided, and the natural scientist who regards music, poetry, and philosophy as adornments or frills is no better. Both are narrow specialists who may be useful and inevitable in our present academic backwardness. But they represent a failure of the schools to unite the general and the specialized modes of knowing as well as a failure of the individual to resist the temptation to close himself to equally valid realms of experiencing reality.

There is a very simple homily in all this for those who learn and those who teach. Though all of us must resign ourselves in this age when knowledge has expanded beyond imaginable comprehension, to life-long ignorance of more than a tiny fraction of that worth knowing, we need not assume that the modicum we do possess has greater importance or validity than that which we do not know. The specialist who has insufficient general education is constantly in danger of the false assumption that his field is more important than others, not only for him but as such. And one of the virtues of the truly general course is that it is fitted to induce humility in the student. Nevertheless, it is a universal and pathetic human tendency to believe that one's own sphere of competence is uniquely fitted to give perspective on the whole of knowledge. Hence, the need for acquaintance with the principles of several fields. The educated man is one who is as deeply aware of his ignorance as of what he knows. Like Socrates, he must know something of the range of what he does not know.

If it is true that range or breadth of knowledge is as necessary to the student in search of an education as depth in one or more disciplines, the question of prescription or required courses in high school and college is of major concern in educational theory. Which courses should be required of all students in school and which should remain elective? Put more exactly, which subject matters are of such importance that every American young person should be expected to demonstrate at least minimal knowledge of them before proceeding to less essential but to him possibly more interesting areas? Rather than losing ourselves in the details of this problem, we should seek for a relatively few general principles upon which to proceed.

First among these is one that has been largely adopted by our American system after considerable experimentation and with which reflective theorists will be reluctant to quarrel. It is that prescribed courses should be all but universal at the elementary level, yielding at the secondary school to a mixture of elective and required courses, and in college or university elective courses should predominate with prescription gradually disappearing, except within departments of student specialization. The justification for this practice is simply that as students mature and discover themselves, they should be allowed greater choice within the curriculum in the interests of their freedom and self-discipline. As they demonstrate competence in the more universal disciplines, they ought to be given opportunity to explore areas of genuine interest in the endeavor to discover those fields in which they may desire to specialize and continue to educate themselves long past the period of formal schooling.

If this principle is sound, as I think it is, it involves corollaries that are not as widely adhered to in practice, however generally they may be agreed upon. Individual differences in ability and in interest are so great in our school population that these prescribed courses can by no means be uniform in difficulty or the same in content. This is particularly true in secondary school, but as more and more of our population enter college, it becomes increasingly true of higher education also. The current response to this enormous diversity in ability is to develop a track system or homogeneous grouping whereby students of different abilities are taught in separate classes. With all its dangers, such a procedure, if we can develop sufficient safeguards against abuse and enough flexibility in administering it, seems to be the feasible solution. A second corollary requires that a difference in required courses be insisted on in high school between those designed for students who are terminating their formal schooling at this level and those who plan to attend college. This is by no means the same division as that between students of high ability and those of average capacity, since at present many of the latter are not terminal and too many of the former do not opt for further schooling. There is and ought to be a considerable difference in the materials of instruction and the manner of teaching of a course which is likely to be the last exposure of a student to it from a course designed as preparation for more advanced treatment of the same material. The stubborn difficulty here, which at present balks all our efforts at a solution, is the indecision of large numbers of high school students regarding attendance at college. So long as this remains, the desirable differentiation between preparatory and terminal education in prescribed subject matter cannot be completely carried out. A third corollary involves no such dilemma, but is most frequently violated and with the most disheartening consequences. Courses that are required of all students stand in need of constant examination and revision, of the most conscientious teaching, and the greatest support of administration and faculty. Because they are nearly always resisted by students, they require those teachers most able to induce motivation and most skillful in separating essential from inessential aspects of subject matter. An elective course that is poorly taught provides its own corrective: fewer students will elect it. But a captive audience must be protected against routine, stale, and repetitive teachers and teaching. Such a course concerns the whole school, indeed the whole community, not simply those who teach it from year to year. And it is not true that the materials of these courses never become obsolete. On the contrary, in a society like ours some prescribed courses should doubtless in time be made elective, others formerly elective should be prescribed. Within every such course, alert and conscientious teachers should continually work to modernize, vivify, and adapt the material to every level of student ability. Administrators should strive to avoid overloading these teachers with too many students and too many required classes. It would be hard to find a more unequivocally right principle than this one or one more frequently violated in practice.

If prescribed courses in any school system deserve primary attention and emphasis, elective courses should, nevertheless, be as numerous, carefully chosen, and rich in content as the resources and interests of the community or individual institution can provide. The virtue of pluralism, the recognition of a desirable diversity in our American life, which has kept us from a federal centralization of schools and curricula, should govern the determination of subject matters to be offered for free electives. The principle to be followed is that the full resources of a varied and incredibly lavish culture be offered to every American student insofar as possible. Many of the curricula in high schools and colleges in too many of our states are in fact impoverished and thin. The student who desires to elect Latin, Greek, geography, ancient history, astronomy, or the like, or pursue these and other courses at an advanced level is all too frequently thwarted in his desires, both in high school and in college. For every institution that offers too many trivial and ill-chosen subjects, there must be dozens that fail to offer important and indeed essential electives. School boards are notorious for desiring to drop those courses that do not attract a heavy enrollment, in complete disregard of the relatively few students who do elect them. If those critics who delight in ridiculing in popular magazines a few courses with silly titles and content in the curriculum of certain institutions, would concentrate instead on the distressing absence of centrally important electives in thousands of schools, they would be doing something inestimably more important. For concentration of prescribed subjects should by no means preclude, in a society as affluent as ours, rich and varied offerings in new and old fields of learning.

Most responsible educators agree on the courses that should be required at the secondary level. The work of James Conant and his corps of investigators has done a good deal to unify public opinion on this very practical issue, on which there is not very great room for philosophical dispute. Perhaps first among requirements most of us would list physical education, despite the gross failures of actual instruction and concept in this area. Second, the English language and literature require continued emphasis throughout secondary schooling. The immense difficulty American students experience in mastering our intricate tongue, one of the enduring discouragements of sensitive teachers, makes constant concentration on this subject matter imperative even beyond high school, sometimes beyond college. That mastery of the language is best attempted through study of our rich literature, English and American, increasingly world literature, goes without saying, though there is much dispute about the details of this interrelationship of language and literature.

Third, everyone would agree that American youth must be acquainted in the schools with the fundamentals of American history and government. This follows inexorably from the nature of a free society in which voting rights and privileges are held in principle by all adults. In our time, rightly called the first global era, this requirement is expanding to include some acquaintance with the history and government of other peoples as well.

Fourth, all students need to acquire as much knowledge of the basic physical and biological sciences as their aptitudes warrant and as our schools can supply. This includes, of course, work in mathematics, universally recognized as the gateway to the sciences. How much of these disciplines should be prescribed depends upon the facilities of each school and abilities of the students; but there is no longer any question of their central importance to the educated mind.

Fifth—and too often last—are the so-called fine arts, music, painting, drama, and the like. Though there is as much endless dispute about the balance of theory and practice in the teaching of the arts as about the relative place of the performing arts over the purely creative, most of us would concur in the necessity of introducing all students to at least one of these disciplines, freighted as all of them are with possibilities of happiness through creative self-development.

The case for requiring at least one foreign language in high school is currently embroiled in controversy. We Americans are notoriously poor at languages and as our country has moved to the front of world powers, this inability has begun to disturb government officials. As a consequence, we are making a national effort to overcome this handicap. With the aid of new methods, machines, and language laboratories, more high school students than ever before are seeking to acquire mastery of a foreign tongue. James Conant has helped to direct this effort by recommending longer concentration on one language rather than a smattering of two or three. It is evident that we are in the midst of an academic revolution in the learning and teaching of other peoples' languages.

What can be said for prescribing the study of one foreign tongue for every American student? It is difficult to avoid personal bias on this issue or to overcome the danger of being influenced too greatly by present propaganda for language study. Certainly acquaintance with a foreign tongue is highly desirable for all and its importance has been greatly increased with the revolutions in transportation and the likelihood that nearly all young persons will travel abroad at some time in their lives. A strong case can be made that even one year of such study is not wasted at all. Veterans of World War II can well recall how those soldiers who knew perhaps fifty words of Italian, French, or German made great efforts to acquire hundreds more, whereas those totally ignorant behaved in the manner of suspicious deaf people toward the inhabitants of the land they were occupying. And anyone who has observed the delight in the eyes of a foreigner when one attempts to communicate in his native tongue will not lightly dismiss the question of required language study for a people, like ourselves, who aspire to world leadership. There are still too many "ugly Americans" who cannot comprehend why other peoples fail to understand English when spoken slowly and distinctly enough. Beyond dispute is the fact that other peoples will more willingly follow our leadership as we demonstrate our *caring* enough to learn their languages and respect their traditions.

On the other hand, it must be acknowledged that genuine mastery of a foreign language is much more difficult than is commonly recognized. It is one thing to be able to communicate orally on matters of simple daily need and quite another to be able to read, write, and speak another language at the level of thought and emotional comprehension. A moment's reflection on the long years of study required for semi-mastery of our own language ought to be sufficient to convince the doubter. Hence, it may well be questioned whether a language requirement for everyone ought to be introduced into the secondary schools. There seem to be many students, able enough in other subjects, who experience nothing but frustration in their efforts to acquire minimal competence in the elements of a foreign tongue. Certainly most high schools should vastly increase the number of foreign language classes, going far beyond the two years usually offered. For those who plan to attend college, foreign language study should be mandatory. Colleges, for their part, ought to insist that all their graduates attain minimal competence in one foreign language as a requirement for the degree. Desirable as such study may be for the large majority of those who do not at present continue beyond secondary school, foreign languages are doubtfully on the same level of importance as the subject matters previously mentioned.

Nevertheless, there is an additional consideration that needs emphasis here. Too often we are taught in America to look upon language learning as the acquiring of a tool. Much of the teaching that is done in our high schools and colleges misses the educational mark widely. Language learning is far more than the acquisition of a skill. There is a wise saying of Goethe to the effect that "he

who has learned a second language has acquired a second soul."
We are human beings largely by virtue of language. Reflect as
long as we will, it is hard to appreciate this simple fact sufficiently. The potentialities of coming to feel at home in a language
other than our mother tongue are enormous. They can only be
realized—and then partially—if we teach students how integrally
the learning of a language is bound up with ways of thinking and
behaving other than our own. The possible contribution of such
subject matter to general education is hard to exaggerate. For all
of us in the tumultuous present stand in need of more than one
soul—all the more reason to protest against the shallow teaching
of languages, much too prevalent, as mere tools or implements.

Within the limits of space of this chapter there is opportunity
to discuss briefly only one of the foregoing requirements, that of
physical education. Because most students today have been exposed to little more than a parody of physical education in our
schools, it may appear dubious to put it as an unquestioned prescription for all. Though we retain the term *education* for it,
what we have is, for the most part, physical *training*, though even
that may be an exaggeration. Yet our traditions of liberal education, stemming from ancient Greece, are unambiguous in placing
gymnastike on a par with the fine arts and the sciences. At the
source of our educational ideals in fifth century Athens lies a
conception of the harmony and unity of body and mind, not the
product of nature but of careful cultivation. There, the educated
man was the end product of a many-sided development, physical
as well as intellectual. He embodied such virtues as grace, proportion, and style, and these qualities were thought to be as truly a
part of physical movements as of mental agility and esthetic perception.

Plato expressed in his *Republic* this ideal of Hellenic education:
"And when a beautiful soul harmonizes with a beautiful form,
and the two are cast in one mould, that will be the fairest of
sights to him who has an eye to see it" . . ."And he who mingles

music with gymnastic in the fairest proportions, and best attempers them to the soul, may be rightly called the true musician and harmonist in a far higher sense than the tuner of the strings." Even then, however, the goal of the education of the body, as opposed to physical training, was threatened by too great emphasis on competition in sports and military defense needs. Plato speaks scornfully of the sleepy athlete who is physically overdeveloped in his youth, and of the weakly, myopic intellectual, of the soldier who is a barbarian and the health faddist who "educated diseases," "who was in constant torment whenever he departed in anything from his usual regimen, and so, dying hard, by the help of science he struggled on to old age."

Perhaps the successive corruptions of physical education are inevitable, but our American society has less excuse for them than had most of its predecessors. We have the facilities and the leisure for a gradual development of physical capacities in our youth, for their early instruction in carry-over sports that can be exercised throughout life. The necessity for hard labor over long hours that earlier deformed the body as well as the mind is long since past. Ignorance of and inability to obtain proper diet for physical development are also no longer a question for the majority of our population. Rapid advance of medicine has made the correction of congenital defects easily possible and has provided us with a knowledge of physiology and the prerequisites of physical and of mental health never before possessed.

What can the schools do to bring physical education closer to the norm of what every reflective person realizes is desirable? First, we require in the public consciousness a clearer realization of the purposes of physical education. These courses are insufficiently related to the goals of liberal education. The potentiality for joy of a well-developed physique, of glowing health, the sense of well-being that comes from control of the body and skill in its performance of difficult feats, is sufficient reason for including physical education among the liberal arts. Even apart from this, the role played by such education, rightly conceived and carried through, in developing self-discipline and consequent freedom of the individual is insufficiently appreciated by the general public. We need to support the schools in their effort to understand physical education as a more integral part of general education than at present. Many of our disquieting problems of sexual promiscuity, of morbid preoccupation with suicide and violence, would be ameliorated if our schools developed physical education courses that were not simply ways of tiring the body or competing in sports.

For physical education is not merely concerned with muscular development, with weight reduction as in "Lady, Be Fit" exercises, or with increasing the competitive spirit in youngsters. It is a discipline rich in theory, embracing the spheres of hygiene, physiology, and the relations of our biological organisms to the environing world. Properly taught, such courses can contribute a considerable share to the Socratic program of "Know thyself." Knowledge of one's body can even promote a kind of wisdom of the body that is as genuinely a part of wisdom as the more purely intellectual kind. And as knowledge is a prerequisite for artistic skill in the moral realm, so is it likewise in the sphere of physical practice.

In the present situation the schools must stand in opposition to two great and related evils. The first of these is the emphasis on competition, often more destructive of genuine education in this realm than it is in more purely academic subjects. Competitive sports have all too frequently come to usurp the time, energy, and ability of physical education departments in high school and college. Often the community is to blame in demanding that gladiatorial entertainment be provided for adults, that publicity be obtained for a local school, and that school spirit or morale be enhanced by fierce contests in "contact" sports. Such practices have become so widespread on the American academic scene that, until recently, few teachers or parents could imagine a school without them. It is cause for wonder that more people do not ask the elementary question of how these competitive contests contribute to the physical education of the participants or to the spectators. The demand for entertainment is naturally legitimate, and in themselves competitive games can be a part, though a subordinate one, of physical education. But the entertainment of the public is surely no duty of an educational system, and when competition becomes an end in itself it defeats the very purpose of all education, which is concerned with intrinsic values.

This evil is by no means easy to overcome. For the competitive spirit is deeply rooted in our American traditions and enjoys ideological support in our economic system and our general mores. Only as the schools slowly build a new conception of the aims of education of the body as inseparable from the mind and assume leadership in propagating these aims will the public permit them to reclaim their departments of physical education. Then the public's need for entertainment can be satisfied by professional sports, and we can expect school children again to become participants, rather than spectators, of intra-mural contests based on the principle of playing well, not of winning, as the goal.

Though this principle is voiced frequently enough in connection with the game element of physical education, it is rarely deeply understood. Teachers and administrators in every discipline can help to restore physical education to a more central place in the curriculum by shifting the stress on victory to the intrinsic values of good form and mastery of the skills of playing. It is a simple fact, yet so difficult for adolescents to grasp at the dispositional level, that the joys of physical activity are in its performance, whereas the satisfaction in winning is transient. Most of us dimly grasp this truth, for we have experienced as children the elementary fact that games are played and enjoyed for their own sake, having no justification beyond themselves. But the corruptions of adult society are such that we must normally wait until we are middle-aged before understanding clearly the implications of this childlike revelation. Hence, nothing is more important in teaching and learning than stress upon doing something correctly for its own sake, upon good form and the acquisition of skills for the enduring satisfactions they yield, rather than for the evanescent pleasures of superiority over others. Since the dangers are greatest in the realm of sports, greatest emphasis should naturally be concentrated there.

The second great evil is the temptation to softness and physical flabbiness in a society like ours where sedentary occupations predominate and where the passion for comfort and ease is a national characteristic, long noticed by students of American civilization. The law of inertia is not simply an abstract generalization in physics; laziness is native to the species *homo sapiens*. It was a theorist of education who coined the witty phrase: "When I feel like taking exercise, I just lie down until the feeling goes away." When these tendencies are combined with the greatly improved diet of average Americans, they result in the phenomenon of overweight as a national health problem, in a kind of physical deterioration by middle age that makes our physical constitutions ill adapted to the psychic strain and stress of contemporary life. Though medicine can keep more of us in existence through the normal life span than ever before, we have not yet discovered the medicine that can keep us truly vigorous and alive. That can only be accomplished when we learn to be in large measure our own physicians.

It is exceedingly unlikely that the easy conditions of physical existence, lately so prevalent in America, will continue indefinitely. If history teaches anything at all, it indicates that physical hardihood and vigor are in the long run prerequisites for any nation. There is no case at all for war, of course, but if there were it would not lie in war's alleged ability to check population growth, for which it has been proved to be inadequate, but in the toughening of a culture's physical fiber and capacity to withstand hardships. Since we dare not rely on this means any longer, physical education, it seems clear, must increasingly stress survival techniques and actively promote in the schools a knowledge of the conditions for survival, which former generations could assume were learned in the home. One trembles to realize how few of our young people know any longer how to prepare a meal without the facilities of electricity and packaged foods, how to keep themselves in minimal health without central heating and air-conditioning, in short how to utilize Nature's bounty and scarcity in their uncultivated state. The marvels of our technological civilization will prove to be a short-term blessing indeed, if we become dependent upon them as an absolute necessity.

Only in very recent years has the danger of physical flabbiness moved our government to undertake measures to combat it. The Kennedy Administration launched a physical fitness program that was widely publicized, designed to call attention to the problem. But the uses of propaganda are limited in this sphere. Long hikes in the country or occasional camping trips in our wilderness areas are insufficient correctives to what has become a deep-seated national problem. Only the schools can undertake the kind of long-range program that will attack the roots of the evil, a program that will be as concerned with knowledge and attitude as with specific skills.

In the right direction certainly are the schools, originating in Britain and now spreading over this country, called Outward Bound. They are a consequence of World War II when millions of students were suddenly asked to condition themselves to a form of life entirely foreign to all their previous training. These schools take young men into the mountains and onto the seas and endeavor to teach them self-reliance and self-discipline as well as the strength and skill to endure genuine hardships posed by the natural elements. These short-term courses are carefully graded in degrees of hardships encountered in the wilds and on the oceans. They are designed to test not simply physical capacities but the will and resourcefulness of the students. And from all reports their greatest value lies in changed attitudes, in the revelation that comes to these young people that they can actually do what had before seemed utterly impossible.

It would be contrary to our educational theory to use arguments for national survival to frighten our population into physical fitness. There is a sense in which every government is properly concerned with the hardiness of its people for the event of emergencies and military necessities. But the point is a wholly different one. The goal of free individuality implies a measure of self-reliance that pertains as truly to physical skills as to intellectual powers. The student in search of an education must come to realize sooner or later that he cannot divorce mind and body. So long as he has failed to test his capacities for physical survival and acquired a full measure of independence in this area, he will find that moral and intellectual autonomy is much more difficult. If our physical education departments ever learn to communicate these intrinsic virtues, this wisdom of the body, they will have begun to assume their rightful place in liberal education, and will no longer be looked upon askance as a kind of necessary appendage in our schools.

Among elective courses in the curriculum, those called vocational form as great a problem for the theory of education as do required courses in physical education. To what extent do courses in typing, home economics, machine shop, radio, and many others belong in the schools? Are they rightly a function of liberal education at all? As everyone knows, the comprehensive American high school is nearly unique in the world in its endeavor to bring under one roof instruction in the practical arts and skills with the more conventional academic subjects. Other nations prefer to separate vocational subjects from the arts and the sciences, not merely in the schools but in the selection of pupils who are to pursue the one or the other. This commonly leads to sharp social and class separations as well. But we Americans, partly under the impetus of our love of equality, have insisted on the principle that schooling should prepare everyone to make a living as well as to make a life. We like to keep a close connection between vocational training and liberal education, a connection that is not only physical proximity but also theoretical and cultural as well. The question for philosophy of education is: are we justified in this preference? Does instruction in the manual or practical arts contribute to education as we have defined it? Or do these subjects represent an unwarranted concession to our national passion for the practical as opposed to theory, to our alleged preoccupation with the "cash value" of education? Though it may be granted that such courses need to be taught somewhere, what justification do they have in the curriculum of nearly all high schools and indeed most of our colleges as well? From the standpoint of the goals of education, one's attitude toward the unifying of vocational and liberal courses can only be affirmative. There is no necessary antithesis in our time between making a living and making a good life. The ancient Greeks were forced in the absence of technology to make a sharp distinction between education for leisure and vocational training, between liberal and illiberal occupations. In some sense our early experience on this raw continent forced the same disjunction on us. But that time is past. For the student who anticipates entering a profession, almost any course, even philosophy, becomes a vocational course. And the old self-evident separations between manual labor and mental labor are increasingly blurred, like the disjunctions of work and play. It may well be that the United States, far from being a lonely innovator in standing for the unity of vocational and liberal studies, will be seen in the perspective of history as a precursor of future universal practice.

For the model of the educated man, whom we have been delineating in the foregoing pages, is one who has overcome, as much as may be, the conventional dualisms of head and hand, of art and science, of theoretical and practical competence. He is not one who is helpless in the practical emergencies of everyday life, driving a car in total ignorance of its mechanical principles or unable to cope with simple repairs of the many implements which make his physical needs easy to satisfy. Nor, on the other hand, is he the merely practical man, jack of all trades, who scorns political, moral, even philosophical problems of theory, and clings to a narrow pragmatic viewpoint. The direction of our whole educational system has been, and with some current doubts and hesitations continues to be, toward avoiding either type as one-sided, ill-educated, and unfitted to responsible democratic life.

At the very practical level, such one-sidedness on either the intellectual or the manual side is proving to be a severe handicap. We are essentially a nation without servants any longer, a trend that seems to be universal among advanced industrial societies. Even the very wealthy in our society feel that they must have an occupation and must perform for themselves everyday tasks that their fathers and mothers would have disdained. Many of them find a satisfaction in knowing how to cook a meal, use a hammer, manipulate complicated machinery, etc., that they would not willingly forego. At the other extreme, parents without intellectual interests or competence find themselves quickly out of touch with their own children, unable to help them with elementary school tasks, bewildered by a wide world that is on their TV screens and in their newspapers. Whatever may have been the case a few short years ago, we are today in dire need of a schooling that can provide some delicate balance between the skills of the hand and the head, the understanding of the heart and the analysis of the intellect.

This is not to say that the schools should not restrict the number of such vocational courses in the curriculum and limit the credits of students electing them. There is too frequently today a positive correlation between the proliferation of such courses in a curriculum and the absence of desirable offerings in languages, sciences, and history. Some of the skills now taught in the schools could be done better by local industries, business firms, and professions. The old apprentice-journeyman guild system of learning is coming again to the fore, and many firms prefer to train their own employees in the skills peculiar to their needs. In this age there is great need for the closest kind of cooperation between school and society, particularly in the vocational area. Students in these courses might well spend part of every school week in actual job training under the direction of skilled personnel from industry, receiving from them grade evaluations and occasional lectures and demonstrations in the classroom. Many of these courses can well be taught during summer vacations, after regular classes in the evenings and on weekends. Others can be acquired by students on "sabbatical leave" from school, who desire or need full-time work experience. Only when our schools become actual centers for the induction of our youth into the skills of adult life, taught by the possessors and users of these skills and not alone by professional teachers will they fulfill the purpose advocated by educational philosophers through the centuries.

The real difficulties with many vocational courses as currently taught are numerous. Too often they are conceived as mere "how to" disciplines with little or no attention to principles or to generalization. When they consist simply of laboratory work without any teaching of the underlying science and technology, their educational value is nearly lost. This leads to the social disparagement of such courses, the oft-heard charge that they are for "dumbbells." Actually, students of limited mentality do not perform better in these courses than they do in more academic classes. Nevertheless, the overcoming of this widespread attitude is one of the real problems of vocational education, particularly in high schools. It has led to an inferiority complex on the part of many such teachers and consequent difficulty in the procurement of imaginative teaching personnel. There is also the expense of purchasing up-to-date and costly equipment for vocational classrooms. There can be little merit in teaching students skills that are no longer marketable in industry. Everyone knows how swiftly these change nowadays. Recently the federal government, recognizing the need, has provided separate funds for vocational education.

Hence the task confronting vocational education is to keep the material of its courses as up-to-date as possible, more closely geared to industry and the community than it is or has been, and above all, to teach their subject matter in as liberal a manner as it can be made. This last requirement signifies an insistence upon the science and theory of such subject matter as well as its correlation with other fields. These courses promise, like few others, a rapprochment of school and community, of learning through doing, of the practical and the theoretical. When properly conceived, they can provide as large a share of the ingredients for individuality as courses in literature, chemistry, or philosophy.

Not all students are fitted to profit from such traditional subjects when studied in depth. Yet the achievement of individuality, happiness, and a philosophical faith is surely as possible for the skilled tradesman as for the intellectual worker—and as difficult.

This survey of some of the philosophical problems of the curriculum, brief and inadequate as it is, has suggested nevertheless certain guiding principles for the student in search of an education. First among them is the necessity for him to keep specialized and general education in balance, not only during his school career but throughout his future life. Difficult as this has become in the age when a floodtide of knowledge threatens to impose specialization upon all who seek mastery, there is no alternative. Lest we become as individuals depressed by the sheer bulk of knowledge, we need to keep uppermost in our minds the undeniable fact that this new knowledge is a blessing, one of the greatest blessings of our time. There is no doubt at all that we still possess far too little for the mastering of our staggering problems as a society. If the schools can only make a beginning on the task of inducting our youth into an understanding of this complex social and natural world, the beginning is, as always, vitally important to the developing whole.

Second, the greatest problem of curricular planning is to develop courses that are genuinely concrete and at the same time general, that is to say, material that will lead students to principles by means of selective illustrations, without demanding of them familiarity with mountains of detail. For an education does not consist in the amount of knowledge we possess, but in its organization and generalizing power as well as its potentiality for effecting understanding. The possibility of promoting general education is present, if largely unrealized, in most of the specialized courses in any curriculum, as likewise is the possibility for specialized and concrete instruction in general courses. Everything depends on the way the teacher understands and presents his material. The best course will always be the one that combines the particular and the general, theory and fact, principle and illustration.

More specifically, however, this unfinished business of curriculum involves a separation in purpose between introductory courses in the various disciplines designed for the later professional and those intended for the general student. Too often at present these introductions are taught by an instructor who assumes that every student before him plans to become a specialist like himself. Such a procedure makes impossible the winning of a knowledge of principles without more work in a given discipline than student time or interest permits. When American schools are sufficiently advanced to distinguish in every subject matter the vast difference between a course designed to teach general principles and a course designed to prepare specialists, we will have begun to cope with the unifying of general and specialized education.

It is, of course, much more than a matter of taking course work. Critics are right in complaining of the widespread notion that in order to know anything about a subject matter one must have had a formal course in it. Our schools are much too course-centered at present. We have as yet hardly begun to make use of the techniques of oral and written examinations of students on material that they may well have mastered on their own. In the age of paperback printing, with more and more good general books, films, and other self-teaching materials easily available in nearly every field, many of the required as well as elective courses in our curriculum might well be passed by the enterprising student without class attendance at all. His ability to balance the general and the particular, the primary and the derivative in such subject matter would be the best possible preparation for his further education beyond the schools.

Finally, the student seeking an education, as far as that may be advanced within the schools, will use the curriculum as a means for many-sided development. He will scorn neither the arts nor the sciences, neither physical development nor vocational courses insofar as they are properly taught. Though youth and inexperience will make him a temporary victim of the prejudices of teachers and the inadequacies of curricular offerings, he will, if persistent enough, be able to attain the foundations of an education in many, if not all, American schools. Frequently all that is required is that he come to know one imaginative and sympathetic teacher who is able to see clearly through the mazes of formal curricula, and can guide him in the selection of teachers and subject matters most likely to further his search for self-realization. The great curricular task, which will be ever unfinished, is to remove as many obstacles as possible from the path of such a student and such a teacher. It has often been remarked that the first duty of a hospital is to prevent the spreading of diseases, if it cannot cure them. Likewise, it is the first responsibility of a curriculum to remove as many hindrances to the pursuit of an education as teachers and administrators are capable of perceiving.

Part V

SCHOOLS AND THE WIDER SOCIETY

I come back to the fact that we are living in a mixed and divided life. We are pulled in opposite directions. We have not as yet a philosophy that is modern in other than a chronological sense. We do not have as yet an educational or any other social institution that is not a mixture of opposed elements.
—John Dewey

9. ACADEMIC EQUALITY AND SEXUAL INTEGRITY

WHEN WE REFLECT on schools in relation to the larger society, philosophical problems of practice are many. But in terms of the educational goals I have selected earlier for analysis, two appear to predominate. First is the development of integrity in relations between the sexes to promote individuality, happiness, and artistic morality. Second is the necessary transformation of attitudes required to cope with the unprecedented reality of living in a world which has become a neighborhood. These two problems, more correctly, complex of problems, are not separate and distinct, for the task that underlies both is one of attaining mutuality among human beings, without which the goal of individuality in community is impossible. These problems represent a kind of ultimate challenge to the schools in contemporary America, the challenge of promoting associations of individuals which will enable them to actualize potentialities hitherto dormant or left to accidental development.

Let us start with the question of integrity in the association of the sexes. We can begin by asserting a simple proposition: we are human beings before we are male or female. That which unites us as a species is more basic than that which divides us into sexes. By integrity I mean the achievement of a disposition by which men and women respect each other's full humanity as a condition of their associations with each other. One of the tasks of education, formal or informal, is to aid boys and girls to win those right relations with each other which will increase their own happiness and the common good of public responsibility in adult life. Both ends are achieved to the degree that the sexes come to recognize, during the process of growing up, their complementary roles and to discover, in the various interrelations where their lives mingle, the fulfillment we are capable of as men and women.

All of us begin existence as children with a predisposition toward the unity of the sexes. In our early years we normally have little difficulty acknowledging each other's equal status. At least the sexual difference is not a hindrance to the winning of friendly relations. Again in the declining years of old age men and women are frequently able to treat each other with full dignity. A married couple who have loved and suffered through the triumphs and trials of a common life are at times able to establish a mutuality where differences of outlook occasioned by sex enrich and supplement the limited wisdom one sex alone can acquire. When we meet such a perfectly mated senior pair, we can gain an insight into something very nearly ideal in human existence. It is matched only by the deep, unconscious attachments of brother and sister while very young. The freedom of children and the very old, before sexual passion has come and after it has departed, is very enlightening. In the absence of strain and self-consciousness one gets a glimpse of the ideally human.

Educating for integrity in attitude and behavior toward the other sex during the adolescent years can be conceived clearly in philosophical terms, though its achievement is extraordinarily difficult. In essence, the goal is to effect a harmony of the biological, moral, and esthetic qualities of male and female nature in which each quality supplements the other, without tyranny of any one of them. The educated person is capable of love in all three spheres and able to blend the three into ever new relations. At the biological level love between the sexes can be completely amoral. It is man and woman coupling, with little regard for the individuality of either partner; Nature's way of propagating the species. Each uses the other for intense erotic excitement and their bodies become hardly more than objects for each other. Though there is apparently great variation in the intensity of such appetites from person to person, such a stage nearly every young person must go through. Unfortunately, many tend to remain bound to this stage. For an indeterminate number of adults, some of a highly intellectual kind, this biological love represents the greatest pleasure they are capable of experiencing. Members of the other sex are habitually viewed in the light of their physical attributes, primarily as imagined or potential conquests. Only by such means are many of us part of the time and some of us all the time able to lose our inhibitions, get outside ourselves for a few minutes, and become little more than representatives of the species.

Fortunately in normal development the biological component becomes suffused with esthetic qualities and with them arises affection in the relations of the sexes, a dawning recognition of the distinctive individuality of this or that person. We speak of the beauty of such relations and learn to cherish a kind of intimacy and tenderness which has little in common with sexual passion in its primitive form. Young people are often at a loss to explain why it is that they enjoy each other's presence so much or what is involved in this complementary character of sexual attraction. But they are conscious, dimly at least, that an entire new dimension has been added by the attributes of masculinity and femininity. The biological urgencies are overlaid with the specifically human attributes of caring and tenderness that appear to be ends in themselves. Something of the possessiveness and object-character of the biological phase has relaxed its hold.

Girls, perhaps more than boys, are likely to consider this esthetic quality of attraction to be genuine love and to concentrate it on one member of the male sex. Actually they may later discover that these affections are not so specific as they would like to believe. If they seize opportunities to associate freely with boys in various relationships, they will learn that esthetic emotions are capable of indefinite extension.

To the degree to which this esthetic factor in sexual attractiveness gains prominence and extension in breadth and depth, par-

ticularly during adolescence, it is possible to determine the
quality of health and naturalness a society attains where sex is
concerned. When boys and girls associate with each other in work
and play, in easy exchange of opinions and in social diversions
without undue strain, then the development of free individuality
is afforded scope. Co-education of the best kind promotes such
naturalness and permits a kind of interrelation impossible to attain
where young people are segregated and allowed to mingle with
the opposite sex only on special occasions.

There is a necessary development in integral relations of the
sexes which can be distinguished as ethical, even though it is
closely allied with the esthetic. The ethical bond, for Western
morality at least, implies a respect for the other person as an
independent being, or in Kant's words, it implies treating everyone as ends and not merely as means. The esthetic relation is thus
subtly different from the moral relation; the latter is not basically
concerned with a person's sexual being. When biological, esthetic,
and moral affections become fixed on one person of the other sex,
there is the birth of romantic love which, if reciprocated, can
make two people happy as can little else in human experience.
Nevertheless, such a love, however momentous, ought to be only
one of many relationships between the sexes. Friendship across
the sexual barrier is possible only when male and female consider
each other as more than love partners. In such friendship there
must be the intention to promote unselfishly the well-being of
the other, to aid the other in growth and understanding of the
human condition. Friends wish each other well and actively seek
to bring about that welfare. What is peculiar to friendship between the sexes is a greater potential ingredient of the esthetic
quality, which can add sweetness and beauty to the ethical relationship without awakening physical desire.

The educated man or woman is able, in short, to associate on a
basis of friendship with other men and women, not in disregard
of their sexual natures but without allowing the biological factors
to undermine the esthetic and ethical. Such an achievement requires the most careful kind of education, formal and informal,

of long duration. It is clearly not the responsibility of the schools to promote romantic love or serve as marriage bureaus, however many young people may find their future mates there. What is a responsibility of education is to aid boys and girls to grow toward the esthetic and ethical relations with each other that provide adult men and women the subtle enrichment not possible to either sex in isolation.

One of the sources of impoverishment of Americans in erotic life is surely our failure in the schools to develop sufficiently the possibilities of freedom in these relationships. Too many marriages are disappointing to both partners because they restrict tenderness and affection to the marriage partner alone and effectively prevent any friendship with other members of the opposite sex. There is a fear, probably justified in the present insecure stage of development, that biological urges will dominate if we indulge our need for wider and freer friendships. But why should we have to wait till passions die before men and women discover the essential humanity in each other's being? A proper education would surely enable young persons to carry over into adult life some of the higher naturalness and liberty in intersexual relations they experienced as children. It would make possible a closeness and intimacy of association reserved at present for comrades and friends of the same sex.

Evidently one of the hindrances to such an education is the growth in this country of the peer group mentality. At a crucial stage of their development most adolescents nowadays look solely to each other for guidance in matters of greatest moment to them. All too rarely does a young girl find it possible to communicate her thoughts and deepest concerns to an older man, not her father, or a young boy form a deep attachment to an older woman, not his mother. Yet it seems clear that especially in these relationships we are able to discover the possibilities inherent in the existence of two sexes. When youth and age communicate across sexual lines, ethical and esthetic qualities can fuse without the danger of erotic attachments in the narrow sense. Even more important, in such attachments each of us can learn from the other the different ways in which every generation conceives the world. The sad consequences of peer group authority are to narrow the range of possible experience available to either sex.

Related to this is the current pressure for early marriage and child rearing, at a time in our national history when too rapid population growth has become of overriding concern. The peer group persuasion is that every girl must be married to be successful; fulfillment lies along this path alone. The counter pressure is for girls to pursue higher education and a career, which in most cases involves postponement of marriage and motherhood. The question of marriage or a career torments maturing girls, making them unsure of their proper role. If they go too far and too long in the direction of independence and career making, their chances for marriage may be missed, condemning them to the social stigma currently attached to the unmarried state. On the other hand, those who put marriage and child-rearing ahead of other goals discover too often that the expected fulfillment does not come. Holding a marriage together and bringing up children can be for them at one and the same time more than they can accomplish and less than they desire.

The bane of these contradictory pressures lies in the loss of potential individuality and happiness they impose. Not every woman is fitted for marriage, just as many women have no real vocation for motherhood. Even those who do have some talent for these are nowadays pushed into what are essentially child marriages before they have more than begun to explore the various possibilities and range of male companionship or developed their own promise intellectually. And middle-class, suburban marriage can be frequently confining, as the endless number of articles by women eloquently testify. However satisfying her husband may be and regardless of the time and devotion he may have for her, many a young wife finds that there are sharp limits to the fulfillment she can find by restriction of free association to one person only. In spite of herself she is all too likely to envy the career girl who can meet and converse with many different men on terms of equality and without unwanted emphasis on the biological relationships.

Peer group cohesiveness also dictates that girls must not show themselves the intellectual superior of boys, in school or out, lest they endanger their chances of getting a desirable mate at an early age. The doctrine runs that boys do not like to be outshone by girls and instinctively distrust the brilliant female who insists on demonstrating her abilities and ambitions. Even if this were not true, the fact that so many girls believe it to be true probably has much to do with the fact that so few women reach peaks of achievement in our society. If we accept the proposition that ability, particularly intellectual ability, is distributed by nature without regard to sex, it is asking far too much that men always marry girls who are their intellectual inferiors. The minority of women who are superbly gifted, given our current contradictory mores, are in peril of not finding mates at all, though they may well desire a career as wives and mothers as much as their less endowed sisters. A woman with a college degree is practically prohibited from marrying a man without one, though the reverse situation is deemed acceptable.

So long as these and many other hindrances to free association of the sexes obtain, there is small chance that women will achieve real equality in our American society. Though we have made great advances in the present century, it is likely that equality of race and religion will be won before all traces of discrimination in sex have vanished.

There is another conservative conviction still prevalent in our society, to the effect that the intelligence of men and women is of a different kind. Though women may be as intelligent as men, their use of it is directed toward the concrete and the practical, rather than the general and theoretical. Women are more intuitive, hence less logical than are men. All of us have heard these and related arguments against academic equality again and again. And since this is a question of primary concern to a philosophy of education, it deserves careful analysis.

Margaret Mead has recently[1] put this age-old persuasion in trenchant terms. She charges that in the effort to achieve equality

[1] In the "Newsletter of the Inter-University Committee on The Superior Student," Vol. 4, No. 4, Boulder, Colorado, May 1961.

for women in education, we have unfortunately assumed that "just as good" means "exactly alike." We have made the old mistake of democratic cultures of confusing being equal with being the same. She goes on to contend that our American conceptions of curriculum have been dictated by an ascetic male tradition, first by monks of the Middle Ages and later by intellectual males. As a consequence girls find it nearly impossible to become absorbed in this male-created body of knowledge. The language of higher education particularly, being formal and symbolic in nature, is like a foreign tongue to the more bodily-oriented, intuitive-minded females. For a girl to succeed with this curriculum, it is necessary for her to adapt herself to this male style and forget her essential femininity, her preoccupation with life and motherhood, and her future role in culture. For these reasons, according to Mrs. Mead, girls are attracted to the "more human subjects" among the sciences like biology and medicine, and to the humanities generally in distinction to the non-human sciences. In short, the accusation is that our educational system reflects male interests and typical male abilities, without consideration of the fact that women are unalterably different in both interests and abilities from men.

In a succeeding issue of the same publication Margaret Mead is supported by a graduate Radcliffe student who complains that Radcliffe's affiliation with Harvard now makes available to girls an education marked by "ascetic intellectuality." Instead of learning to speak her native language and concern with what is most real to her, namely "the physical, perceptual, the emotional realities," the Radcliffe girl must learn "the artificial language of the sterile, masculine academic culture."

It should be added that neither Margaret Mead nor her supporters want a return to an earlier type of education for women in which women studied the decorative and domestic arts, presumably appropriate for their future roles as homemakers. They demand instead a reform of academic curricula which would permit women to give full play to their unique kind of intellectual abilities, which are less abstract and symbolic than those of men. Women should have a career and marriage, too, like men, but a different kind of career in line with their biological and inherent differences.

What are we to think of this demand? Are there really intellectual differences of the kind alleged between the sexes?

There is, in my judgment, just enough truth in these charges to be haunting. That our curricula still bear the marks of their ancient origins is doubtless correct. The contribution of men to the storehouse of knowledge is out of all proportion to their numbers. And that many of these men were little concerned with sexual realities, like reproduction of the race and family cares, is likewise undeniable. Intellectualism is a preoccupation of our Western society that may well have had its origin in renunciation of the flesh, the heritage of both Greek and Christian influences.

It is surely not true that this intellectualism has been "sterile." To it we owe many of the greatest discoveries in the natural sciences and some of the grand metaphysical systems of ancient and modern times. Much of our pure poetry and painting, architecture and music have been a consequence of this one-sided intellectuality as well. We would hardly possess the wealth of modern culture in either the technological or the humanistic fields without the one-sided concentration on abstract and symbolic structures which men, renouncing the flesh and "the world," have painstakingly worked out for us over lifetimes of concentrated effort. The theoretical, as opposed to practical, wisdom embodied in them is immense.

The mistake Margaret Mead makes is to assume that curricula emphasizing these symbolic systems are any more appealing to the majority of male students than to women. The vast majority of both sexes, for better or worse, are directed toward practical life. They want from their studies instruction in how to perform well in the various duties and privileges of personal, social and political activity. Experience for them is a combination of intellect and feeling and the concrete seems to them unquestionably the real world, as action is the only test of theory. When a course in high school or college centers on symbolic or abstract structures, most students, male and female, are certain to find it lacking in vitality and relevance. Only a tiny minority can draw meat and drink from such fare; only those with a passion for theoretical truth can be sustained by considerations very remote from daily life. Such intellectuality becomes "sterile" only when the teaching of these symbolic structures is mechanical and merely repetitive or when students lack the imagination to invest these symbols with meaning.

It is ultimately foolish to complain about this situation. Most of us are simply not fitted for the life devoted to pure theory, and perhaps fortunately so. Practical wisdom is our aim and courses in the schools should be largely directed toward that purpose. With secondary and higher education becoming ever more available to all our youth, there is a growing need to avoid excessively intellectualized subject matters. Or put more positively, materials of instruction should combine the concrete and general, the rational and emotional, theory and practice; they should endeavor to lead students to the concrete universal, starting from where they are.

To allege that women are less able than men to find satisfaction in purely intellectual pursuits seems to be simply a confusion of a cultural with a biological fact. These opportunities have for ages been denied women and it is hardly surprising that as a sex they have contributed relatively little to the highest achievements in these spheres. My experience over many years as a teacher of philosophy has helped to persuade me that women are as likely to be competent in the abstract and analytical as men are in the intuitive and concrete. In logic and metaphysics, for example, female students can become as absorbed and able as males. The venerable notion that such subjects as physics and geology are inherently more fascinating for men, whereas literature or languages attract women, is surely being disproved by contemporary experience. Even in our own society, which is more backward in this respect than many others, such a generalization becomes ever more suspect. The number of women who can do superb work in mathematics should give people like Margaret Mead pause, for mathematics is surely the most abstract and symbolic of all academic disciplines, the farthest removed from human, physical "realities," alleged to be the primary concern of the feminine gender.

Most women, it can be granted, are willing to give up their careers as mathematicians, physicists, or public figures to become wives and mothers, if the "right" man comes along. But this is a consequence of our peculiar mores and our lamentable inability to discover a solution to the double role of women, not because they find the worlds of scholarship, the professions, or intellectual endeavor unreal or finally unsatisfying. In a society which would expect women to reach the heights of creative achievement as frequently as men, none of these differences based on gender would appear. As things now are, women are too often faced with the alternatives of pursuing a career or a mate and it is not surprising they prefer the latter. Were men confronted with the same alternative, who can believe they would choose differently? After all, attaining competence, not to speak of excellence, in any discipline is nowadays a long and difficult road. It is to be expected that most of us, men and women, choose the easier path of biological ambition. That men are required to follow a vocation before and after marriage accounts for their pre-eminence in nearly every field, including even the art of cookery.

I would not want to deny entirely that male and female capabilities are in any way different. What I do assert is that women can achieve superlatively in any field that men enter, once the social expectations permit. The sexes do apparently have their particular outlook on many problems; this makes discussion in mixed groups often superior in insight and judgment to that of one sex alone. Male and female minds can complement one another. But this is easily exaggerated and usually of secondary importance. We are so blinded by our traditions that what we ascribe to intuition of women or male powers of reasoning are simply individual differences or cultural conditioning. The longer boys and girls are educated together and the more that equal performance is expected of them, the less distinguishable will purely intellectual differences of the sexes become.

There is another notion deeply embedded in our culture to the

THE PROMISE OF WISDOM

effect that women's creative needs are in large part satisfied by child-bearing and child-rearing. These functions are supposed to substitute for creativity of an intellectual or social kind. The analogy of being pregnant in the body with being pregnant in mind is an old one and like most analogies is unreliable as a tool for reasoning. It serves to transfer to the biological realm what is, I think, another effect of cultural conditioning. In order to give birth to children, women are supposed to be in their prime, the early middle years of the life span. Before the children have grown beyond their ministrations the better part of their most creative period has vanished. Nature, it is often said, intended it that way. Hence for a woman biological creativity is basic in a way that is not so for the male.

I do not believe it. Its probability derives from the circumstance that at present we are persuaded that women who bear children are the only ones who can best nurture and sustain them till the onset of puberty and beyond. The American cult of motherhood is largely responsible for this. In other societies, the British for example, children are frequently sent away to boarding schools where they remain for the largest part of the year. Elsewhere nursemaids and governesses have for centuries been entrusted with the nurture and care of infants and children. The idea that young women of intellectual promise—or without any, for that matter—must devote the better part of their lives to the care of their own children, even if they do not want to, is far from a universal practice. The American *ethos* holds, however, that only the mother is able to give her children the sort of love and devotion they require. If a woman bears a child she becomes automatically responsible for its nurture and early education. It is a sovereignty that is thought to be indivisible, i.e., not to be delegated.

The fallacy lies, I think, in a confusion of bearing and rearing. Without doubt, there is a deep-going satisfaction in the experience of parenthood for most people, for men hardly less than women. In Aristotle's phrase, it is "the perpetuation of one's image" and in a limited sense the model of all creativity, whose goal is the human search for immortality. Being available to nearly all, however, and largely the work of Nature, the creation of children is hardly sufficient for anyone who has more than a modicum of education and ambition. And rearing children well is something very different from bringing them into the world. Rearing gives creativity great play, of course, but is of a very different sort and hardly related to the biological kind.

The idea that mothers are the best teachers of their own infants is clearly refuted by innumerable observations every day. They may or they may not be. That they can give their own offspring a special sort of love and care, especially during the infant stage, I would not be inclined to deny. When it involves, as it often does today, constant solicitude, presence, and limitations on interests of highly capable young women in their twenties and thirties, it seems to be a gross mistake. Even the most devoted mothers grow weary of the repetitive tasks of child-tending and bitterly resentful of a social system that ties them to the home and the company of childish minds for months and years. Motherhood becomes not an important episode in their lives, but a career and a destiny. Without any special aptitude or preparation for instructing the young, many are forced into the role of teachers.

For those women who wish homemaking and motherhood to be their vocation in life, there is no problem. But in our society, where young women are receiving as much formal education as men, it is unrealistic to believe that husband, children, and a suburban home will be sufficient for vast numbers of them. Many of the ablest ones still imagine it to be until they try it, misled as they are by our long traditions and cultural expectations. But the demand for meaningful professional work—as opposed to the busy work and play many now engage in rather desperately—will not be stilled. Nor should it be. Most men expect to live the double life of husband and worker, of private and public person, of home and office, shop, or farm. If they are puzzled by the discontent their wives display with the single, private role of home and children, they have not come to grips with changes in the modern world.

A basic problem, therefore, in achieving integrity on the sexual question is to effect a basic change in male attitudes about the role of the sexes. What we have hitherto often taken to be fixed by Nature, we must learn to be largely a matter of custom and culture. What we once thought to be determined by genes and unalterable laws, we must now recognize to be within the scope of human freedom. To change these attitudes, often hardened into dispositions, will not be easy. On such matters of sexual roles, it is almost easier, in our present state of scientific development, to alter biology than to alter tradition.

Many of the injustices in relations between the sexes will probably be with us after every trace of racial prejudice has disappeared. After all, discrimination against women is historically more ancient than discrimination on the basis of race. Not only must one reconcile himself to patience on this question, but also one must take the long view. Tragedy is in any event an inescapable fact of the human condition. The task of building a satisfying and satisfactory life is the hardest of any for human beings to resolve.

Meanwhile, there are certain things those of us engaged professionally with American education in this generation can seek to accomplish. All are implicit in what I have said so far. Though none of them goes to the heart of the problem of integrity in the relation of the sexes, they have the advantage of being meliorating measures which effort and intelligence ought to accomplish within the foreseeable future.

First, we must provide in the teaching profession a far better balance of men and women at all levels from kindergarten through graduate school. This will mean fewer women in elementary education and far more in college and graduate school teaching. That our children under present conditions are normally taught only by women until they are in the seventh and eighth grades and then increasingly only by men through college is an intolerable situation. Young people need models at every stage of their development and teachers are naturally models. Boys have no male models in school in their early years, and girls few women models in their higher education. For this reason, among others of course, boys frequently become behavior problems in early education and girls drop out of school at the higher levels. Until we achieve a more equitable balance in our teaching staffs, we shall not measurably improve the rates of juvenile delinquency or avoid the shameful waste of superior feminine talent in our professions. Though this reform is increasingly recognized as urgent by critics of our academic order, we have as yet hardly made a start on effecting it. Other societies, most of them opposed to ours, are well ahead of us in this respect. Their motivations may well be suspect. But the interests of closer and more integral relations of the sexes require that we follow after them and, if possible, overtake them.

A second reform, perhaps more controversial, is the elimination of sexual segregation in education. In our public schools and universities this has already been effected, but our private schools, where many of our ablest youth are educated, lag behind. If anything is reminiscent of a medieval ascetic tradition, surely this practice of separating boys and girls in adolescence for educational purposes is such an anomaly. There are, of course, arguments for the social separation of boys and girls at certain age levels and for particular individuals. Many of them are based on presuppositions of natural differences of the sexes which we have already considered and rejected. And even though others are valid, the question is one of relative advantages and disadvantages, as always in matters educational.

Those of us who have taught in both kinds of institutions have had opportunity to weigh this question. Leaving aside the alleged advantages of social separation for some boys and girls in adolescence, most of us prefer, I believe, the intellectual give-and-take of classroom discussion in co-education. More important by far is the fact that only when both sexes learn that intellectual superiority has no regard for sex will our society abandon the foolish tendency for men and women to avoid serious intellectual discussion in mixed company.

Nothing is more therapeutic in the classroom, I have learned from experience, than to see a brilliant male student overshadowed in argument by a still more brilliant female. His admiration may be reluctantly given, but his respect for her ability is unavoidable. And it is not only males who tend to feel superior. There is some truth in acid European observations about our matriarchal culture. When either sex is segregated during the formative years, there appears to be an inevitable tendency to claim exclusive virtues. Only when they are given opportunity at all levels to experience directly that the spectrum of abilities is no respecter of sexes will we have a chance of modifying the dominance-submission patterns that erode integrity in human relations.

Of course, we are moving toward co-education as the rule in our society. Even the more conservative of Eastern institutions are seeking to transform themselves into a co-educational pattern. It would be illegitimate to argue that what is increasingly being done is therefore desirable. Yet those of us who oppose segregation in any form note with satisfaction that fewer young Americans wish to divide their school lives into weekdays of classes and studies, weekends of social life and dating. Without pressure of propaganda, students are bringing about this change by their choices of institutions. In a land as wealthy as ours we can afford both kinds of school, and doubtless the secondary male or female school and college will continue into the indefinite future. There is a positive value in diversity of educational opportunities and few of us would want to ban such institutions. There are always students who are probably better off when temporarily isolated from members of the opposite sex. The principle of co-education, both on teaching staffs and student bodies, however, should be asserted as the norm and the ideal.

Third, we who teach must learn how to combat the deep-seated feeling lurking in many male and female hearts that women who aspire to equality and a career lose something essentially feminine. Anyone who tries to define femininity in any exact way will find the task most difficult. Nevertheless, most people do mean something by it and to have this something disappear in the quiet struggle to give women full status as human beings would signify a loss of diversity and happiness in the career of our species.

In the feminist revolt of a couple of generations ago, when women fought for the ballot as a symbol of other rights, some went too far in trying to become like men. Aggressive, shrill, and coarse in talk and behavior, they gave some justification to the fear that women in public life might well lose the qualities of charm and refinement usually associated with their sex. We are living in a period of reaction to some of these extremes. In many instances, women themselves are in the vanguard of this reaction. Many of them will say that they wish to be dominated by men, though what they mean by "dominated" is often hard to determine. The old patterns of submission, supported by tradition and in some sense by biological factors, are proving difficult to overcome. Most girls seem to desire husbands who will be more "intelligent" than they, though how this is to be possible when intelligence is equally distributed they are at a loss to say. They are also reluctant to vote for other women for leadership positions, even when the superiority of the female candidates is not in question. And so on.

Perhaps this femininity issue will be partly resolved for us by the example of other countries. As everyone knows, Soviet Russia has proportionately many more professional women than we do; their medical profession, for example, is overbalanced by females. There is considerable testimony to the fact that women physicians and physicists in that country have not sacrificed any of their femininity or their chances of marriage by becoming professionals. Though Americans are not fond of learning anything from Communists, we could take lessons from other peoples whom we respect more. In the last analysis, the only way the schools can help to overcome this inchoate anxiety is by the power of example. When more and more of our own women demonstrate that they can lead the double life of public and private persons, without losing essential qualities, this prejudice will gradually disappear.

For the question of femininity is not a matter of role but of style. It is not a question of function, except in a biological sense, but of outlook. It is not a question of intelligence but of taste and temperament. When women learn how to discover their appropriate style in public life, in the professions and in the trades, how to bring their peculiar strengths to bear on the solving of social, political, and economic problems, their male counterparts will recognize the complementary character of female abilities. Then they will gradually learn to cherish these abilities.

Our society badly needs the special talents of women, now too often wasted and frittered away. Plato lamented long ago that Athens was using only half its potentialities in relegating women to the roles of child-rearing and homemaking. His cure for the problem may well have been worse than the disease. But our society should adopt a better way than to trivialize women's capacities after they have borne children and to stigmatize those who decide to omit the marriage and motherhood role. After all, we hardly need children in the numbers that are being produced today. But no one has claimed that we have an overproduction of insights and new ideas for the solution of most of our overwhelming social dilemmas.

Achieving integrity in the relations of the sexes is nevertheless not only a question of pressing social needs, perhaps not even mainly so. It is a question of the progressive attainment of individuality and happiness. For this, much greater freedom and closeness of association of male and female of all ages are required than exists today. Until men and women learn to associate with each other on a basis of equality that does not disregard differences but cherishes and enjoys them, we will continue to have the so-called war of the sexes, to the detriment of both. The schools can do a great deal by keeping together the rising generations from kindergarten through graduate schools, by providing teachers of both sexes in roughly equal numbers at all levels, and by teaching directly that women, no more than men, have a "place" unless it be the wide world itself.

10. AMERICAN STUDENTS AND WORLD TRAGEDY

A SECOND PROBLEM of practice in relating schools to the wider society is as new and unprecedented as the sexual problem is recurrent and perennial. We live in the first era of global history. The world has suddenly become a large neighborhood. As one of the most powerful and most wealthy nations, our people have come to feel responsible for large sectors of this neighborhood, in some sense, indeed, for all of it. Even if our ability to alter events whose causes antedate this era is sharply limited, we must nevertheless assume economic and political responsibility for areas and peoples we understand poorly or hardly at all.

If we are not to remain a nation merely prominent and predominant by the accidents of history, the rising generations need to gain relationships of closeness to these foreign peoples. Geographical nearness makes such relationships necessary, without alas any certainty that they will come to exist. Physical proximity is something quite other than psychological nearness, as all of us know from experience. How to attain the necessary closeness to these teeming millions, many of whom are undernourished, illiterate, of a different skin color, resentful of our wealth and pale faces, fired by passionate new nationalisms and ideologies, is by any reckoning the most comprehensive task our educational system has ever faced.

Why must we undertake it? For one thing, our American technology has contributed to making this planet fantastically dangerous for human habitation. For another, our culture has helped to erode age-old traditions and customs of other peoples, causing them to ape our ways and to be fiercely envious of our material advantages. Without our wishing it, American cultural patterns have penetrated everywhere and created myriad new demands and appetites that demand satisfaction out of proportion to the resources of other countries. Harlan Cleveland, some fifteen years ago, coined an apt phrase for this new situation. He spoke of The Revolution of Rising Expectations. More recently, he has added a new slogan: The Evolution of Rising Responsibility. But neither he nor anyone else can do more than hope that evolution will not be swallowed up in revolution. Our nation has the greatest stake in the evolution of responsibility because we have most to lose by revolution. Hence there is no alternative for us but to accept the duty of relating ourselves to nations, new and old, whose existence could be safely ignored a couple of decades ago.

Education's first task is understanding this new world scene as a preliminary to effective action in it. Our young people must somehow be prepared to cope intelligently in the future with human beings, whose individual and collective experiences have had hitherto little in common with theirs. The materials of education in the arts and sciences have long been international in scope, but politically our education has been provincial. Emotionally we are still nationalists, responding to atavistic appeals to local and familiar habits of action. Loyalty to home and homeland has always seemed the most natural and inevitable value to instill in our children. Yet it is now all too clear that a democratic education must urgently find ways to resolve the conflict of national allegiances and wider social goals. Unless our children learn to overcome provincial patriotism as a kind of ultimate good, we are assuredly lost.

Similarly, on the problem of race. It is one thing to teach scientific findings on the equality of all ethnic groups, quite another to make Americans feel equal and to seek community with yellow and black and brown on the same basis as they seek it with white. Yet we must raise up a generation who will transcend these ancient prejudices and become eager to discover what visions these colored peoples, who vastly outnumber us, have to communicate. Most difficult of all, perhaps, education must attempt to persuade our youth that their high standards of consumption will progressively isolate them from the majority of mankind who, still near the subsistence level, struggle to keep body and soul together and to feed and clothe their children in minimal fashion.

In soberest perspective, these are the demands on American education vis-à-vis the world scene. In the light of this problem, the internal issues of education look small indeed. The needs of a vocational education appropriate to rapid economic change, the issue of state versus federal support and control, the balance of liberal and professional curricula, progressive and traditional methods of instructions—all are of secondary or derivative importance by comparison. In order for us to live successfully with the world as one neighborhood requires of the new generations almost a different kind of character, for which there exist precious few models.

It is certain that we as educators are not prepared for these demands and that those we teach will not accomplish what the times require. The essence of tragedy consists, as I have had occasion to mention earlier, in the recognition of what one must do yet is prevented from doing by weakness within, either preventable or beyond the power of man to alter. We shall not succeed in overcoming national, racial, and class pride in our children because we have not overcome them in ourselves. Consequently, we shall fall short of being equal to the tasks imposed on us, and our children will pass on to succeeding generations a tangled skein of unresolved contradictions and predicaments. Nevertheless, it is an element of philosophical faith to hold that there is direction in human affairs, and the stumbling progress we make—or fail to make—in our generation will not be without effect. Once we grasp the true dimensions of our situation today, as many increasingly do, we will be more able to seek the road of amelioration, that is, of reducing the dilemmas of future offspring.

It is well to reflect at the outset on the difficulties which we Americans experience in understanding other peoples. Those of

us who have lived through the Great Depression and the Second
World War, or those who have had intimate and prolonged
acquaintance with desperate social conditions here or abroad, are
struck by the sheltered character of student life in the 'fifties and
'sixties. How can these fresh-faced youth sitting in our classrooms possibly know what hunger is when they have always
known plenty? Or being cold, when they move from one centrally heated building to another in warmed automobiles? How
can they begin to grasp imaginatively the gnawing fear of want
and destitution, of pain and exposure to the terrors of war, so
common to other peoples in their youth? What in their experience is remotely similar to the primitive conditions of existence,
typical of most of their counterparts in Africa and Asia and
South America? They read about such lives in classrooms and see
them on their television screens; increasingly as tourists they gaze
upon the youth who lead their lives under these conditions. But a
wide gulf lies, as Archibald MacLeish has remarked, between
knowledge of the fact and the "feel" of the fact.

Those of us who teach these youngsters in school and college
and are their parents are likewise shielded, for the most part one
step removed from the experience typical of the world's peoples.
Even if we had imagination sufficient to bridge the chasm between knowledge-about and direct acquaintance-with common
realities, we ourselves too often lack primary experience. Not
since the Civil War have Americans been exposed to the harsh
facts of history in anything like the measure meted out to other
nations. Our soldiers have always had the prospect of returning
to a prosperous and peaceful homeland after wars on foreign soil.
We have had room to expand, a dynamic economy to improve
the lot of every generation, and, until the last decade, the feeling
of security through natural borders and boundaries. How few of
us have any vivid memories of really desperate conditions of life
such as are constantly faced by more than ninety percent of the
peoples in other lands, many of them only an hour or two distant
by air travel!

As a consequence the generation now in school has acquired

unconsciously—with their mother's milk, so to speak—three kinds of pride, all of which serve to unfit us for the world civilization now emerging: the pride of wealth, the pride of race, and the pride of national power. Before turning to the educational resources we possess for their control, we may well reflect on the strength of these forces and the degree to which they separate us from genuine understanding.

What does the possession of material comforts and physical ease do to the human psyche? The question is a provocative one which only a few clear-sighted observers have been able to answer in approximate fashion. It is fatally easy to underestimate the role of wealth and property as universal human concerns. Polls have been taken which indicate that money shares with the themes of love and death an equal place in the desires and anxieties of the world's population. Perhaps it is a more constant and enduring concern than either love or death. Those with an idealistic cast of mind tend to shrink from this insight. They want to believe that more internal issues are paramount in the human condition, that material security is a secondary consideration. Most commentators today are inclined to place the threats of global war and of overpopulation above the threat of want and need as the more basic problems. Yet it is surely true that until we have relieved the huge and growing disparity between the few nations which enjoy superfluity and the many which are in fearful want, neither war nor overpopulation will be withdrawn as spectral shadows darkening our future.

Both our Christian and our classical heritages speak with a divided voice on the role of possessions. On the one hand, the possessionless life has been held up as alone making possible the kind of sympathy and understanding required for true service. The Hebraic scriptures are filled with polemics against wealth; they reveal a tendency to equate the poor with the good man. And in the mosaic of Christian history, the strain of blissful, voluntary poverty is very prominent. The founder of Christianity rejoiced in his freedom from possessions and established an ideal of saintliness as renunciation of everything but "the one thing needful." Property stands in the way of man's recognition of his dependence on God. A rich man is constantly tempted to the illusion that he has other security; wealth brings pride and imminent danger of losing one's soul. The vow of poverty enjoys equal status, even today, with those of chastity and obedience in many Christian orders.

Similarly in ancient Greece the ascetic ideal was early present among a people who were far less explicitly religious than the Hebrews. Socrates was a standing reproach to the wealthy Athenians by virtue of his poverty. His pursuit of knowledge and of the care of his soul and those of his fellows left no time, he claimed, for amassing private goods or even for providing minimal security for his family. His example inspired followers in succeeding centuries to renounce possessions and seek virtue and self-sufficiency in complete neglect of bodily comforts and the amenities of civilization. Socrates' greatest pupil, Plato, built his masterpiece, *The Republic*, on the idea that the good society can only be attained when its founders and guardians have given up the striving for possessions in the interests of harmony and justice. Plato was convinced that the appetite for wealth inevitably divides all states into "the haves" and "the have-nots"; until this appetite is strictly subordinated to reason and a proper education, community even in a small city is rendered impossible.

Though the Christian and the humanistic motives for distrust of property were different and sometimes diverse even among themselves, there is a common element: possessions hinder the development of the requisite bonds between man and man and so obscure the vision of one's destiny. They prevent the simple and terrible awareness of Job, after he had been deprived of everything: "Naked came I out of my mother's womb and naked shall I return again thither."

On the other hand, our tradition also contains the concept of property as an aid and support to a life devoted to ideal ends. The influential Aristotle taught that the good life was possible only when man was freed from providing the basic necessities for himself and could devote his days to political activities and pursuing scientific truth in leisure. Too much and too little wealth, according to him, are equally destructive of the goal of community and of genuine wisdom. Even in the Christian heritage, this middle class ideal of a modest sufficiency of goods has never been absent. Man as a steward of the things that Nature and Nature's God have made available is an early theme. Not the possession but the improper use of possessions is conceived to be the barrier to fruitful communion. Though voluntary poverty is a requirement for some of God's chosen, others may serve Him as truly in more conventional ways, provided they subordinate the pursuit of wealth to other ends. Hence, there is ample support in both taproots of our tradition for either beneficent or baneful interpretations of the role of property.

The American experience has been influenced by a pervasive idea that material success and divine favor tended to converge. The Puritan virtues of hard work, thrift, and self-reliance helped to spread the notion that material prosperity was compatible with God's governance of the world and sometimes a mark of His special dispensation. And from a wholly secular standpoint we have been driven by a need to settle this raw continent and realize its rich resources. A large proportion of our immigrant ancestors came here to improve their material fortunes, which were normally minimal upon arrival. The ascetic impulse has not been absent in our short history, but from the overall perspective Americans have been known for their preoccupation with "getting ahead." Success has become for us often synonymous with large income and material goods. If other peoples seem to be at least as materialistic as we, they have better known how to profess other values. It must be admitted that few of them have made as overt attempts at uniting moral and material values as has been our custom until recent times.

In the twentieth century there has arisen a different justification for the material plenty with which Americans have long since learned to live. Economists assure us that unless we remain economically strong and preoccupied with consuming, we cannot help the underdeveloped areas of the world to improve their economies. Our wealth is pictured as the only sound underpinning of freedom. The miserable majority of mankind look to us, we are told, for concrete evidence of how freedom and prosperity converge. Moreover, with our surpluses we enable them to get started on the road to full industrialization and mechanization. Hence, we find it comfortable to consume luxuries to the point of satiety and boredom while other peoples are struggling hard to find the bare necessities. Not only has the ascetic ideal nearly vanished, but also the ideal of a modest sufficiency. Middle-class standards of property today would have signified great wealth a few generations ago.

Under these conditions it is hard to exaggerate the difficulty of Americans reaching a sympathetic understanding of the poor in other lands. The pity is that we do so little in our schools to analyze the hindrances to fruitful dialogue between rich and poor of whatever country, including our own. A little reflection should reveal some of those hindrances which are relatively universal and which change little from age to age. If our well-fed youngsters were made aware even of these at some level, much might be accomplished.

Perhaps the threat to human dignity in any dealings between persons whose possessions are radically unequal is primary. Without sensitivity the man who has from childhood been assured of enough to eat, of a comfortable bed, and protection against Nature's extremes is certain to be unaware of this threat. Such a man is simply unable to understand why poor people do not accept his proffer of friendship and equality at face value. If he is eager to disregard material differences in status as external and inessential, why cannot they?

Why not, indeed? There are many reasons. The poor are normally proud and their pride conceals certain resentments. In our equalitarian century, they are unlikely to feel inferior to the rich, least of all to admit inferiority to themselves. Yet they suspect the well-to-do man of feeling superior and carefully concealing it by false heartiness. For this reason they are frequently unable to hear the direct meanings in conversation because they are listening to the overtones and undertones. Anything like friendship is possible only where frankness rules as an implicit force. Between rich and poor there are nearly always unspoken issues. The rich are able to withdraw into seclusion whereas the poor must spend the greater part of their lives exposed to public gaze. The rich can go elsewhere; they are not bound to locality. This reminds the poverty-stricken that unpleasant consequences of behavior can be easily evaded by the rich by virtue of this freedom.

Frankness is impeded on the part of the privileged person because he senses the resentment of the unprivileged with whom he associates. He suffers from a sense of guilt which he rarely wants to analyze. At some level he suspects that his advantages are accidental. Consequently, he is kinder and more generous than his nature warrants. Try as he will, he is likely to slip into a patronizing attitude, however little he may feel superior. Pride of nation and of class and of education arises as his defense against the suspicions of the poor and of his own guiltiness. Often he yields to their image of him and generates resentment by so doing. The slow process of understanding one another is thus thwarted by the intrusion of alien feelings on both sides. To discover and hold fast to the common elements of humanity in such situations is a triumph of will over instinctive powers.

Americans are warned that they must not expect gratitude on the part of other nations for aid extended by our country. Many of us can accept this, at least at an intellectual level. But this is merely the beginning in understanding those whom the chances of history require us to aid, because we are currently in a position to do so. Such material aid imposes subtle obligations on the recipients and threatens their freedom. They resent the necessity of being helped and fear they will fall into the power of those aiding them. The suspicion of our motives is unavoidable. It is, unfortunately, hard for any of us, rich or poor, to believe that others intend our welfare from motives of benevolence. How much more difficult is it for other nations to believe in unselfish acts from powerful strangers!

In their turn, the poor are far from guiltless for the interrupted dialogue. There is a corruption in poverty as deep as any corruption that wealth is able to effect. Deprivation, long sustained, schools its children in habits of deception and of self-interest which exceed all normal bounds. The poor man is rarely capable of revealing his whole mind and finds it fatally easy to cheat and lie to his privileged neighbor. Both excessive surliness and undue obeisance come more naturally to him than do openness and frankness. He is all too ready to believe that no one can understand what it means to be poor. Bitterness often renders him unwilling to make the attempt to explain. In his dealings with the privileged, he is likely to see affronts and reproaches where none are intended. Evasive, frequently rapacious, and cunning, in his materialism he is far from virtuous. It unfits him for the kind of trust on which community among human beings must be founded.

When one considers this oldest and possibly deepest division of mankind, occasioned by wealth, and reflects on the requirements of the world neighborhood, one gets some imaginative measure of the task of education in our age. How are our inexperienced youth to be made aware of what awaits them in this expanded world that is suddenly so contracted? Unacquainted with tragedies except those occasioned by family quarrels and separations, how will they react when they discover themselves in locations where they are cordially disliked, even hated, simply because they are rich Americans? As well-to-do, privileged adults how will they adjust to the revolution of rising expectations of the world's masses from which we, their elders, have been shielded and to which they will be fully exposed? The answer is still missing and can hardly be guessed.

Material privilege is by no means the only burden they will have to carry. Scarcely lighter is the burden of color. We in the United States have already earned the ill will of the colored majority, an ill will that will be slow to die under the most altered conditions. Every generation has had to suffer not only from its own mistakes and stupidities, but from the sins of the past as well. It is asking too much to expect a black or yellow man to forget history when speaking with one who is white. Whatever progress our children make in overcoming racial pride, they must be taught to expect that the wounds their fathers have inflicted are slow to heal. Victims of injustice have much longer memories than do the perpetrators. Members of the white race will increasingly have to experience being disliked on sight because of their skin color, before they can understand what Africans and Asians have had to endure for generations. The elementary injustice of being hated, not as a person or for one's deeds, but as a member of a race, can become branded into consciousness as a rule only when it happens to oneself. Again one wonders how our children will take such treatment.

We have heard so much of the psychological, economic, and sociological causes of racial prejudice that we are likely to forget the philosophical basis of it in superiority feelings. Why does the white man feel superior to other races? The answer is naturally complex, compounded as it is of historical events and different rates of cultural advance and advantage. At the root, however, is the irrational preference for one's own tribe and fear of the alien and the strange. As evolutionary creatures we cling to the familiar and the familial; our feelings pursue a different course from reflection. Closeness is much easier with those who look alike, talk like us, and share our desires. Racial pride is thus the most natural and elementary of prejudices. It resides in all of us as children, however obscured it may be by the accidents of culture. The white race is, of course, no exception. Only when reason has been mixed with much experience of common work and common goals can we hope to modify this elemental prejudice. Necessary is a kind of educational conversion, no sudden phenomenon, as in Christian conversion where God turns the soul about and sets it on new paths. Educational conversion is not of the instant, nor is it single, but of duration and continuity. It is the attainment of progressive levels of transcendence, requiring a life time for most of us and realized imperfectly even then.

Though superiority feelings are not peculiar to Westerners, it is we who, at this juncture of history, have a special responsibility for their suppression. For ours are the power and influence granted by myriad inventions and the transforming capacities of technology and science. For better or worse, it is our culture which is undermining ancient practices. As a newcomer to Western civilization, America has been lately saddled with the task of leadership in its worldwide dissemination.

Here at home we have sizeable racial minorities, as many European states do not, and hence a decided advantage in the struggle to overcome racial pride. Our maltreatment of these minorities in past and present has hardened the hearts of Asians and Africans and weakened our own confidence in the possibility of eradicating racial strife. Yet we are only on the threshold of the global era and the realization is slowly dawning on more and more Americans that there is no alternative at all to overcoming prejudice in this sector. Though the hour is late, most white Americans are hopeful that there is still time. Millions of our youth are able to feel strongly about this problem when they are still lethargic about other issues of social injustice. The suffering and tragedy that are almost certainly in store for the youngsters now growing up may well enable them to include these minorities into full membership in our society. If so, they will be more able to endure the hostility of colored peoples abroad with some understanding and tolerance. American education has a clear-cut, if enormous, task in the moderating of racial pride, perhaps more easily solvable than that of teaching rich and poor to communicate with one another.

In the world neighborhood that is struggling toward minimal community, it is conceivable that we shall master these two burdens and yet fall under the third, the pride of provincial nationalism. How are young Americans to learn that the sentiments of their fathers regarding love of and allegiance to one country—in moments of crisis overriding all other sentiments—are sadly inappropriate today? Though nationalism has no biological basis similar to pride of race, in modern times it possesses a force and fury able to unite classes and races temporarily and hold all other passions in abeyance. There is something unbearably pathetic about the willingness of youth to abandon all private enjoyments and occupations while under the sway of patriotic sentiments, to give up their lives or their health or moral convictions, with no assurance that their sacrifices accomplish anything substantial. If other causes of war are more basic, nationalism is clearly a pervasive contributing one, able to prolong conflict beyond any reasonable limit. To clear-sighted men, few things are more evident than the necessity of curbing and controlling this sentiment. In its place must be instilled loyalty to more inclusive groups than the political nation; love of country must be integrated with other values of equal importance.

What attitude toward our country is appropriate to encourage in our school children if they are to come into intimate and meaningful communication with the people of other lands? Two extreme positions on this question today seem clearly wrong. On the one hand, there are those who contend that patriotism is anachronistic and must be abandoned entirely in the interests of loyalty to a world order that is consistent with human dignity. They oppose our government's position on nearly all problems. Deeply alienated by our national self-righteousness and frequent belligerence in the Cold War, they incline to the view that our motives as a nation are essentially corrupt. Their attitude may be only slightly caricatured in the slogan: "My country is always wrong."

Much more numerous are those who believe that America is the greatest country in the world and must be defended at all costs, even at the cost of destroying mankind. Patriotism is the only practical absolute they recognize and its indoctrination in our youth they consider a self-evident necessity. Their attitude is as old as human history. Our country has succeeded because of inherent virtues of her citizens. Other nations hate us because of our success, consequently we must defend to the death the only enlightened civilization that remains. All internationalism that is not based on self-interest is suspect in their eyes.

If the rising generations are to achieve community with other peoples, they will surely need to be resolute in avoiding both extremes. The ideal is not to make world citizens, without local and regional ties of loyalty. Nor is it to prolong the lamentable fiction of national superiority in virtue. What is wanted is a type of man who can belong to a nation and share its values without absolutizing them, a kind of citizen who can hold a proper pride in his country without thereby denying its limitations. We require a generation who can rise above provincial nationalism without condemning its virtues yet recognizing their partial nature and the equal right of other national preferences. For a democratic people it should not be impossible to educate at once for local and universal loyalties, though the task of holding them in balance is, of course, enormously difficult. With the world as a neighborhood, no other course is feasible than to teach simultaneously attachment to our own and the world's other peoples. He who is estranged from his homeland is as unlikely to gain the trust of others as he who would transform all others in his own image.

The practical dimensions of this educational task are likely to appear overwhelming to one who allows himself to ponder them enough. How can our comfortable, white-skinned, power-conscious American youngsters possibly communicate in depth with the poverty-stricken, colored, passionate, proud youth of foreign lands? Is not physical proximity as likely to breed psychological estrangement as it is mutual sympathy or spiritual closeness?

The question of the time needed for such an educational reformation also plagues the reflective observer. Education is a slow process and the machines which bind us ever closer as a world population are incredibly fast. Given sufficient time, an optimist will assert, American ingenuity can remold the thinking of our youth along world lines, teach them to understand sympathetically diverse peoples, and leaven the inequalities that now divide us. But there is an urgency about the task, generated by atomic weapons and the Cold War, which can weaken the optimism of the stoutest heart. The doubt that infects us like a physical disease for which no cure is discoverable is a consequence of the consciousness of so little time for such momentous changes.

What is to be done? Since the task is an educational one in large part, we ought to start with those elements of strength and weakness in our present system and seek to reflect on the changes necessary to bring it more in line with the dimensions of the new task. Then we can move beyond formal education to the kind of experiences which can provide our young people with the "feel" of the fact as a requisite supplement to knowledge of the fact.

Let us begin with school curricula. Of all the subjects taught in American schools, history is perhaps the most crucial for the dawning global era. Far too long our youth have formed nationalistic values on the basis of sectional and partisan views of the past. Though history can never be written with the objectivity of a science, it is not impossible to produce texts that are not simply reflections of provincial patriotism. It is not impossible, given the will and the knowledge to do so. Unreflective loyalty to American values has been induced by confusing American ideals with practices, by reading our history in terms of "the American dream" and other peoples' history in terms of their deeds. The amount of dogmatism found in most texts concerning inner motives of the principal actors on the national and international stage is simply intolerable. So much of our national self-righteousness is generated by the subtle indoctrination of the idea that our statesmen have been a nobler breed than others. At present most of us advance in knowledge and wisdom only by unlearning many of the prejudices about American virtues which school histories have instilled. Those of us who do not remain curious long enough carry for life a black-and-white version of past events. Others become cynical and alienated from our tradition by the conviction that history is not different from propaganda.

The attempts to write history from a supra-national perspective, advocated for some time by UNESCO and other organizations, will no doubt continue to meet obstacles. Such attempts will have to battle the perennial impulse in us toward simplification of the complex, toward national self-justification, and the abuse of the past for present political aims. There is also a justified fear that such history writing may be dull and colorless, a mere chronology. Yet there is no necessity for an unbiased history text to lack vibrancy and point when its authors are motivated not only by the will to truth but also by the vision of a new order of interdependency among nations. Thucydides was an Athenian historian who wrote of the most bitter and momentous war in Greek history but who nevertheless achieved something approaching a just evaluation of the rights and wrongs on both sides.

Hitherto we have conceived the teaching of American history as one way to weld our immigrant population into a national unity. To "make Americans" has sometimes been held to be not simply the purpose of teaching history to our children but of education as a whole. Understandable as this motive has been in the past, its persistence in the present and future will be calamitous. In one sense, the overcoming of narrow loyalties should be easier for us than for Europeans. Our history is not only shorter; we are also inheritors of many other cultures. We are an amalgam of other nations, owing much of what we are to others. Europeans have an infinitely more difficult task, on which they are making rather spectacular progress recently. Nothing less is required of us, though we lack the apparent urgent necessity of the small European states which serves to hasten the process abroad. Nevertheless, our power and wealth are negative factors of great force. No one can predict the outcome of this required effort at national self-transcendence. Yet it is hard to see how any other course is open to us, if we are to help to moderate the fearful nationalisms which are tearing our world apart.

Scarcely less important in the overcoming of pride of race and class and power are the social sciences in our curricula. Conceived broadly, they are the subjects devoted to understanding the human career in its collective, institutional manifestations. As such, they reveal the interdependency of peoples and the universal structures of cultures and civilizations. Young as they are and still struggling for the prestige and recognition of the older scientific and humanistic disciplines, they surely represent one of our best hopes for a future generation which will be relatively emancipated from crippling prejudices.

It is true that they have been till the present something of a disappointment in view of their optimistic beginnings and boundless aims. Many of our youth find their study unexciting; many of their practitioners are too frequently led astray by inappropriate methods and inadequate theory. Yet their future holds great promise, for they are dedicated both to knowledge of the complexity of group life and to action for its improvement. Unlike the natural sciences or the humanities, social science should find it easier to avoid the cleavage between knowing and doing that has weakened formal education in previous epochs. Many of the myths about race and culture that have held us captive for centuries have been exploded. Each succeeding generation now carries around with it, in this respect at least, fewer superstitions and old wives' tales.

The relativizing of values, which subjects like sociology and anthropology have engendered, is frequently criticized. Foreign patterns of behavior are conceived to be equally justifiable with the ones our culture has evolved. Students become aware early that social habits often serve as hidden absolutes which oppose critical intelligence and individual freedom. There is a sense in which many of the social sciences have been destructive in their impact on immature minds. Yet against this we must remark that a strong medicine is required for overcoming ethnic and cultural egocentrism. Surely in the present situation it is preferable to have young people believe that nations are equally justified in their beliefs and actions than to have them hold the far more common conviction that ours are inherently superior. In any event, there is ground for confidence that social science will move beyond this first stage and achieve a better evaluation of descriptive and normative factors. Relativity of values among groups, which is a simple fact of life, need not imply either the desirability of this state or the helplessness of individuals to move beyond subjective judgments of good and evil.

In their efforts to advance knowledge about foreign cultures as

well as about the nature of culture as such, both history and the
social sciences can give our youth an intense consciousness of the
worth of diversity. Older generations have seen no path toward
union and amity among nations except to play down differences
and seek a future of greater homogeneity of peoples. But the
newer ideal, surely superioɪ, is to teach our youth to exult in the
variety they discover among cultures. The solution to our own
race problem in America is not to induce the Negro or the
Spanish-American to abandon his distinctiveness in cultural habits.
Similarly, in the larger world we cannot but impoverish the
future by using our power and wealth to make other nations more
like ourselves. The immense contribution the social sciences can
make is to stimulate lasting curiosity in school children about
other visions and different life-styles than those of our homeland.

Nothing could conceivably overcome the hostility of foreign
peoples more effectively than the realization that American
youth are eager to learn the secret of their ways of experiencing
and thinking, not with a view to making them over in our image.
Perhaps our children and grandchildren will learn with the aid of
the social sciences enough curiosity and humility to approach
other nations in this spirit. Most of us today do not know enough
to be properly curious and are not open enough to other alternatives, even when we have the requisite information.

It is my hope, too, that the study of the human career will
make our people, or at least the articulate minority, more aware
of the precarious ground on which all cultures stand. Civilization
has always been a perilous affair, at times, even in the brief period
of written history, nearly disappearing altogether. To the student
of history its survival appears to have been more a product of
natural renewal than of human design. At present, civilization is
again threatened as it was at the opening of the Christian era. We
stand like prairie dogs poised at the surface of their burrows,
uncertain whether to duck below ground or to emerge into the
light of the mutual world. Our landscape, as the poet Rilke put it
beautifully, has not yet been persuaded. We have not yet come to
trust one another sufficiently to live in the sunlight of full day.

At such a juncture of history no change in curriculum is as important as a pervasive and subtle alteration in the teaching and learning of every subject. I mean by this that American education needs to become more philosophical. In his great study of America, Tocqueville remarked that "in no country in the civilized world is less attention paid to philosophy than in the United States." Perhaps this is still true, if we mean by philosophy what we should mean, a habit of reflection on ordinary and extraordinary daily events. Becoming aware of the possibilities and predicaments of men today means becoming philosophical. Such a change would not only affect the teaching of social sciences and history, but the humanities and natural sciences as well.

Since the term "philosophical" is likely to be misunderstood, it may be better to speak of the need for reflective thinking. For I certainly do not mean that American educators should introduce more courses in philosophy into our curriculum. The academizing of the philosophical spirit has done it no good. As I have earlier remarked, philosophy is not so much a subject matter as a way of looking at all subject matters. In fact, what we require are fewer isolated courses in philosophy and much more reflective teaching of the standard courses already in every American school.

What would it mean to make our youth more reflective? At the outset of this study, I suggested that education is the endeavor to rise from information through knowledge to wisdom, with the aim of living life rather than squandering it. To live one's life at this time of splendor and misery in history involves becoming aware in an intimate way of the new dimensions that have been added to our existence.

To become reflective, in the first place, suggests the struggle to acquire perspective on what we are doing, as individuals and as a people. Perspective in turn implies vision, vision in the comprehensive sense of the early Greek word *theōria*, insight and theory. Without such insight and theory we shall hardly be able to fathom the complexities of foreign psychologies; we shall hardly understand the delicate tasks of coming close to other peoples. Our youth will continue to be taught that the solutions to intractable problems lie at hand, that they are simply a matter of technical "know-how." Over-simplification is an inherent weakness of our American emphasis on practicality.

In our generous country we have had manifold opportunity for the experimental, the second chance, the wasteful folly. Our thinking is constructed on the idea that few acts are irreversible and few choices irrevocable. But the rest of the world is unaccustomed to such margins for error. The perspective we need would help to persuade us that more thought before action on the world scene would guard against fateful blunders. It would prevent us from uncreative improvisation in the face of unexpected crises. For our eagerness to do something about immediate urgencies stands in the way of our seeing long-term solutions that would prevent future disasters.

Philosophical perspective enables the individual to build emotional reserves against the unpredictable calamities of history. Many of us are living on our nerves from day to day and teaching our children alas to do likewise. Frenetic activity and restless haste suggest too often an attempt to cover up inner voids. And they suit us ill as would-be leaders of the free world. Robbed of the confidence of continuous progress in the solution of world problems, we are too likely to betray panic. A modicum of reflection would convince us that there are no single resolutions to such problems. We live in an age of continuous crises, no one of which is likely to be decisive; they require of us a steadiness of nerve and a calm courage that only the mature can display.

Though analogies between the individual and the nation are only roughly valid, something of the same sort is surely required for the personal crises which have cumulative impact in a fast changing environment. How to build these inner reserves in our youth is a query of contemporary education which can only be answered by the need to make all schooling more reflective.

In the second place, philosophical reflection alone can help us to distinguish the novel from the perennial elements of our contemporary situation. We are more tempted than were earlier generations to regard our age as unprecedented, a temptation which the preceding chapters have hardly resisted. I was shocked to read in the introduction to an issue of *Daedalus* (Fall 1961) the following paragraph by its editor, the historian Stephen Graubard:

> There is no idea more congenial to the twentieth century than the one which suggests that it is an epoch unique in world history. No previous generation experienced comparable dilemmas; statesmen were never more sorely tried; hazards were never more imminently lethal; the burdens of office were never so onerous and never of such transcendent importance. The age insists on its uniqueness. It will abide no comparisons. This is the badge of its inordinate pride; also, perhaps, the symbol of its ignorance. It is the source of its most primitive myths.

That has the ring of simple truth and something of its bite. We may well reflect on it long and hard. For the discontinuities of modern experience are one of our greatest threats. Too often we are unwilling to learn from the past because of the suspicion of irrelevance. Parents and children, teachers and students, adults and adolescents, are estranged from each other when they too hastily conclude that the unique elements of the present far outweigh that which is common. Such convictions underlie our fondness for innovation in education, our impatience with any curriculum that has continued unchanged for a decade, our distrust of the older teacher or administrator.

Probably the oldest division among civilized men is that between the conservative and the reformer, most simply stated as the tension between the advocates of inherited tradition and the proponents of the untried. In politics this conflict may appear clear-cut, enabling us to take sides with one party or another without anguish. But in education, as in some other areas, wisdom counsels a proper admixture of conservative and reformist ingredients in every change. Attractive as extremes are, especially for Americans of the twentieth century, they promote the dissociations and the voids which cause us to lose our way. Clearly we must discover altogether new ways to relate privileged, racially proud, and patriotic young Americans to impoverished, frequently resentful, tradition-bound youth of other lands. But we cannot afford to neglect the hard-won lessons of earlier epochs before nationalism divided us and before technology made so acute the inequities of wealth and poverty. Once it was possible to blame God or Nature for some of these disparities in individual or collective destiny; now in a society of vastly increased power and freedom of action we are without excuse. Whatever else has changed, the simple claim of man on man for succor and support in the search for meaningful fulfillment has not changed. And the record of the past can teach us, at the very least, the pitfalls we must skirt. The oft-quoted insight of Santayana can stand one more citation: "He who does not remember the past is condemned to repeat it."

The greatest gift of philosophic reflection, however, is likely to be the measure of equanimity of spirit it could bring to our anxious age. Among the multiple uncertainties of the future one thing is hardly uncertain: the meed of suffering and tragedy in store for all of us. How well we succeed in instructing the young to endure this suffering and tragedy will be a final test of the soundness of our educational foundations. Such equanimity of spirit is at the farthest remove from the restlessness and impatience that beset so many of us adults, as it is equally far removed from the stagnation and boredom that threaten our whole society. On the contrary, equanimity makes possible a basic cheerfulness in the face of unresolved problems which do not yield to effort. It helps us to live in the half light that continually plays over human affairs when seen in longer perspective. It teaches us that victory and defeat are seldom ultimate, that power and weakness are always struggling for the upper hand.

The equanimity, so constantly praised by poets and philosophers, is formed by our human capacity to rise above both petty and great vicissitudes of existence and find the irony and humor inherent in them. It enables us to forego the solemn and cleave to the serious, to cherish the drama even in tragedy without yielding to the absurd. If the happiness we dream of as youngsters eludes us continually, the balanced mind learns to discount some of the fictions of such dreams.

It is most important not to confuse such equanimity with detachment or imperturbability. The prevalent image of the philosopher as impervious to the passions and impulses of everyday life is the heritage of Stoicism and not that of the real founder of Western philosophy, the man of the marketplace and companion of all and sundry, namely Socrates. Detachment as a stance in life is like isolationism in American foreign policy; it separates what belongs together. The reflective mind does not seek to escape the joys and pains of protean experience but to absorb them and to profit from them. Equanimity is the fruit of self-possession and discipline in the pursuit of more comprehensive experience.

That such philosophical reflection can be taught in any classroom may well be doubted. Enough if the flame can be kindled there, to be nourished and grow strong by experience beyond the academic walls. In the matter of coming close to the world's peoples, nothing can substitute for working with them directly, sharing their common tasks and games, seeing the world their way. In this area of education it is most important not to overestimate what formal knowledge of the fact can do nor to underestimate what "the feel" of the fact may bring about.

In the last two decades there has been something like a diaspora of American youth over the world. Many of these youth understand better than the older generation that nearness to others involves sharing their physical labor as well as discussion with them; teaching their children, learning their languages and traditions in addition to governmental aid and the dubious blessings of tourism. I receive letters from former students who are in Africa and Asia, remote places from my perspective. They write enthusiastically of cities and states whose very names I barely know and whose location I have to trace on a world atlas. They are teaching or working there with organizations like the Peace Corps, Vista, Crossroads, etc., which did not exist a few years ago. This is a dimension of education that holds great promise for breaking down provincial nationalism and alleviating wounds of wealth and color.

Those of us who have been Fulbright students or scholars caught an early vision of the transforming power of such experiences. We learned to study at foreign universities and to discuss issues with the elite of other lands. When the history of this tragic century is finally written, the Fulbright Program may well be regarded as far more important than we think now. Studying with others is a first step in coming to know them intimately. But present-day advances like the Peace Corps hold still more promise, for they involve the hand as well as the heart and the rank-and-file as well as the elite. It is a truism that the change in the Peace Corps members themselves is likely to be greater than anything they accomplish for the disadvantaged groups they are seeking to help. But it is a welcome and enlightening truism, for it is we who need to alter our views as much as other countries require economic and educational help.

All these programs are still in their infancy. If they are increased in scope and many others of different but allied objectives join them from other lands during the remaining years of this century, prospects are good. They require, of course, not only considerable intelligence but great sensitivity on the part of administrators and participants alike. It is wise indeed to keep the financial remuneration for such service to a bare minimum. But American colleges could well afford to extend academic credit for work in the Peace Corps, Vista, and other approved efforts. Certainly a year of such work is far more likely to educate our youth than two comparable years within ivied walls. And our government must sooner or later allow this service to substitute for military training.

Military training itself can well afford to alter its character in the first global era. That we will continue to require armies in this revolutionary world is nearly beyond question. But the primary needs of defense are not inconsistent with the promotion of education, formal and informal, within the military services. It has long been an unrecognized scandal that millions of our youth are rejected by the military as educationally unfit. The school dropouts, the untrained, and those of below average intelligence are as unwelcome to the Army, Navy and Air Force as they are everywhere else. Yet it is surely possible that with some basic educational training, under the strict discipline common to military tradition, many of these rejects could be rescued from the blight which today is their adult fate. Moreover, they could be later returned to civilian life in possession of certain basic skills that would enable them to earn a respectable livelihood. If we must have armies—and it seems we must—let them at least help in the vast endeavor to educate our populace for the new global era. It is not unthinkable that armies may be gradually transformed into educational institutions of an informal kind. For opportunities to educate oneself in military service are legion. Yet we still think of soldiers and sailors as spending large portions of their time in enforced idleness, miscalled readiness, or in endlessly repeating outmoded drill and exercises that have no carryover value whatever to civilian life. The concept of military organizations as educational institutions, even though of modest dimensions, is slow in coming, but it has large implications for the future.

There is something more, something likely to be increasingly controversial. I believe in the concept of required national service for all our youth, of which military training should be only one segment. There is an elementary injustice in demanding this only of able-bodied young men. Why should not young women also serve their country and the larger world? Those who are physically unable or intellectually opposed to military service could be required to meet their obligation in one of numerous other ways. If we regarded this service as an extension of formal education and gave proper academic recognition to it, I see no reason why it should be more repugnant to our American traditions than is compulsory, universal, free schooling. For millions of our youth such service would be far more educative than the reading of books. Whether carried on at home or abroad, it would have a good chance of bringing our world together, as required schooling once created Americans from a diverse immigrant population.

There is something drastically wrong with the equation: schooling equals education. As I said in the first chapter, the learned man is by no definition an equivalent for the educated man. In this area of world understanding, the gap between learning and true education is particularly wide. We need informed hearts today as much as informed heads and the need is urgent. For this, direct experience of other classes of people, other races, other cultures, within the United States and abroad, is an absolute prerequisite. The ancient Greeks understood very well that the educated man required first *Lernjahre* then *Wanderjahre*. The minority of our young people are increasingly impatient with formal education alone. The majority could easily be persuaded to embrace a conception of education that would bring them face-to-face with a large world to which their adult lives will have to be oriented, whether they want it or not. If they could look forward to a period of active service as a capstone of their formal education and as a requirement for their diplomas and degrees, it would make more meaningful the years spent in classroom, library, and laboratory. It might well give more direction and discipline to their lives as well.

I would think of such public service as basically a work and study program, an integral part of our educational system. There ought to be as much choice of the kind and location of service as now exists in our public school system. Perhaps the time of such service should also be a matter of option insofar as possible. Certainly a minimum of compulsion, a maximum of choice are in line with the overriding objective of bringing our own people close to one another and to other peoples on this crowded globe. Closeness to each other in a psychological sense requires acquaintance with realities. Such acquaintance is not only a matter of knowledge, it is also found in work with the hands and the acquisition of basic skills. It is the capacity to see the diversity of the world, to be not only appalled by conditions in this world but willing to alleviate what we can, and the ability to acquire the necessary skills with which to implement this willingness.

I began this study by quoting John Dewey's definition of education as "the process of forming fundamental dispositions, intellectual and emotional, toward nature and fellow men." After analyzing this definition, I found it insufficiently concrete and expanded it to include "dispositions of closeness to nature and fellow men." The succeeding pages have been attempts to specify what closeness signifies in school and out of school, in learning and in teaching. Gradually it has become clear to me that the search for an education is man's age-old search to become at home in his world. In this respect all of us are schoolchildren throughout the course of our lives. The world in which we have to make our home today and tomorrow seems to us of an older generation, despite all efforts, strange and uncanny still. Yet it takes on more home-like qualities as we persist in our struggle to make it not only more understandable for our successors but also more habitable than it has been for our predecessors.

INDEX

abstractions:
  danger of analysis and, 83-85
  general principles vs., 1-3
  notions of practicality and useful-
    ness as, 48
  relationships as, 79
  single persons as, 58
  study of, 2
  theory as, 1-3
absurdity, 74-75
adolescence:
  indoctrination in, 174-175, 177
  rebellion in, 36, 102-103, 175, 180
  religious faith and, 178, 179-180
  sexual integrity in, 232-234
Arendt, Hannah, 147
aretē, 98-99
Aristotle, 5, 39, 51, 90, 158, 174
  on equality and education, 120,
    131, 135, 150
  on happiness, 67, 68
  on parenthood, 242-243
  on wealth and property, 254-255
artist, use of term, 96-97
artistic morality, *see* moral character
authority, 147-169
  of adult figures, 150-151
  freedom and, 147-148, 152, 159-
    160, 170-171, 192
  physical punishment and, 152-157
  pseudo-, 157
  respect and, 163-166
  of state, 173-174
  subject matter and, 157-161
  unappealing subjects and, 158-159
  undermining of, 75-77, 150-151,
    169, 180
Autobiography (Mill), 83-84
automation, 4-5, 90, 95, 199

Bergman, Ingmar, 46-47
Brown, Harrison, 79

Bruner, Jerome, 160

censorship, 173-174, 183, 192
Challenge of Man's Future, The
  (Brown), 79
childhood:
  adjustment to new environment
    in, 49
  critical abilities in, 60-61
  death recognized in, 73-74
  dispositions toward education in,
    31, 174-175, 178
  early relationships in, 47-49
  family needed in, 48-49, 56
  idealization of, 72-73
  indoctrination in, 173-174, 176-
    179
  sexual integrity and, 232
child-rearing, 236, 242-244
Christianity, 72, 153-154, 176-177
  morality as viewed by, 94-95
  property as viewed by, 253-255
Cleveland, Harlan, 250
co-education, 234, 241, 245-246
collectivism, 45
  individualism as polar opposite of,
    45, 58
college:
  discipline in, 147-148, 162
  indoctrination in, 174-175
  intellectual independence in, 140-
    141
  required courses in, 210-211, 215
Comenius, John Amos, 9, 205
communication, 52-55
  feelings essential for, 85
  with gifted students, 138, 162-163
  in global era, 256-258
  lack of, 55
  silence as, 53, 189-190
  true self masked in, 53-54
  verbal vs. written, 54-55

280